WHAT IF THE SPIRITS COULD HAVE SPOKEN

THE AMITYVILLE HOUSE & THE CONJURING HOUSE

BRUCE HALLIDAY

BEYOND THE FRAY
Publishing

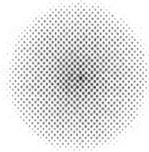

BEYOND THE FRAY

Publishing

CONTENTS

This book, as my last book was, is dedicated to my loving wife. I could not think of a more deserving person to dedicate this book to. My wife, Melady, has been a constant supporter of my work in the paranormal and has served as a confidante, partner, and sounding board throughout our twenty-some-odd years together. Melady has never imposed her opinions or beliefs on me either as a wife or best friend, especially when it came to my work in the paranormal. She has always been the supportive and encouraging rock on which I have built the last twenty years of my life. Without her, there would be no me.

FOREWORD

WRITTEN BY AUSTIN MAYNARD, ITC
RESEARCHER, INVESTIGATOR, AND PREMIER
GHOST BOX BUILDER.

What if the spirits of the most infamous cases in paranormal history could have spoken during the height of the havoc they wreaked? What if the spirits had had access to a ghost box to communicate their messages? Bruce Halliday brings you this book, which involves two very well-known paranormal cases, the "Amityville house" and the "Conjuring house." You are invited on a fantastic journey to discover what might have happened if the spirit entities in those two haunted locations had had the chance to speak live through a ghost box. Bruce is a longtime live spirit ghost box communication researcher and gives readers an authentic perspective of both the true history of these cases, and offers his perspective on the possibility of what the outcome might have been if the spirits had had their chance to speak.

My name is Austin Maynard, and I've been in the paranormal field for seven years, and an ITC experimentalist since 2018. I've seen the passion that Bruce Halliday brings to live spirit ghost box communication, and I believe others will see that while they read his new book, *What If The Spirits Could Have Spoken*. The reader will ponder the "what-if" scenarios and be drawn into the exploration of the possibilities!

PREFACE

My name is Bruce Halliday. I started my journey in the world of paranormal research over two decades ago. My journey began as a novice paranormal investigator running a modest team of like-minded individuals conducting investigations of reported haunted locations in and around New York City and southern New Jersey. I worked exclusively in the field of traditional EVP research for several years before being introduced to the device that would lead to my sole area of study and research within the paranormal field of live spirit ghost box communication.

I began my research into live spirit communication with the use of a ghost box in 2006; at that time there were only a handful of individuals who actually owned a ghost box, and very few more who even knew what the device was. I am one of two original creators of live spirit ghost box communication research. I am personally responsible for formulating the majority of theories and working protocols accepted in the field today, which are based on years of extensive research. I am the creator of two of the more popular ghost box "hack radios," the Radio Shack 12-470 and the Jensen SAB-55. I have written many articles, which have been published in magazines as well as on popular paranormal websites, and have also hosted two of my own internet radio shows dedicated to live spirit ghost box communication. I am the owner and sole administrator of the popular Facebook group "Live Spirit Ghost Box Communication Learning & Sharing," with over 1,200 members, along with my YouTube channel "Halliday Paranormal."

With the writing of this book, I attempt to convey what it might have been like if paranormal investigations of two of the most popularized hauntings in history, the Amityville house and the Conjuring house, would have unfolded had the paranormal investigations been conducted using a ghost box and live spirit communication as the primary tools for contacting and communicating with the entities that were reported to be active in these two paranormally historic locations. This book combines both fact and fiction; the stories of both haunted locations start with an account of the publicized reports of paranormal activity given by the residents who occupied these two homes and were the alleged victims of disturbing paranormal activity. The stories then meld into a fictional account of a paranormal investigating team whose lead investigator is based on myself. The team takes on the task of conducting a paranormal investigation in each of the locations using a ghost box as the primary tool. The two chilling stories take the paranormal team through dark and dangerous encounters with malevolent entities, as well as emotional and rewarding encounters with spirit entities who were victims of the dark forces that reined over these two publicized haunted houses.

CHAPTER ONE

THE AMITYVILLE HOUSE INVESTIGATION

I n the wee hours on the morning of November 13, 1974, Ronald DeFeo Jr. systematically shot and killed all six members of his family in their spacious waterfront home at 112 Ocean Avenue in Amityville, Long Island, New York. On that chilly fateful morning, Ronald DeFeo Jr. crept silently through the hallways of the large Dutch colonial home, carrying a .35-caliber rifle. Without provocation and unbeknownst to his parents and siblings, DeFeo Jr. opened fire, killing both his parents, his father, Ronald DeFeo Sr., his mother, Louise DeFeo; his two brothers, Mark, twelve, and John, nine; and his two sisters, Dawn, eighteen, and Allison, thirteen. All six DeFeo family members were executed while they slept.

Ronald DeFeo Jr., also known as "Butch," was known to be a violent person given to fits of rage that were often exacerbated by his use of LSD and heroin as well as other narcotics. A friend of DeFeo Jr. was once heard saying that the DeFeo home was a "crazy house." Ronald DeFeo Sr. was known to be verbally and physically abusive, especially when it came to his oldest son, Ronald Jr. Ronald DeFeo Jr. confessed to the murders of his parents and siblings after being confronted by police with the murder weapon and undeniable evidence found at the scene. DeFeo Jr. had originally tried to blame the murders on a friend of his father, who was reported to be a professional hitman. The lawyer for Ronald Jr. entered a plea of insanity as the defense for his client, whose testimony now was that he was ordered to commit the grisly murders by an evil voice that had commanded him to do so and that he was not in control of his actions when he brutally killed his entire family. Ronald DeFeo Jr. was subsequently found guilty of six counts of second-degree murder in November 1975 and sentenced to six consecutive twenty-five-years-to-life terms. Ronald DeFeo Jr. died on March 12, 2021, at the age of sixty-nine; he was still incarcerated at the Sullivan correctional facility in Fallsburg, New York.

After the DeFeo family's untimely departure from their home at 112 Ocean Avenue, the house was purchased by George and Kathleen Lutz for the bargain price of only $80,000. George and Kathy married on July 4, 1975. Kathy had three children from a previous marriage: Daniel, ten; Christopher, seven; and Missy, five, all of whom George insisted on legally adopting. The Lutz family moved into their new Amityville home on December 18, 1975. On the day that the Lutz family moved into their new spacious home, Kathy Lutz arranged for the new home to be blessed by a local Catholic priest named Father Ralph Pecoraro.

| The Lutz Family

Upon entering the home, Father Pecoraro reported experiencing extraordinary cold despite it being a relatively nice day outside. As the good father proceeded to bless the home with holy water, he reported being startled by a loud and gruff voice behind him ordering him to "get out." The priest also reported being slapped in the face by an unknown hand while he was alone in one of the home's many rooms. Following the blessing of the home, Father Pecoraro, disturbed by his experiences during his visit to 112 Ocean Avenue, decided to telephone the Lutzes and voice his concerns. Father Pecoraro attempted to call the Lutz family numerous times, only to have the calls blocked by a loud static hiss.

From the day the Lutz family entered their new house, they began to experience strange happenings; all family members reported the house always being extremely cold, colder inside than outside. One of the Lutz children remarked in a later interview that their father, George, was having to continuously keep the home's fireplaces supplied with wood in an attempt to combat the ever-present chill. As the days went on, various members of the family, including the youngest child, daughter Missy, began reporting troubling incidents of alleged paranormal activity. There were reports made by both George and Kathy of an alarming number of flies that would occupy a specific room; the flies were eradicated on numerous occasions only to have them immediately reappear. The oldest son, Daniel, reported having his hand smashed by a window in the home that was inexplicably slammed down on it. Daniel stated that the injury to his hand was severe, but upon examination of the injury moments later by his father, George, the hand was completely healed as if nothing had happened.

The troubling reports continued, such as black ooze appearing in the home's toilets and dripping from the keyholes in various doors about the house. The Lutzes claimed that doors and windows in the home would open on their own and then slam shut; one incident involving the home's front door occurred when the door opened by itself and was then slammed shut with such force that it was dislodged from its hinges. Kathy Lutz was noted as claiming that at one point there was green slime that could be seen dripping down a wall in the home. George Lutz reported being awakened every night at 3:15 a.m., the exact time that it was believed Ronald DeFeo Jr. murdered his family in the home.

One of the most startling reports of paranormal activity came when George Lutz claimed his wife, Kathy, had levitated above their bed on several occasions and transformed from herself into an old hag woman right in front of his eyes. One of the most intriguing claims of supernatural incidents came from the family's youngest member, Missy Lutz, as well as from other family members. Missy claimed to have interactions with what was claimed to be a spirit entity that called itself Jodie. It was reported that this entity would manifest itself in different forms and appear to Missy and other members of the family as an angel and a pig.

These and other alleged incidents of paranormal activity in the home were so disturbing and frightening that it led to the entire Lutz family fleeing the home in terror a mere twenty-eight days after moving in. The Lutz family's entire experience at 112 Ocean Avenue lasted less than a month; they entered their new home on December 18, 1975, and fled the home on January 14, 1976. George and Kathy Lutz later agreed to take individual polygraph tests pertaining to their claims about the incidents at their Amityville home. Both passed their respective polygraph tests. Following the Lutz family's hasty departure from the spacious waterfront home in Amityville Long Island, the house fell into foreclosure.

| Ed and Lorraine Warren

Twenty days after the paranormal incidents that allegedly occurred at the Amityville house reported by the Lutz family, paranormal investigators and researchers Ed and Lorraine Warren were called upon to investigate the reported haunting and deliver their assessment of whether the house was truly occupied by entities that were not of this world. Ed Warren was a self-proclaimed demonologist as well as an author. Lorraine Warren claimed to be a clairvoyant and light trance medium. Both Warrens were considered to be extremely experienced in the field of paranormal investigation and research.

The actual photograph that was taken during the Warren investigation

When the Warrens arrived at the Amityville, Long Island, house, Lorraine Warren was immediately overwhelmed by a feeling of dread and the sense of an evil presence. Lorraine reported that she was almost overcome by a strong malevolence in the house and experienced a feeling of being swept backward by a strong wave as she ascended one of the staircases in the home. Lorraine also reported instances of being physically pushed by unseen hands. Ed Warren claimed that he was in the basement of the house, performing a religious invocation, when he was forcefully pushed to the ground by an unseen force. The most compelling piece of evidence produced at the now famed paranormal investigation was a photograph taken by a member of a news crew who accompanied the Warrens on their investigation; the photo was reported to contain the image of a small boy with stark white eyes peering around a door frame. It was suggested that the boy captured in the photo was the spirit of the youngest DeFeo boy, John Matthew, who had been murdered by his brother in the home.

The Warrens, Ed and Lorraine, after completing their investigation of the Amityville house were reported as saying that they emphatically believed the house was haunted by an evil entity. In a later interview, Lorraine Warren was quoted as saying, "Amityville was horrible, honey, it was absolutely horrible; it followed us right straight across the country. I don't even like to talk about it. I will never go to the Amityville house ever again."

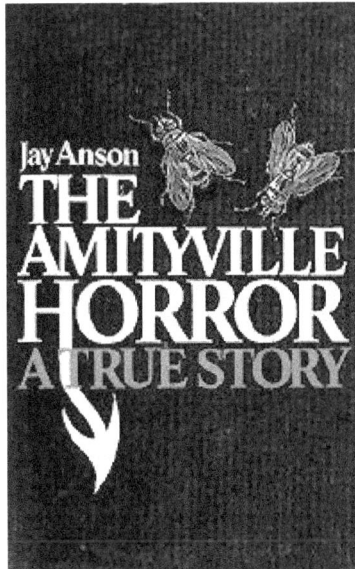

| The Book by Jay Anson, *The Amityville Horror*

The incidents at the Amityville house and the reports of paranormal and demonic activity reported by the Lutz family and the Warren investigation associated with it caught the attention of the author Jay Anson. Jay was a newspaperman prior to penning the now famous book *The Amityville Horror*.

Anson collaborated with George and Kathleen Lutz, detailing their accounts of the incidents that took place in the Amityville home. The book enjoyed runaway popularity and became Jay Anson's most celebrated work. Jay went on to write other horror books, including the work entitled *666*. Jay Anson died on March 12, 1980, at the age of fifty-eight.

The popularity of Jay Anson's book *The Amityville Horror* caught the attention of producer Samuel Arkoff, who purchased the rights to Jay Anson's book with the intention of producing a motion picture, which inevitably gave birth to the now classic 1979 film *The Amityville Horror*. Released by American International Pictures in 1979, the film was directed by Stuart Rosenberg and starred James Brolin as George Lutz and Margot Kidder as Kathleen Lutz.

The film was an instant box office success and went on to gross over $80,000,000 nationwide and went on to be among the highest grossing films of all time. The film's major success was in spite of the negative backlash it received from individuals and groups who claimed the film portrayed incidents of evil paranormal activity that had never occurred in the actual Amityville horror house. The filmmakers countered with statements that the film was never meant to be a work of factual events, just a loose portrayal of the events reported to have occurred by the former occupants of the home.

As per the purpose of this book, I will now give my interpretation of how a paranormal investigation of the Amityville house might have unfolded if I were to conduct the investigation with the primary investigative tool being a "ghost box." I will also attempt to give an account of any interaction that might have occurred between myself, my team members, and any spirit entities that were possibly in attendance at the infamous haunted house, including any audible, visual, and physical experiences of paranormal activity reported by myself or my team members.

CHAPTER TWO
MEETING GOOD AND EVIL

I was preparing to leave my home on a spring morning in the not too distant past when my phone rang. I had been expecting a particular phone call and hoped this was it. I picked up the call and said hello; the voice of a friend and colleague in the paranormal field came across.

"Hey, buddy, how's it going?" my friend asked. "How's the weather down there?"

I snapped back, "Stop playing around," knowing this was the call I had been waiting for. "Did we get it?" I asked.

With a snicker in his voice, he said, "Yeah, you got it."

I let out a resounding, "YES!" This particular call was to inform me that my paranormal investigating team and I had secured permission to investigate one of the most popularized hauntings in American history, the Amityville horror house. My paranormal investigating team consisted of four individuals: myself as the lead investigator and live spirit ghost box communication researcher; Tom, who was the investigator in charge of all evidence review and documentation; Bill, who was the equipment manager/investigator and on-site coordinator; and Sue, who was an investigator/researcher.

I called a team meeting at my home one week prior to the Amityville investigation. Team meetings were crucial to the success of any paranormal investigation but especially important for this particular high-profile investigation. The purpose of a team meeting was to form a solid plan for the entire investigation, such as target locations within the house, time parameters, available equipment and any additional equipment that might be needed, assigning specific areas of the house to certain team members for investigation, what type of methods of evidence gathering would be used, and a plethora of other small details to be worked out. I suggested that all team members familiarize themselves with the history of the Amityville horror house and the alleged incidents that had occurred there, and to be mindful not to formulate any opinions on those reported incidents either for or against. I wanted the team to approach this investigation with completely open minds and let any and all evidence gathered decide whether the Amityville horror house was haunted or not.

The big day had arrived; it was an early Friday afternoon when we arrived at 112 Ocean Avenue in Amityville, Long Island, New York. Pulling up the driveway and seeing the infamous Amityville horror house in person was kind of surreal; the whole team admitted to feeling slight butterflies in their stomach as well as the hint of a chill running down their spines. We pulled up in front of the house and got out of the car. The old Dutch colonial home was impressive, as was the surrounding waterfront property. At first glance the house and its surrounding property appeared very well maintained and did by no means seem ominous or foreboding in any way as one who knew its history might imagine.

As my team and I started to unload our equipment from the vehicle, the front door of the home opened. Out walked an average-looking middle-aged woman; as she made her way toward us, it struck me that her face was expressionless. I stopped what I was doing and walked a few steps to greet the woman. I extended my hand and introduced myself. "Hi, my name is Bruce Halliday. I am the lead paranormal investigator."

The woman was able to muster a faint smile as she grasped my hand. "Hello, my name is Sarah. I was sent to meet you and to explain the conditions of your investigation."

I replied, "Nice to meet you, Sarah—"

Before I could finish my sentence, she informed me that she would be waiting just inside the house for us when we had finished unloading our equipment. As I looked at the amount of equipment that was now placed neatly on the driveway, I could not help but wonder if we had brought too much or not enough. I reached for my case containing the two ghost boxes and some other essential equipment I would personally need, and instructed my team members to come with me into the house to receive the instructions that our liaison, Sarah, I'm sure, was eager to deliver.

I reached for the front door handle and realized I was doing so very cautiously like I was expecting one of those static electric shocks you get when you have been walking on a rug in socks and then touch a metal surface. It was not a feeling I had anticipated but more like an instinctual thought. My team and I crossed the threshold of the Amityville horror house, and I was instantly aware of the temperature difference between the inside of the house and the outside. Although the weather was relatively mild, it was very noticeable that the temperature inside the house was lower than that of the outside temperature. The woman, Sarah, was waiting just ahead of me in the foyer; her look was now more a look of mild concern or discomfort. I assumed it was caused more by the reputation of the house she was standing in than actual fear.

Sarah began to immediately give us the conditions we were to adhere to during our stay at 112 Ocean Avenue. She began by saying, "Please do not take any of what I am about to say personally; these are general conditions set by the homeowner."

I smiled and nodded understandingly.

She continued with, "Please do not move anything that is not absolutely necessary, do not alter the thermostat setting, please do not move any furniture, do not leave any windows or doors open, and please wipe your feet before entering the house from outside, and please make sure to turn out any lights after leaving a room." She finished with, "The homeowner would appreciate it if you did not make any public or media statements about any information pertaining to this house without presenting said information to the homeowner beforehand." Sarah then asked if I agreed to these conditions. Of course I agreed. She then presented a paper containing the conditions she had just explained and asked me to sign it. I smiled and rendered my signature. With a slight look of relief now on her face, Sarah said goodbye and informed me that she would return at the predetermined time of conclusion of the investigation to check on and lock up the house. I thanked her and said goodbye.

With the formalities out of the way, we were ready to bring in the equipment and eager to set up and start the investigation. It was late afternoon by the time we finished hauling in the equipment and unpacking it. As I looked at all we had brought, I felt like someone who had really overpacked for a weekend vacation; however, on an investigation of this importance, the motto was "It's better to have it and not need it than need it and not have it."

Bill, our resident equipment manager and site coordinator, had chosen the dining room as our base of operations for the investigation. The dining room table would hold the video monitors, the laptop computers, and any and all equipment that would serve to record and store data from the investigated sites throughout the house. Before we began to set up the equipment, I called a short team meeting to go over our investigative plan of attack and which team members would have what responsibilities as far as location and method of investigation, time parameters, and set periodic check-in times during the investigation. We had decided that the entire investigation would be conducted from Friday night to Sunday morning, it was also decided that we would stay in the house the entire time, and the investigation would be ongoing for the full time we were scheduled to be there. The team would alternate rest periods to catch a few winks and have something to eat and drink, these marathon investigations were not very common, but we had done them before.

As the team went about setting up for the investigation, running extension cords, setting up video cameras and monitors, placing motion sensors in strategic locations, etc., I decided to take a preliminary walk through the house and check out the locations I had chosen for my live ghost box sessions. I proceeded to the living room on the first floor. It was large with a set of two windows on either side and a large fireplace. As I entered the living room, I had the uneasy feeling of being followed. I turned to see if one of my team members was possibly behind me, but as I kind of suspected, I was alone in the room. I shook off the feeling and headed for the staircase that led to the second floor; to the right of the staircase was a bathroom. I stuck my head in to check the toilet. I had remembered that one of the reports of paranormal activity made by the Lutz family was that the toilet bowls in the house had an inexplicable black sludge in them. As I peered into the toilet, it was absolutely clean. I climbed the stairs to the second floor. As I reached the top of the stairs, the first room I could see was a dressing room; it was almost devoid of furniture except for a chair, a small table, and an armoire. As I entered the room, it was brightly lit by daylight and had an almost pleasant feel, kind of cozy.

A few steps down the hall was the master bedroom. As I entered, I noticed something a bit strange. Although having the same amount of windows and facing the same direction as the sewing room I had just left, the master bedroom was considerably darker; the light coming through the windows seemed to be diffused somehow. I took a quick look back at the sewing room and noticed it had the same type of shades and curtains that the master bedroom had, and both sets of shades in each room were drawn basically the same. I checked outside the bedroom windows to see if a tree could possibly be blocking the light, but that was not the case. I stepped into the master bathroom, which was a part of the bedroom, and peeked into the toilet, no black. Other than the difference in illumination, the room was average and normal; nothing felt out of the ordinary. Due to the room's past history of paranormal activity and the light anomaly, this room was definitely on my list for a live ghost box session.

I proceeded to cross the hall and enter what was called the sewing room, which was located directly opposite the dressing room. This room again was sparsely furnished, with a comfort-able-looking chair, a sewing machine, and a stuffed torso manikin; like the dressing room, it had a pleasant aura about it. I stepped out of the sewing room and went a few steps to the second-floor bathroom. As I went in, the only thing that I noticed that was out of the ordinary was not the color of the toilet but that the left side of the bathroom was colder than the right side. I stepped over to the wall that contained the bathroom sink and placed my hand on it. The wall felt cold to the touch as if you'd placed your hand on an outside-facing wall in the dead of winter. I looked up to see if there was an air-conditioning vent at the top of the wall or in the ceiling close to the wall, but there was not. I thought that maybe an air-conditioning duct might have been directly behind the wall, which could explain the temperature difference; that was not the case. I made a mental note of the temperature anomaly and exited the bathroom.

Directly adjacent to the second-floor bathroom was a smaller bedroom that had belonged to the Lutz family's young daughter, Missy Lutz. I entered Missy's bedroom; no sooner had I stepped into the room than I felt a twinge of nausea and a bit light-headed. This feeling was not foreign to me, I had experienced it on other investigations, and I knew the cause was not something I had eaten. This feeling I knew was associated with the presence of paranormal energy. I quickly remembered as a kid whenever I would feel nauseous, my mother would tell me to "Look up and take a deep breath." Believe it or not, this helped to alleviate the feeling, although in this instance not totally. As a seasoned paranormal researcher, I knew this was an occupational hazard, and I would have to tough it out no matter how intense it became. This bedroom was one of my main focus locations. I looked around the room; it was nicely furnished although not as if it were a child's bedroom but more like a guest bedroom. There was a bed, of course, a nightstand with a lamp, and a digital alarm clock that read 6:05 p.m. The room also had a chair, a small television set, and a dresser; there were two windows and a small closet. I left the room acknowledging to myself that this would be the location for my first live ghost box session.

I headed to the last set of stairs that led up to the house's third floor. I walked up the stairs, and even though I had a hundred things on my mind as I ascended the staircase, I noticed that almost the whole length of the stairs creaked as I walked up. This was more of a subconscious awareness, not something that overpowered the other thoughts in my head, until I reached the landing at the top of the stairs. I stopped in my tracks, becoming coherently aware that the steps I had just walked up were still creaking one at a time as if someone else were walking up the staircase after me. I turned to look down the stairs, they were empty, and as soon as I had turned, the creaking sound stopped.

We had been in the Amityville house for around four, four and a half hours now. I had not experienced any direct paranormal activity; the temperature differences, inexplicable noises, and physical anomalies were indications of paranormal activity, but only that, indications. In order to declare any solid paranormal activity, we needed documented evidence. I didn't know it at that moment, but there would be no lack of solid evidence by the time we left the Amityville horror house.

I walked onto the third floor; there was a bathroom directly in front of me, a bedroom to the right, which had belonged to the two Lutz boys, Daniel and Christopher. To my left was a room that was used as a "playroom." I made my way to the bathroom; it was clean, quiet, and uneventful. I left the bathroom and made my way around to the back of it, which was used as storage space. The area was relatively clear except for an old cardboard box and some small artificial Christmas wreaths. I made my way to the room known as the playroom, entered the room, and focused my senses, attempting to detect any anomalies in the room as far as temperature, sound, or physical discomfort, but none were forthcoming. The room was empty; the only thing that occupied the room in the far corner was an old dusty chalkboard that looked as if it could have been used when Abraham Lincoln went to school.

I left the room and walked directly across the hall to the Lutz boys' bedroom. I stepped into the room fully expecting some indication of a presence since I had experienced indications of a paranormal presence in the other bedrooms that had been occupied by members of the Lutz family. I was disappointed; the room was bright and clean and devoid of any hint of paranormal anomalies. I looked around and realized there was access to another storage space in the boys' room that led behind the third-floor staircase. I walked through the opening and immediately got a very eerie feeling, not fear, but the feeling that fear was not far away, if that makes any sense. The storage space was completely empty, so I exited and made my way out of the boys' bedroom and back to the staircase.

I made my way down the staircase to the second floor and made the turn around the banister to head for the adjacent stairs that led down to the first floor. As the second floor came into my view, I saw the figure of a man pass the doorway in little Missy's bedroom. I immediately thought it must be one of my team members setting up equipment, so I casually walked in, fully expecting to see either Tom or Bill. I looked around the room and saw no trace of my team members or any equipment that was in the process of being set up. I had been a paranormal researcher and investigator for many years at this point and knew the difference between what could have been a light anomaly or a trick of the eye. This was a distinctive figure I saw; sadly, without any equipment set up, there would be no evidence.

As I walked down the last flight of stairs, my team member Bill, the equipment manager, passed me going up, carrying a bunch of extension cords and two video cameras. I stopped him and apprised him of my sighting of a figure in the Missy bedroom. Before I could suggest it, he told me he was just on his way there to set up a video camera.

As I arrived on the first floor, I made my way to the basement door. When I opened the door, there was a trace of mustiness that you would expect from any basement. I flicked on the light and went down the basement stairs. The walls were covered in old wood paneling; it was neat and clean with a few boxes and old suitcases. I searched for what was known in the book and the movie as the infamous "Red Room." I opened the only door in the basement, which led to a small storage space that had remnants of red paint on the walls. The room was empty and cramped; it was clearly only a small storage space located under the stairs and not a demonic room as depicted by Hollywood. Like in any dimly lit basement, it had an eerie feeling. The temperature was lower than in the rest of the house, which was not uncommon for a basement. I felt no ominous presence and experienced nothing remotely paranormal while I was in the basement.

I left the basement and arrived back at the base of operations. Sue was sitting at the table, checking the battery power in her handheld equipment. I asked her how the setup was going, it was around 6:45 p.m., and I was anxious to go dark and begin the investigation. Sue informed me that all the necessary equipment had been placed and was about to go live, it should be about ten or fifteen minutes, and we would be ready.

I opened my personal equipment case and removed one of the two ghost boxes I had chosen for this investigation. The box I had chosen to use first was my primary ghost box; this was the ghost box that I used most often and that had the strongest imprint on it. Back in the early days of live spirit ghost box communication, I was able to extrapolate a theory. From experience and with the help of information given by my spirit technicians Mike and Lisa, I discovered that the continued use of a specific ghost box for live spirit communication would allow said ghost box to absorb the physical energy of the ghost box operator as well as the spiritual energy of the communicating spirit entity, thereby strengthening the connection between the two worlds and facilitating a higher quality and quantity of live spirit communication. I named this process "imprinting."

I checked the battery power in ghost box #1, my digital voice recorder, my flashlight, the EMF detector, and the temperature gun; all were at full battery strength. Just as I had finished checking my equipment, Tom and Bill returned to the operations room. Tom informed me that everything was a go and that we were ready to go dark. Sue would be investigating the first floor, Tom and Bill the third floor, and I would be conducting the first live ghost box session in the second-floor bedroom that had previously been occupied by Missy Lutz.

I instructed my team members to avoid the second floor while I was conducting the live ghost box session so as not to pollute the session recording with any ambient voices or noise that may have been created by the team members. As I entered Missy's bedroom, ghost box in hand, I checked my watch; it was 6:51 p.m. I sat on the bed and placed the ghost box on the small nightstand. I checked my digital voice recorder for any remnants of prior recordings to make sure it was clear of any. I wanted this ghost box session to be the only recording saved to the device. As part of the preparation for this investigation, I had prepared a ghost box session plan for this particular bedroom, questions I would ask and statements I would make, how long the session would last, and of course, time allotted for any impromptu questions that may arise during the performance of the session. I was ready.

I turned on the voice recorder, hit the record button, and stated my name, the name of the investigation, the name of the session location, the time, and the date. I reached for the power switch on the ghost box and flicked it to the on position. The ghost box came to life; as it picked up the existing radio broadcast signal, it began to sweep the dial. I had the box set to the AM band. I preferred AM as opposed to FM because it contains more speech in the broadcasts and less music and song. As I prepared to ask for my spirit technicians Mike and Lisa and greet them, I noticed the sweeping sound of the ghost box began to get lower in volume. This sometimes happens when the incoming radio signal fluctuates in strength; however, I also noticed that the content of the sweep was deteriorating. The initial sweep had been relatively clear with a decent amount of radio broadcast fragments; it was now turning to almost all static hiss and getting lower by the second.

Before I could react, the ghost box went dead, completely devoid of power. I checked the voice recorder, and it was still running normally. I switched it off and picked up the now silent ghost box. I checked the box for any electrical malfunctions. It was good; the only cause could be dead batteries. Since I had put fresh new batteries into the ghost box prior to coming to the bedroom, it was not very likely that the cause of the problem was six completely dead batteries.

There was a battery tester on the operations table, so I removed the batteries from the ghost box and made my way back downstairs to the operations room. I proceeded to test all six batteries, and lo and behold, all six were completely dead. This was not an unheard-of occurrence. I had experienced this before, not many times but a couple. The theory regarding this type of incident was that a spirit entity or entities that are in proximity to an electrical device powered by batteries are capable of draining the energy from batteries in an effort to either strengthen their own energy or to hinder any attempts by the physical investigator to gather evidence of their presence. I believed this to be the case; since the ghost box was in working order and I had just placed brand-new fully charged batteries in the ghost box, all indications pointed to paranormal interference. To avoid the risk of this happening a second time, I decided to run the ghost box using the power cord as opposed to batteries. This would hinder my ability to move around the room with the box in case I needed to try to obtain a better signal reception, but it was the only way to ensure that the ghost box would remain running. I also grabbed some fresh batteries for the digital voice recorder just in case.

I went back to Missy's bedroom and retrieved the ghost box, which I had left lying on the bed. I attached the power cord and plugged it into a wall socket behind the night table. As I inserted the plug into the outlet, the ghost box boomed to life, which completely startled me and sent me onto my butt. I had forgotten to turn the power switch off when I removed the ghost box batteries. Oh well, so much for the brave seasoned paranormal investigator. I lowered the volume of the ghost box so I could restart the voice recorder. With the voice recorder running again, I raised the volume on the ghost box; no sooner did I hear the sweep of the box than a voice came through: "Bruce." It was very common to hear my name called during a live ghost box session. I didn't think I have ever done a session without hearing my name called at least once. I responded to hearing my name with, "Yes, I hear you; go ahead." After my allotted twelve seconds of response time, I did not hear any clear spirit communication live.

I then asked for my spirit technicians Mike and Lisa. "Mike, Lisa, are you there? Can you help me with this session?" A few seconds passed, and I heard a clear, "Yes, here," delivered in a male voice. I responded with, "Mike, is that you?" and received the answer, "Yes." I said, "Great, Mike, thank you for being here."

I then asked if Lisa was also in attendance, Mike and Lisa have aided me in pretty much every live ghost box session I have ever done, they are always together, and I have come to rely on their assistance and protection during my live ghost box sessions. Lisa answered my query with a simple, "Yes," delivered in a female voice. I greeted Lisa and Mike and asked for their focus, as this was a very important live ghost box session. Now that I had established the presence of my trusted spirit technicians, I could proceed with the session.

I asked my first question, which was always a generic one. "Are there any entities here who would like to communicate?" No direct answer was forthcoming, but I did hear what sounded like a faint child's voice that seemed to be coming through behind the ghost box sweep, not as part of it. This was a common occurrence; through experience I knew that when I heard something like this, it was most likely a spirit entity who wished to communicate but was either apprehensive or lacked the knowledge to communicate through the ghost box. In this instance, it was probably both. Whenever I encountered this situation, my first reaction would be to elicit the aid of Mike and Lisa to assist the entity wishing to communicate; that was exactly what I did.

After asking my spirit techs to help, I asked the shy spirit to come through and tell me their name, but there was no response. I asked my techs if the spirit entity I heard in the background was there and willing to communicate. A male voice came through and said, "Yes, Bruce, here." I knew that was my tech Mike answering. In an attempt to alleviate the spirit entity's apprehension at communication, I spoke in a calm, soothing voice, as you would when speaking to a child. "Hi, don't be afraid; you can talk to me. Can you tell me your name?" A few seconds went by, and I heard the voice of a child come through with a timid, "Yes."

"Ok, that's good. What is your name?" The timid voice came through once again clearly with, "John." I heard this live but was not able to hear any further responses before I went on to my next question; however, later in a review of the session recording, I discovered there was a second response immediately following the name John. The response was Matthew. My next question was, "John, are you here in this room with me?" To which I received the answer, "Yes." I acknowledged the answer and asked, "John, are you John DeFeo?" I was listening now, of course, for the child's voice; instead, I received the answer of "yes" in an adult male voice. This was a frequent occurrence due to how live spirit ghost box communication works. Since the spirit communication is formed by the entity using whatever sound fragments are being produced by the ghost box sweep at the second they need to form the communication, it can come in any form, male-, female-, child-, or old-person-sounding speech. The answer I received indicated that the communicating spirit was that of John Matthew DeFeo, who was murdered by his brother Ronald DeFeo Jr. in the Amityville house; however, as an experienced live spirit ghost box communication researcher, I knew you should never take the communication you are receiving at face value. It could very well be an entity claiming to be John DeFeo, perpetuating the deception for its own purposes.

At this point in the session, I would need to try to confirm the communicating entity's true identity. My next question was, "How old are you, John?" About ten seconds elapsed without my hearing an answer. I repeated the question, and a few seconds later in the midst of the ghost box sweep I heard, "Nine." Knowing this to be the correct answer from my research of the Amityville house history, I proceeded to the next question. "Ok, John, I heard you say nine. Are you alone here?" Almost immediately I received the answer "NO" in an excited-sounding voice; I heard it clearly. "John, if you are not alone, can you tell me who is with you?" As soon as that question left my mouth, a loud gruff and almost growling male voice came through the ghost box speaker with the response, "NOOO." It took me aback. I was not expecting to hear that voice.

Before I could continue, I became aware that the temperature in the room had dropped considerably; this was accompanied by the hairs on my arms and the back of my neck standing on end. It took me a few seconds to absorb these feelings. I took a breath and asked, "Who just said no in that angry voice?" I received no answer. I asked, "Is there anyone here besides John DeFeo?" The response of "behind you" came through in a low deep male voice. I quickly snapped my head around to look behind me; there was nothing there; the room was empty. I turned my attention back to the entity claiming to be John DeFeo. I said, "John, are you still there?" I received no response. I continued, "John, if you are still here, please let me know you're here."

As I listened intently for a response, I could once again hear the sound of a child's voice faintly in the background but could not understand any of the words. During this ten-to-twenty-second period, a male voice came through. "Mike." I heard this clearly and knew it was my spirit technician Mike. I said, "Mike, is that you?" In order to confirm it was him, he answered, "Yes," which was immediately followed by the word "evil." I recognized this to be a message from Mike letting me know that there was a negative presence communicating through the ghost box. The reason I was able to determine that from the one-word communication "evil" sent by my spirit tech was that experience had taught me my spirit technicians knew that if there was a message they needed me to be able to hear live at the time they sent it, it would have to be very short and to the point; otherwise they ran the risk of my not catching the pertinent communication live in real time.

My tech's message of evil could mean one of two things: either there was a negative spirit or a demonic entity on the other side infiltrating the live ghost box session, or, and I hoped this was not the case, there was a negative or demonic entity present here in the house. My next question to my spirit technicians was crucial in my understanding of where this negative-sounding communication derived from. I asked Mike and Lisa, "Is there a negative entity here with me now?" I received a "yes" in a male voice, which I attributed to Mike, and immediately following, a "yes" in a female voice, which I knew was Lisa. The thing that troubled me most at that moment was that the two answers of "yes" I received were faint and buried in static noise. I was barely able to catch them live. This was troubling because I had developed a very strong connection with my spirit technicians, a bond that allowed for a very high quality of live spirit communication when delivered by them. This stifling of their communication indicated a strong presence that was able to interfere with their efforts. Receiving the two confirmations from my techs of "yes" told me that the negative presence was not on the other side but here in the house and most likely right in this room with me now. Part of the job of a spirit technician is to do their best to protect the live ghost box session and its operator from the influence and/or interference from negative or evil entities; because the odds were that this malevolent presence was here in the physical, it would be that much harder for my spirit techs to try to intervene and protect against the negative interaction.

Normally if I were convinced of a negative presence during an average live ghost box session, either from the spirit realm or in proximity to the live ghost box session, the protocol would be to end the session immediately so as not to afford the negative entity any further opportunity to emit or gather any more energy; however, this was not an average or ordinary live ghost box session. I decided to continue the session in hopes that I would be able to garner further live spirit communication from the spirit claiming to be the child John DeFeo, and if possible, to attain information as to who the negative entity was, why they were here, and what they wanted. I proceeded with the live ghost box session as planned, intending to deal with any negative interference as it arose.

I called out, "John, are you still here with me?" I waited for a response and heard the answer, "Yes, here," in a low timid voice. I heard this answer live and replied, "Ok, John, are you here alone?" to which I received the response, "No." I heard this and asked, "John, can you tell me who is with you?" A few seconds went by without a response. I repeated my question and listened for ten to twelve seconds, but still no response. I try not to make a habit of doing this because the lack of a response usually means that the communicating entity either cannot or will not answer the question, but I repeated my question a third time. As I listened, I could hear that same child's voice attempting to send communication; the attempt was being made but was not successful. I knew there was an attempt being made by John to respond to my question, but he was simply unable to form and send the words he intended to.

Through years of experience in listening to live spirit communication and a ghost box sweep, I had finely tuned my ear to be able to discern what was live spirit communication or an attempt at it, from what was merely a ghost box sweep. There could be many reasons why the spirit John was unable to complete his communication: lack of the correct sound fragments, insufficient energy, lack of knowledge and experience in communicating through a ghost box, or intimidation and interference from a negative presence.

My next statement was, "John, I was not able to hear your answer. Can you please say it again?" After a few seconds I heard the word "no" in the child's voice John was using, and following that, I heard what to me at that moment sounded like the word "monster." It was not clear, so I could have been mistaken. I would have to wait till the review of the session recording to be able to focus on it. With this interaction in mind, I decided to call on Mike and Lisa. I asked, "Mike, Lisa, is the entity John being intimidated or stifled by another entity?" The forthcoming answer from Lisa was expected but very unwelcome. Lisa answered, "Yes, evil." At this point, hearing that answer from Lisa live, I decided to bring this live ghost box session to an end, realizing that any further attempts at communication with the child entity of John DeFeo would be fruitless, and also not wanting to give this negative entity a further opportunity to gather energy or further intimidate and oppress John. I informed my spirit techs Mike and Lisa that I was going to shut the session down, to which I heard the reply, "Yes, Bruce," loudly and clearly.

As I switched off the ghost box and the voice recorder, I could not help but empathize with my two trusted spirit technicians Mike and Lisa, fully knowing that their job was not an easy one under normal circumstances, and unbelievably hard under these circumstances. My thoughts also turned to the spirit entity who claimed to be little John DeFeo, the fear he must feel, and the nightmare of confusion and loneliness that was compounded by the presence of an evil entity. I knew I needed to help him. I also knew that would be a monumental task and a test of all my and my team's knowledge and experience. With my ghost box and recorder in hand, I headed back downstairs to the operations room.

CHAPTER THREE

I MEET THE EVIL SPIRIT JOHN KETCHUM

I entered the operations room to find Tom sitting at the table, his attention directed at the three video monitors sitting in front of him. As I put my ghost box on the table, Tom was startled; he had not heard me come in due to his focus on the monitors. Tom's gaze snapped quickly toward me, and he said, "Oh, hey, didn't hear you come in. How did it go?"

"Interesting to say the least," I replied. I started to give Tom the highlights of my live ghost box session in the Missy bedroom when Sue entered the room.

She walked over and greeted us. "Hey, guys, how'd it go?" She realized that she had interrupted my replay of the ghost box session and apologized.

"No problem. I would rather wait till everyone can hear it than repeat it three times," I said with a smile. It was now around 7:45 p.m. I told Tom to give Bill until eight o'clock and then call him on the walkie-talkie and have him return to the operations room. I wanted to bring everyone together after the first hour or so of investigating to get everyone's feel for the house and to hear about any paranormal activity or experiences any of us may have had. This short meeting would be a sort of barometer for the rest of the investigation.

Eight p.m. came, and Bill made his way back to the operations room. As he walked over to the table, I could tell he was a bit flustered. Bill was a seasoned investigator who had years of experience under his belt; it was not like him to get flustered. I asked, "Bill, are you ok? You look a bit out of sorts."

Bill assured me he was fine and added, "You won't believe what I just saw." That was two team members who had obviously experienced something in the initial hour of the investigation, not to mention the solid live spirit communication I had received during my ghost box session and the inference that came with it. We all sat at the operations table.

Tom said, "Ok, guys, I know everybody is chomping at the bit to tell what they experienced; let's keep it orderly so that we can optimize the time spent and get back to the job at hand." I agreed. Tom said, "Bruce, you go first, Sue second, then Bill, and then me."

I started by saying, "I'll give you the highlights of my ghost box session. Of course, only what I was able to hear live in real time, as I have not listened to the session recording." I started with the incident of having my batteries completely drained, which I thought they knew about already since I had gone back down to the operations room to check them. I went on to give a condensed version of the live ghost box session, the main questions, and the important pieces of live spirit communication I had heard. I, of course, emphasized the part of the session where my spirit technicians warned me about a malevolent presence that was in the room I was in.

As I continued my report, Tom broke in; he said, "Sorry to interrupt, but I have some video capture that is relevant to what you're explaining."

I paused in my recounting of the ghost box session and said, "Go ahead."

Tom proceeded to tell us that during my ghost box session in the Missy bedroom, he had been watching the video monitor that had been placed in the second-floor hallway. He went on to explain that the video camera was positioned in such a way that it was able to view through the doorway of the bedroom I was in and also part of the room; the camera could see part of the bed but not me. Tom went on to say at one point he saw a dark figure move across the doorway inside the room toward the bed. I realized that if that had been a person walking where Tom explained, and headed in that direction, the person would have been directly behind me as I sat on the bed performing the live ghost box session. I immediately remembered that at one point a live spirit communication had come through the ghost box saying "behind you" in a low male voice. I waited until Tom had finished and then apprised the team of the message I'd received and its correlation to the video Tom had seen. Tom told me that the video was time stamped and that if we could narrow down the time that I received that particular live spirit communication and it coincided with the sighting Tom had on camera, it would be a very strong and validating piece of evidence.

I went on to finish my recap of the ghost box session. We did not elaborate on any experiences we'd had at this point in the investigation; this was simply a quick meeting to ascertain whether anyone had experienced anything they thought to be paranormal and to get an overall consensus of what we might be dealing with. It was now Sue's turn to give her account of her initial experience.

Sue began by saying, "There is definitely a presence here. What it is, or how strong it is, I don't know, but I definitely sense something." Sue went on to say that although her initial investigative efforts were uneventful as far as any tangible paranormal activity, she did record temperature fluctuations and EMF spikes. Sue concluded by saying, "Whatever is in this house, I don't think it wants us here."

Bill was up next; he had started his initial investigation with Tom on the third floor. Bill started with, "Tom and I went up to the third floor for our initial investigation. I had a digital voice recorder; I wanted to try some EVP captures. Tom had a handheld digital video camera and a still digital camera. We spent the first five or ten minutes looking around, checking out the rooms and the storage areas. Tom was on one side of the floor; I was on the other. I could see quick flashes of light, so I knew Tom was taking photos. I saw Tom walk into the playroom and continue to snap pictures. I walked into the bathroom at the far end of the hall. I looked around the bathroom and took an EMF reading; there was nothing to speak of in there except I did notice that it was cooler than the rest of the floor. I made my way to the bedroom that had been used by Danny and Christopher.

"As I was about to walk into the bedroom, I suddenly heard the faint sound of water running. It took me a couple of seconds to process it, in which time Tom came out of the playroom and asked me if I heard anything like water running. I said, 'Yeah, I hear it,' and we both followed the sound to the third-floor bathroom I had just left. As I entered the bathroom, I could plainly see that the faucet of the bathroom sink was running full on. Tom quickly asked me, 'Did you turn the water on and forget to shut it?' I told him I had not touched the faucet, and that the water had not been running a minute ago when I left the bathroom.

"I turned off the faucet, and both Tom and I stated at the same time, 'Wow, it's pretty cool in here.' I took out my temperature gun and stepped back out of the room, pointed the laser dot at a nearby wall and took a reading. The temp gun read 78 degrees F. I quickly stepped back into the bathroom and took a temperature reading; the temperature in the bathroom read 66 degrees F. Tom and I both noted the temperature variant. Tom snapped a few still pics and then turned on the handheld video camera and stepped back to get the whole bathroom into the camera's view.

"I decided to turn on the digital voice recorder and ask a few questions in hopes of capturing some EVPs. As the digital recorder began running, I asked, 'Is there anyone here in this room with us?' I allowed about ten or fifteen seconds for any response that may have been delivered. I then asked, 'Did you turn on the water faucet?' I allotted the same amount of time and proceeded to ask two or three more similar questions before turning off the voice recorder.

"We had been on the third floor for about fifteen or twenty minutes when Tom told me he was going to head downstairs to operations to check on the video and motion feeds. I told him to give me a call on the walkie when he needed me to come down. As Tom made his way down the stairs, I made my way back to the boys' bedroom. I walked in and turned on my EMF detector; the reading was midrange with quick up and down fluctuations, nothing to write home about. I decided to make some provocative statements to try to elicit some kind of tangible activity. Before doing so, I turned on my voice recorder and the handheld video camera Tom so graciously left with me. I placed the running voice recorder on a stool that was next to me and turned on the video camera, hit the record button, and began to scan the room back and forth slowly. I held the camera in one hand and picked up the voice recorder with the other.

"Now that I had audio and video covered, I stated in a semi-loud voice with a provocative tone, 'If you're here with me, show yourself, say something, let me know you're here.' I continued with, 'You're good at turning on little water faucets, but what else can you do? Even a little girl can turn on a water faucet.' No sooner did the words leave my mouth than the small stool I had just taken the voice recorder from started to vibrate, then shake. I took a few steps backward and aimed the video camera at the stool. Just as the stool came into view of the camera, it quickly slid along the floor about five or six feet and toppled over. I won't lie, it shook me up. I managed to keep my composure and silently commented to myself, 'I got that on video.' I guess whoever was there was not too happy with the little-girl comment.

"I gathered myself and my thoughts. The voice recorder continued to run. I picked up the small stool and placed it back in its original spot. As I proceeded to make a few more provocative statements, I decided to place the video camera on the stool, running, and take some still images. I snapped digital images of every area of the room. I made my way to the back of the room and went through the small open space that led to the storage area and snapped some pics there. It was pitch dark, and the repeated flash of the camera reminded me of a strobe light effect. In an instant when one of the camera flashes erupted, I was a bit startled by what I could have sworn was a dark figure in the far corner of the storage area. I backed my way out back into the bedroom, turned off the digital camera, and placed it in my pocket.

"As I walked over to the spot I had previously occupied, I was startled again by the crackle of my walkie-talkie; it was Tom informing me that we were all gathering in the operations room and to come down."

We were all excited to hear Bill's recounting of his experience on the third floor and were looking forward to reviewing all the data he'd captured, but that would have to wait. We still had a long investigation to conduct and tons more data to collect. Tom was last up; his account of the initial investigation was short and sweet. Tom told us other than the experience in the third-floor bathroom with Bill and the water faucet, and the anomaly on the video he'd seen during my ghost box session, his time had been uneventful. I stood up and said, "Ok, use the bathroom, grab something to drink, and let's get back to work." Sue walked toward the downstairs bathroom, Bill grabbed a water bottle, and Tom checked the video feeds and other equipment. Everyone had their new investigating locations and was on the move.

I grabbed my personal equipment bag and removed my alternate ghost box. I decided my next live ghost box session would take place in the master bedroom that had been occupied by George and Kathy Lutz. With my ghost box in hand, as well as my voice recorder, EMF detector, and temperature gun, I headed back up to the second floor. I entered the master bedroom at approximately 8:45 p.m. Upon entering, I had no uneasy feeling, the temperature was in sync with the rest of the floor, and now that it was twilight outside, the difference in illumination was not noticeable. There was a chair in the far corner of the room, facing the entrance. I decided to sit there to perform my live spirit ghost box communication session. The chair stood alone; there was no place for me to rest my ghost box and voice recorder. I promptly made my way back down to the operations room to retrieve a box for my equipment to sit on.

I walked into the operations room and looked around for a box or something I could use as a makeshift table. There were no cardboard boxes, so I took one of the empty equipment cases and headed back up to the master bedroom. I placed the equipment case next to the chair and placed the ghost box on it. I took no chances this time around and used the power cord for the ghost box. Before I started the live ghost box session, I decided to check the conditions in the room. I turned on my EMF detector and took a reading; there were nominal fluctuations but nothing out of the ordinary. I took a temperature reading; it was a comfortable 72 degrees. I proceeded to turn on my digital recorder and voice the initial session information, and placed it on the case next to the ghost box. I was ready to start my live ghost box session.

I knew from reports made by the Lutz family that there had been extensive paranormal activity in this bedroom. George Lutz had claimed at one point to have seen his wife levitate above their bed and transform from herself into an old hag woman, among other activities. I planned this session accordingly. I flicked the power switch on the ghost box, and it sparked to life. I noticed the radio signal reception at this time in this room was a bit better than that of my first ghost box session in the Missy bedroom. As always, I asked if my spirit technicians Mike and Lisa were present and able to assist with the session. I immediately received the response, "Here, Bruce." I acknowledged the response and said hello.

My first question was basically the same one I always asked. "Is there anyone there who would like to communicate with me today?" A few seconds passed, and I received the answer, "Me." Whenever I receive a response of "me" when asking for a communicating entity, I always follow it by saying, "I'm sorry, but I don't know who me is. Can you tell me your name?" Sometimes I will receive a name following that statement; sometimes I will not. This particular time I received the name "John." I remembered receiving the name John in the last ghost box session from a spirit entity claiming to be little John DeFeo. The voice that came through the ghost box to deliver the name John this time by no means belonged to a small child. The voice clearly gave the indication of being a full-grown adult male; it was deep in tone and forceful sounding.

I went on to ask, "Is this the same John I spoke to earlier tonight in Missy's bedroom?" There was no answer forthcoming. I altered the question and asked, "Is this John DeFeo who just told me his name?" I waited about fifteen seconds and was about to go on to my next question when a loud, clear, and strong "NO" came through the ghost box speaker. I replied, "I heard you say no; is this a different John?" I received the answer "yes." The voice that came through with these short one-word responses was a male voice but altered in its pitch and tone, giving the impression that it may have been different entities who were delivering the communication. I knew by experience that this was not necessarily the case. Because the ghost box supplied the communicating entity with a cacophony of jumbled sound fragments with which to form the communication, I knew that it was possible for the same entity to deliver communication in different-sounding voices. A single entity could even deliver, say, a four-word phrase and have two of the four words delivered in a male voice and the other two in a female voice depending on the sound fragments that were available to the communicating entity at the moment of formation of the live spirit communication.

I was relatively certain at this point that the communication I was now receiving was not being sent by the same spirit entity I had spoken with in my last ghost box session in the Missy bedroom. I knew from the reports of encounters and experiences with a malevolent entity by Ronald DeFeo Jr. and the Lutz family what type of entity I could possibly be dealing with. I decided to continue this live ghost box session with extreme caution. I called on my spirit technicians Mike and Lisa to render any and all the protection it was in their power to give to me and my team members. As spirit techs and dear friends, I knew they would employ whatever energy and power they could to guard against any negative incidents that were aimed at my team and me. I had learned early on from ongoing communication with my spirit techs that a significant part of their job was to protect against negative entities and negative energy that attempted to infiltrate a live ghost box session; however, I was not really sure how much assistance they could provide concerning an evil entity that was in the Amityville house here in the physical world. I also did not know if the alleged evil entity was a spirit or demonic in nature. If the entity was the disgruntled spirit of a former human being, interaction with it would be completely different from that of a demonic presence.

I continued my ghost box session. "John, are you the spirit of someone who lived a physical life?" I heard the answer, "Yes." My next question was, "John, can you tell me your full name?" I did not hear any response; actually, I noticed at that moment that I was not hearing the usual random words of attempted spirit communication that were common and always present during a live ghost box session. I repeated my question. This time I received what I believed to be an attempt by John at an answer, but I was unable to understand it live as he delivered it. I stated, "John, I did not understand you; can you repeat your answer and try to get it through more clearly?" As I listened for his response, a loud and very angry growl came through the ghost box, "ARRRGH." Hearing this, I paused for a second and asked, "John, was that you who made that sound?" I heard the answer, "Yes." I followed with, "Are you angry?" I knew the entity was frustrated with not only my repetitive questions, but also with the fact that he was not familiar with communicating through a ghost box. He responded with what I heard as, "Too many." There was more to his response, but I was unable to hear it all live. Normally with a regular spirit exchange through the ghost box, my spirit techs would assist the communicating entity in the formation and delivery of their communication. They would either assist the communicating entity to form the communication on their own, or they would in the most difficult instances relay the communication from the struggling entity by forming it and delivering it themselves.

I had come to realize that this was not an ordinary live ghost box session. I had not received the familiar interaction from Mike and Lisa that I was used to in a normal session; they were noticeably quiet, which made me a bit uneasy. I had to try to keep the communication with this entity John going; after all, this was what I was here for. At the risk of further exacerbating the situation, I continued with, "John, I'm sorry, but I did not catch all of that communication. Can you repeat it?" A few seconds later the now familiar male voice came through with, "Too many times," and then the word "answered." I surmised that John was telling me that he had already answered my request for a full name and that I was asking the same question too many times. Taking John's feelings into account, I, unfortunately, had to ask again. This time I asked, "John, can you please just tell me your last name, your surname?" hoping that it would be easier for him to communicate and easier for me to hear live. I allowed a longer period of time before my next question in order to give John ample time to send his last name. About twenty seconds passed, and I was able to discern an attempt at communication but yet again did not understand it clearly. I decided that rather than ask John to once again state his last name, I banked on the chance that the attempted communication I recognized was the communication of his name and that I would find it and recover it in my review of the session recording.

Part of the reason I pressed for John to give me his full name was that I had recalled an individual whose name was John who was associated with the Amityville property before the construction of the house I was now investigating, and that this individual was allegedly involved in nefarious and demonic activity perpetrated on the property. I wanted to see if I could establish that the spirit entity I was communicating with was the same individual in those reports. Of course, like almost every carefully planned ghost box session, this one, because of the received communication and circumstances that occurred during the performance of the session, forced me to throw the session plan out the window and improvise as the session progressed.

My next question to John was, "John, did you live here?" I received the answer, "Yes." I then asked, "Did you live in this house?" I received the simple answer, "No." I paused for a second to mentally form my next question before verbalizing it. I had not remembered at that moment that spirit entities sometimes have the ability to, during a live ghost box session, receive the ghost box operator's thoughts and actually know the intended question or statement before the operator actually speaks it. I have experienced this phenomenon countless times over the years and had formulated the theory early on that the physical and cerebral energy of the ghost box operator that is emitted during a ghost box session can be picked up and deciphered by a spirit entity who is interacting with the operator, thus allowing the entity to know the intended question or statement that the operator is about to deliver. I called this "precognitive spirit communication."

Before I could state my next question, I received the answer of, "Yes, I did," through the ghost box. I heard this live and realized it was an instance of precognitive spirit communication. My question to the entity John was to be, "Did you live on this land?" which John answered before I could ask it. My next question would have been to state John's full name and ask if it was, in fact, that individual whom I was communicating with; however, for the life of me, I could not recall the full name of the individual who had reportedly occupied the land before the Amityville house was built and who allegedly practiced demonic rituals here. Knowing I could not very well put John on hold to go and refresh my memory with his full name, I decided to pause and call Tom on the walkie-talkie and ask him to retrieve the name and to call me back with it. Tom agreed, and I waited for his response.

As I sat there waiting for Tom to render the name, I was able to hear garbled voices and spirit communication attempts as they came through the speaker of the ghost box. In this short period of time, which seemed like an eternity, two words came through the box that I could understand clearly. The first was my name "Bruce" delivered in a male voice; when I heard it, I responded, "Yes, I'm here; go ahead." The next word came in the faint voice of a child; it said simply, "Help." I could not help feeling a rush of empathy for that entity; however, my experience has taught me not to take every live spirit communication at face value.

Not five seconds after hearing that pathetic cry for help, and before I could respond to it, my walkie-talkie crackled, and Tom's voice came through. He gave me the name I was searching for; I thanked him and put away the walkie. I had to decide whether I would address the request for help or resume my communication with the entity John. Since the entity John was coming through loud and clear and his communication could be vital to drawing a conclusion as to what was plaguing the Amityville house, I decided to pursue my efforts with John and address the plea for help later.

Now armed with the full name I needed, I called out to John, "John, are you still here and willing to communicate?" I received a casual but stern, "Yeah," followed by, "Here." John sounded a bit perturbed at having to wait for me to resume our interaction. I asked, "Are you John Ketchum?" In the few seconds that passed, I could swear that I heard the sound of a snicker come through the ghost box. I then received the answer, "Yes," in an uncommonly loud and gruff tone of voice. I realized at that moment that this was the first and only tangible evidence ever captured in the Amityville house confirming the identity of what was believed to be an evil entity residing in the home. My following questions, if answered by John, would shed even more light on the circumstances surrounding the reported activity at 112 Ocean Avenue.

"John, are you the spirit responsible for some of the activity in this house?" As I asked the question and before I received an answer, I could hear the sound of a child's voice faintly calling out in the background behind the sweep of the ghost box noise. That feeling of empathy returned and a twinge of regret from not acting on the child spirit's request for help immediately. I had made an experienced decision and would stick to it. As these thoughts and feelings ran quickly through my mind, I was able to hear a response from John to my current question. The response was, "Me, yes, all me." Before I could ask my next question, a loud, booming, and angry voice came through the ghost box speaker; it shouted, "GET OUT!" I was taken aback a bit. I immediately responded with, "John, did you just tell me to get out?" The response to this was in the same angry voice: "DIE." At this point I realized that what had been up to now a relatively civil interaction had turned ugly.

As I contemplated my next action, I became aware that the temperature in the room had fallen dramatically; given the immediate circumstances of the live session, I was not about to stop and start taking temperature readings. I did, however, know there was a real and noticeable change in the temperature of the room. The chair I sat in while performing the ghost box session faced the entrance of the room, which led to the second-floor hallway. Out of the corner of my eye, I caught a glimpse of a black silhouette standing in the doorway. I quickly snapped my head in that direction to confirm my view, only to see that the doorway was clear of any anomalies. I did remember, however, that there was a video camera situated in the hallway facing the entrance to the room and hoped that it had caught whatever it was that I saw. About a minute had passed since I received the communication "die." I gathered my thoughts and fired my next question. "John, I thought we were having a nice conversation. Why would you tell me to get out and die?" This question was not off the cuff; it was meant to provoke a greater response from John and to possibly be the catalyst for some other form of paranormal activity.

I awaited a response and/or reaction from John. The ghost box was running effortlessly and receiving a strong radio signal. As I waited for a reply from John to my somewhat provoking question, I noticed the bedroom door moved ever so slightly. This could be attributed to a few things: a draft in the room, vibration, even the unfelt motion of an old house trying to get comfortable. I made a mental note of it and turned my focus back to the ghost box. I felt at that moment that an answer to my last question was not immediately forthcoming, so I reiterated my previous question. "John, why would you tell me to get out and die?" After a few seconds, a male voice came through; it was low and guttural in tone and very to the point. "My land." I was able to hear this ominous spirit communication live, and I responded with, "John, we are not going to stay here, we are only visiting." To that statement came the repetitive reply of "GET OUT," this time delivered in a higher pitched and more aggressive voice. It became very obvious that the spirit entity John was finished with any semblance of civil interaction.

I decided to end the ghost box session for fear that further prodding by me might diminish any chance of further live spirit ghost box communication from John Ketchum. I turned off the ghost box and the recorder and rose from the chair I was sitting in at the far corner of the room. I started to walk towards the door on my way down to the operations room. I was about two or three steps from the entrance when the bedroom door swiftly and abruptly slammed shut with a loud bang. I stopped in my tracks; the flashlight I had turned on to help me find my way in the dark began to flicker and then go out. I shook the flashlight in a vain attempt to get it working, but my effort was fruitless. I didn't mind admitting that even with all my years of paranormal experience and considering myself to be pretty much unshakable, I was scared.

I took a couple of steps in the same direction I was facing. I reached out in the darkness and felt the door. I fumbled around for the doorknob and finally grasped it, fully expecting the door to refuse to open. I tugged on it; the door swung open freely. I could see the hallway bathed in faint ambient light that was entering through the hallway window. I clutched my ghost box, quickened my steps, and reached for the banister of the staircase. As I did this, the flashlight, which I was still holding and minutes ago had gone completely dead, beamed to life and illuminated the downward set of stairs in front of me. I breathed a short sigh of relief and made my way down the stairs.

As I stepped onto the first-floor landing and turned left to head into the operations room, I saw a figure standing directly next to the operations table but out of the field of illumination coming from the active video monitors. I immediately assumed this was Tom or Bill checking the data-collecting equipment. I looked down for a split second in order to place my ghost box and the flashlight on the table, and when I looked up again, I was alone in the room. I looked around, scanning the room in search of the person I just saw standing almost directly in front of me; the room was empty.

I glanced at my watch, which should have read about 9:45 or 10:00 p.m., but the time on my watch was exactly 3:15 a.m. I knew the watch had not stopped because I was looking at it when the time turned to 3:16 a.m.; the watch was running. I thought for a second. Did I bang it against something as I fumbled for the doorknob a few minutes ago? Did I inadvertently hit one of the adjustment buttons? I couldn't be sure. I did know, however, that it would take a few steps entailing the use of a couple of the settings buttons on the watch to alter the time so dramatically. I stood up and checked the time stamp on one of the video monitors; it read 9:51 p.m. I proceeded to set my watch back to the correct time and waited for the other team members to arrive in the operations room.

As I sat there waiting, I decided to flick on my ghost box, which was sitting right next to me on the table. I retrieved the voice recorder from my pocket and turned it on. I hit record and placed it next to the ghost box. In my experience, an impromptu ghost box session often produced good results. I turned on the ghost box and lowered the volume a bit so as not to disturb any of my team members who might have been within earshot. The box began to sweep. I asked, "Are there any spirits here who would like to communicate?" I avoided asking for John Ketchum directly.

From the chaotic sound of the ghost box sweep came a familiar voice and name. "Me, Lisa." I enjoyed communicating with Lisa; she would always make the extra effort to deliver her communication in a female voice and try to make the voice as pleasant as possible. I actually harbored a little secret about Lisa: over the years and all the time I have spent communicating with Lisa during live ghost box sessions, I had developed a slight schoolboy crush on her. I had often imagined her to be around thirty-five, sandy-colored hair, slim, with the air of a Sunday school teacher about her. I often found myself using a sort of flirtatious tone when communicating with her. I kept this to myself, but could not help but be reminded of it every time I spoke to her. Hopefully, I would get to meet her when I made my transition to the next existence.

I responded with, "Hi, Lisa, how are you, sweetheart?" Usually, I would receive a response letting me know she was doing ok, but this time she responded in a highly excited and almost panicked tone of voice. She said only two words: "Bruce, danger." No sooner did she deliver that communication than the sound of the ghost box changed from a normal and fluid ghost box sweep to a rumbling and growling sound buried in the middle of static white noise. I realized what was happening: the evil presence in the house was infiltrating and domineering the ghost box. I didn't fear for Mike or Lisa because, one, they were in the spirit realm on the other side and the malevolent entity was here in the physical world in this house, and two, I believed they, as experienced spirit technicians, were more than capable of handling the situation should the need arise.

I did something next that I try never to do during a live ghost box session. I lost my cool. I turned off the ghost box and proceeded to slam my fist on the table and shout, "That's enough. I will not allow you to dominate this investigation." This type of outburst on my part was not a good idea. It was a direct and aggressive challenge to a spirit entity whom I really knew nothing about; my only experience with him was during my previous live ghost box session and was basically negative and unsettling. I no sooner made my bold outburst than the voice recorder, one of my favorites, by the way, flew off the operations table, smashing against the dining room wall and shattering. It shocked me for a moment, and then I remembered the voice recorder held all the audio from my two ghost box sessions —irreplaceable data. I jumped to my feet to inspect the damage. Thankfully, the guts of the recorder were intact; only the recorder housing had smashed. This particular recorder, as well as my others, was equipped with a memory card, which was a safeguard to house the data in the event of damage to the recorder's hard storage device, so even if the audio recordings from the unit itself were unrecoverable, the data could be retrieved from the memory card.

With a sigh of bittersweet relief, I gathered up the pieces and placed them on the table; the recovery of the recordings would be Tom's job. As I sat back down, it dawned on me: what if this aggressive entity would have thrown my ghost box and not the small voice recorder? This would have been an irreplaceable loss; this was a custom ghost box, one of a kind. I swallowed hard and thanked the powers that be that it was not the ghost box. I promptly placed it in my equipment case for safekeeping. All this commotion had alerted my other team members to a potential problem, and one after the other they hastily appeared in the operations room.

Tom was the first to arrive. "Hey, are you ok? I heard some loud noise and shouting."

I assured him I was ok and started to render an explanation when Bill and Sue arrived; both inquired if everything was alright and asked what had happened. I explained the incident that had just occurred, and they seemed to be concerned and excited at the same time. Tom suggested that from now on we set up a camera either in or overlooking the operations room just in case something tampered with the equipment either with or without one of us being present. I agreed that was a good idea. I took a breath and said, "Now that we are all here, let's go over any noteworthy experiences in this last round of the investigation."

I went on to say that I would speak last and for Tom to go ahead.

Tom had decided to go back to the third floor. He went on to explain that he had chosen to go back up to the third floor not only because of the activity he and Bill had experienced there earlier, but also because he just had a gut feeling. Tom had arrived on the third floor with the intention of doing an EVP session and taking some video and still images. He had decided to employ the provocation technique where he would provoke any entities verbally that may be present into reacting to his verbal prodding in hopes of capturing any paranormal activity perpetrated by said entities. Tom explained that he'd turned on his digital voice recorder, which he had attached to a short lanyard around his neck. He had thought of the hanging recorder idea on a previous investigation where he had encountered activity while holding a running voice recorder and was unable to hold the recorder and operate a still or video camera simultaneously, a great idea to which we were all subscribed; however, we were all still waiting for Tom to craft one for each of us. Tom concluded his short report by saying that his time on the third floor had been uneventful and that he would have to wait and review the audio and visual data he'd collected to see if he'd captured anything he was not physically aware of.

Bill and Sue went next. Bill stated that he and Sue had decided to investigate the basement together. Sue looked at Bill, and he looked back at her and asked, "Would you like me to explain?" Sue nodded, and Bill began recounting the last hour or so spent in the Amityville house basement. Bill explained that he and Sue had decided she would initially take atmosphere, EMF, and temperature readings, then turn on a digital voice recorder and sit in the space known as "the Red Room" to perform an EVP session. With a stationary video camera covering most of the basement, there would be little need for handheld video, so Bill decided to place a couple of target objects and an interactive object around the room and have his still digital camera at the ready. Target objects are inanimate items that are placed in certain spots around a room in an attempt to elicit paranormal interaction with the object such as having a ball be moved or rolled. Interactive objects are usually electronic items that can be manipulated by a spirit entity, like a flashlight that can be turned on and off, or a K2 meter that can have its light indicator go up and down.

Bill went on to say that one of the target objects he had placed was a rubber ball about twelve inches in circumference at the center of the room. He sat quietly and spoke in a low-level tone of voice, asking for any spirits who may be there to roll the ball or move one of the other objects; about thirty-five minutes had passed with no activity at all. Bill could hear Sue's muffled voice asking questions for her EVP session. Normally the room would be dark during the investigation; however, since there were the target and interactive objects to be visually monitored, Bill had set up a low-light-level lantern, which supplied enough light for him to see the objects placed about the room. Bill told us he had placed a K2 meter a few feet to his right and that he noticed a quick fluctuation in the meter's colored light indicator. He focused his attention on the meter and asked in a low tone, so as not to pollute Sue's EVP session with his voice, "Did someone just activate the electronic meter here? If so, can you do it again?" He immediately followed with, "The meter has colored lights; can you make them move?"

Bill readied his digital camera and pointed it in the direction of the K2 meter. No sooner did he get the camera up than the lights on the K2 meter went from white at one end to red at the other and back again. Bill started snapping digital still photographs one after the other in the direction of the meter. As he did this, his attention was caught by the rubber ball. It rolled about three feet directly toward him. Bill turned quickly to the area of the ball and snapped more photos. It was not a common practice for an investigator to immediately review any data, audio or visual, on the spot during their live investigation, but Bill decided to quickly scroll through the pics he had just taken to see if there was anything blatantly apparent in any of them. The main reason we try not to immediately check any of the data we captured while still in the act of conducting the investigation is simple: if the investigator focuses his or her attention on looking at or listening to any suspected evidence captured, they run the risk of potentially missing any paranormal activity that may occur during that time. Regardless, Bill scanned the photos he had just acquired. As he looked at them, he stopped on one photo that showed what looked like a gray mist in the shape of a human form standing over the rubber ball. The rest of the photos showed nothing apparent.

When Bill finished checking the photos, Sue emerged from the crawl space known as the Red Room and walked over to where Bill was sitting. She leaned back against the paneled wall and asked in a low voice, "Anything?"

Bill replied, "Oh yeah," and then asked, "You?"

Sue replied, "I think so." As she prepared to give him a short explanation, they heard a loud noise and muffled yelling coming from upstairs on the first floor; that was when they decided to leave the basement and check on what was happening.

After Bill had given his account of the events of his and Sue's investigation, he turned to Sue and asked, "So what did you experience? When I asked, you said you thought so. What did that mean?"

Sue explained that as she was doing her EVP session in the

Red Room, she felt a sudden chill as if someone had turned on an air conditioner. She said a few seconds later she believed she heard a faint child's voice whisper in her ear; it said, "Hi." She admitted that at that moment she experienced a severe case of goosebumps, and the hair on the back of her neck tingled. I stated that we would have to pay extra close attention when reviewing the data from Bill and Sue's basement investigation.

It was now my turn to tell my tale of the master bedroom live ghost box session I had performed. I began by saying, "I'm sure we can all agree that there are spirit entities present in this house." I received a unanimous YES. "Ok, I performed my live ghost box session in the master bedroom on the third floor." I went on to explain that I had received some great eye-opening live spirit communication, and that I had experienced some disturbing poltergeist activity. As I recounted the events of my ghost box session and the ensuing activity, my team members listened intently with open mouths. I told them I believed the spirit entity who had communicated with me and perpetrated the activity I experienced was that of the original owner of this property, John Ketchum. I went on to say that the communicating entity confirmed through ghost box communication that he was, in fact, John Ketchum and that he did not want us here. I finished giving the details of my encounter with the disgruntled spirit and asked for opinions.

Tom was the first to offer one. He said, "I for one definitely believe there is a malevolent presence in this house. I also believe there are other spirits grounded here who have no evil intentions."

Bill spoke and pretty much reiterated what Tom had said.

Sue weighed in last with her opinion of the events so far. "I think there are entities here; however, that being said, I think we should reserve judgment on who exactly those spirit entities might be." Although Sue had the least experience of all of us, she had a keen sense of the paranormal and had taken to paranormal investigation like a duck to water.

I stated that I agreed with Sue, and that our efforts from this point on should focus on gathering evidence of the actual identities of the spirits in residence here and what their intentions were. All agreed. I suggested we take an hour break and recoup, have something to eat, and relax. The next phase of the investigation would start at 11:30 p.m.

CHAPTER FOUR

THE EVIL ENTITY JOHN KETCHUM IN THE BOWELS OF THE AMITYVILLE HOUSE

I glanced at my watch; it was 11:35 p.m. Sue was checking photos on her digital camera. Tom and Bill were seated at the end of the table, talking casually.

I sat up in my chair, raised my arms, and stretched. "Ok, gang, it's time to get to it." Before we all dispersed to our desired locations, I told everyone we would investigate until 1:30 a.m. and then meet back here in the operations room for a short debriefing.

All agreed, grabbed their respective equipment, and headed out of the room. I retrieved my number one ghost box from its case, grabbed the rest of my equipment, and headed to the basement. My intention was to contact and communicate with the spirit entities who created the activity Bill and Sue had experienced earlier. I quickly called Bill on the walkie and asked if he had left his target and interactive objects in the basement. He informed me that he had taken the K2 meter but had left the target objects, consisting of a ball, a teddy bear, and ten children's wooden alphabet blocks, on the floor in the middle of the main room. I thanked him and signed off.

I made my way to the basement, making sure my flashlight and the rest of my equipment had full batteries and were in working condition; all was well. I made my way down the basement stairs, flashlight illuminating the way. As I reached the bottom of the stairs, I paused to get a feel for the room: nothing out of the ordinary, the temperature was about normal for a basement, and no abnormal physical feelings. I shined the flashlight in the direction of the floor in the middle of the room; there sat the target objects Bill had left as if they were simply waiting for ethereal hands to play with them. I scanned the whole room with the flashlight and noticed that Bill had also left the low-light lantern that he used. It was on the floor at the far end of the room. I walked over to the lantern and turned it on; the immediate area became bathed in a dim yellow white light.

There was no furniture in the basement, so I would have to sit on the floor. I took a seat and placed my ghost box and video recorder directly in front of me. I had a small equipment bag that I wore around my waist, really just a glorified fanny pack. I used it to carry my EMF detector, a temperature gun, and a few other small essentials. I took out my EMF detector and took a reading: nothing extraordinary. I pulled out the temperature gun and fired the laser beam at the far wall: 70 degrees, cool but comfortable. I was aware of the running stationary video camera that was placed opposite me in the left corner of the room and knew it had a good field of view and would capture anything abnormal in the room. I sat quietly for a moment before initiating my live ghost box session. I had suddenly recalled the basement scenes from the movie *The Amityville Horror*. At that moment the fleeting thought of, *Please don't let anything like that happen to me*, did cross my mind, only for a second though.

I focused my attention back on the task at hand. I picked up my digital voice recorder and flicked it on, held it up, and stated, "This is Bruce Halliday, Amityville house basement live ghost box session number three." I placed the recorder next to the ghost box and turned the ghost box on. The sound of the ghost box sweep was predominantly white noise with intermittent bursts of sound fragments. This was to be expected due to the fact that I was in a basement, not the ideal place for radio reception. I decided to move around the room with the ghost box in an attempt to find a more suitable spot where the ghost box would pick up a better signal. I walked the perimeter of the room, and in the corner opposite where I started, I found a spot that delivered the best reception possible in this basement. I could now hear that the ghost box had the sound of a normal sweep but still contained more static white noise than average. I parked myself and my ghost box there. I knew I would have less of a chance of understanding any live spirit communication that may be delivered due to the extra white noise interference; this was an occupational hazard I have dealt with on countless occasions. I still had a clear view of the whole room; however, the stationary video camera did not have a view of me. For the sake of receiving better radio signal reception, I would have to be absent from the video for the duration of the live ghost box session. I was now ready to begin the session.

I, of course, asked for my spirit technicians Mike and Lisa, and as I listened intently, I heard a male voice say, "Mike here." I acknowledged it by responding with, "Hey, buddy." I next heard the response of "Lisa. Hi." It was buried in static noise, but I was able to catch it. I greeted Lisa and thanked them both for overseeing the ghost box session.

My next question was the generic one that usually followed my confirmation of Mike and Lisa's presence. "Are there any entities here who would like to communicate?" I let the twelve seconds elapse without hearing an attempt at a response. I repeated the question, but still no response. I decided to try to elicit communication from whichever entity had manipulated the target objects during Bill and Sue's basement investigation. I made a statement out loud. "Any spirits who are here with me, you can use this device in front of me to speak to me," followed by, "Can the spirit who moved the ball earlier speak to me using the device making the sound?" As I listened for any response, I saw the rubber ball, which was on the floor directly in front of me, move about six inches. While I focused my attention now on the ball, a loud childlike voice came through the ghost box, which sounded like "Ha haaaa." I heard this loud and clear and immediately went back to concentrating on the ghost box session. I said, "I heard you laugh," and then asked, "Was that you who rolled the ball?"

After a few seconds, a timid voice came through the speaker. "Yes, me."

My next question was the obvious one. "Can you tell me your name?" I heard what sounded like the same child's voice attempting to answer, but I could not understand what was said. I asked again, and this time I received the response of "John Matthew." I heard Matthew live but not John. My next question was to confirm the previous communication. "Is this John Matthew DeFeo?" In the same child's voice, I heard, "Yes, me, me." I acknowledged hearing little John's answer.

At this point, I was hoping I could continue my communication with little John and not have it interrupted or interfered with by the aggressive entity John whom I had dealt with in my previous ghost box session. I was aware that the video camera now to my right was active, so I asked little John—I had decided to refer to this child entity as "little John" because the other disgruntled entity was also named John—if he would please move the ball again or play with one of the other objects on the floor. I kept my ear on the ghost box and my eye on the target objects. After a few seconds, as I watched, the small teddy bear that was sitting upright next to the wooden blocks fell over on its side. I immediately said in a somewhat loud voice, "Good, John, very good." I then asked, "John, that was you who moved the teddy bear, right?" I promptly received the answer, "Yes, me," followed immediately by, "Like it." I was surprised by the fact that I was able to hear and understand as much of little John's communication as I did, given the poor sweep conditions and extra static white noise, but hey, never look a gift horse in the mouth.

Before I could continue with my next request of little John, a loud and angry male voice came booming through the ghost box speaker and said, "NO MORE!" When I heard this, I knew the malevolent entity John had discovered my and little John's inter-action. I became somewhat deflated, and my emotions went from the anticipation of further communication and activity with the child spirit to more somber and serious. As I was about to address this communication from John of "no more," I heard the voice of little John in the background shout, "Mommy." I then heard a couple more attempted words by little John that I did not under-stand, as his voice became fainter and then nonexistent. At this point, I knew this live ghost box session would go one of two ways: either John would concede to a back-and-forth interaction of communication, or he would growl out short one- and two-word, anger-fueled responses to anything I said or asked. The next few minutes would determine whether I continued with this live ghost box session or would have to bring it to a premature end.

I decided to elicit my spirit technicians in an attempt to garner their assistance in my dealings with John. I asked them to protect against any negative energy that might be used to infiltrate and otherwise disrupt the session, and I asked that they extend that protection to the spirit little John and help guard against any negativity directed toward him. I heard what I believed to be an attempted response by my tech Mike. I was unable to understand it and knew the entity John was managing to impede my spirit techs' efforts to deliver their communication. I realized that if his negative influence was strong enough to muffle the attempts of my technicians to communicate, he was stronger than I thought. However, any spirit entity, be it negative or not, does not have an endless supply of energy. A spirit attempting any activity in the physical world, be it audible or the manipulation of physical objects, needs to expend energy. In doing so, their energy becomes depleted and needs to be restored, like recharging a battery. I would have to enlist all my experience during my interaction with John to try to gauge his level of energy. If I could recognize when his energy reached low levels, I could take advantage of that period of time to attempt communication with my spirit techs and with the spirit of little John. Keeping this in mind, I decided to try to get John to use as much of his energy as I could.

My first comment directed at John was a request. "John, if you are here with me, show me you are here and move one of the objects that are on the floor in the middle of the room." I focused my attention on the target objects. I watched intently for around a minute, but nothing moved. I then asked John, "Are you stopping the child who is here from communicating with me?" After a second or two, came the forceful response, "Yes, I am." This communication was loud and clear. "John, can you tell me why you will not let the child communicate with me?" John then repeated his earlier response of, "No more," which I heard clearly. To further my plan of trying to get John to deplete his energy by sending a strong anger-fueled response or perpetrating some other type of poltergeist activity, I structured my next question to antagonize the already disgruntled entity. "John, are you afraid of the child? Or are you jealous of him?" That did the trick! A booming and guttural sound came through the ghost box. "ARGHHHH." This loud growl was followed by a loud and forceful bang on the wood-paneled wall directly to my right. I knew it was not a very good idea under ordinary circumstances to provoke what was believed to be a negative and potentially evil entity, but these were not ordinary circumstances, and this was certainly not an ordinary paranormal investigation.

During the time that this activity was taking place, I realized I had not heard anything through the ghost box that remotely resembled communication or an attempt at it. The ghost box sweep was steady and still receiving a decent signal. I was relieved at that. I could only surmise that the entity John had enough energy to dominate the session and hinder any attempts at communication by other spirit entities. I had to continue my campaign to drain the malevolent entity's energy. I decided to speak to John as if I were speaking to a physical person who was in the room with me. "John, come on, calm down. Why are you so angry?" After a few seconds passed, I heard the answer, "Off my land," followed by, "NOW," a second later. Keeping with my plan to have John drain his energy without him realizing that was my intention, I stated, "This is no longer your land, and we are not leaving until we are finished here."

As I sat there rigidly awaiting John's next response, I received what felt like a sharp but not very forceful slap across my left cheek. It was not enough to hurt me, but it did startle me and cause me to assume a defensive posture. I had not been on the receiving end of a physical attack by an entity in a long time, and frankly, I was not expecting or prepared for this slap. It took a moment for me to regain my composure and thoughts. What was my next move, did I provoke John further, did I try to defuse the situation, or did I abruptly end the ghost box session and return to the operations room? I decided to do none of the above. I assumed a calm but concerned demeanor. I knew I had to address the attack and try to do it in a way that would not provoke another physical response. All my experience had told me that at this point the right thing to do would have been to conclude the ghost box session and remove myself from the basement. I also knew this would put a checkmark in John's victory column and strengthen his resolve. I had waited too long for this investigation to let some harsh responses and a little slap in the face deter my efforts. I stayed put.

I was ready to address John again. "John, did you just hit me?" I heard what sounded to me like an almost smug, "Yes," as if he was proud of what he did and wanted me to know it. At this point I had two options: I could respond to his answer with a sarcastic and antagonistic response, keeping to my plan to have him use his energy, or I could ignore his obviously condescending answer and try to move in a different direction. If I gave a sarcastic response, I could be risking further physical reprisal. Since I was not sure of the extent of John's power, I decided to try to respond generically and try to gauge John's current energy level. I said, "John, let's both try to be gentlemen and treat each other civilly." I awaited his response through the ghost box, but none was sent. I continued, "John, since we both know you are capable, can you please move one of the objects on the floor?" I watched the target objects intently. As I did, I heard an answer of, "Yes," come through the ghost box, followed by the rubber ball that was lying there suddenly flying across the room and hitting the wall. I was actually elated by this because I knew everything was being recorded on the live video camera placed in the corner of the room, not only visual but audio as well, which would serve as a validation of the communication I received through the ghost box.

It seemed by his displays of physical activity that my efforts to have John deplete his energy supply were in vain, but then I heard a male voice come through the ghost box that was music to my ears. It said, "Bruce, here." I instantly knew it was my spirit technician Mike; he was able to get his communication through clearly enough for me to hear and understand it live. This was an indication that contrary to my last thought, John's energy was fading. I did not acknowledge Mike's communication. I did not want to alert John to my directing my attention away from him. Mike had simply seized the opportunity to let me know he was still with me and would understand my lack of a response.

I continued to engage John. "John, that was great, nice job." I did not hear a response, nor did I expect him to respond to that statement. I continued with, "John, have you been here long?" I waited. Just before I spoke my next question, I heard the answer of, "Yes," come through the box. It was John responding, but his tone and the forcefulness of his response had changed; it was somewhat subdued. I took this as another indication of his waning energy level. I knew I had to try to keep John engaged until he did not have enough energy to continue in this session let alone hinder any other communication between myself, my techs, and the spirit of little John.

I noticed some grumbling sounds among the sweep coming

from the ghost box. I asked, "John, are you still with me?" To this question I received the answer, "Yes, I am here." At the risk of again potentially invoking John's ire, I asked, "Are you ok, John? You sound tired." I did not receive a response to this question from John; however, I did receive a response in a female voice, whom I knew to be my spirit tech Lisa. She said one word that not only answered my question to John but gave me the gratification of knowing I had accomplished my goal. She uttered, "Weak." I knew John could not fuel his energy by drawing from my physical energy alone, and he would have to retreat from further interaction with me until he could either find a source to replenish his energy, or remain inactive until his energy level returned.

I looked at my watch. I had been in this session now for close to one hour and knew I was pushing the limits of a productive live ghost box session. In order for a live spirit ghost box session to work, there must be an exchange of energy between the ghost box operator and the participating spirit entities. This mutual energy exchange is what makes live spirit communication with a ghost box possible. I knew that even though my spirit technicians Mike and Lisa and the spirit little John were not actively sending or receiving communication for the majority of the session, they still had to keep the energy connection with me going. In doing so, they, like John, would be slowly depleting their supply of energy. This would start to hinder their ability to send and receive communication through the ghost box, hence giving the live ghost box session a limit on which it was productive.

I decided to continue the session in an attempt to garner whatever communication I could before conditions brought it to an end. My first statement was to thank Mike and Lisa for their efforts and for sticking with me and the session despite the circumstances. To this statement I received the response, "Love you, Bruce." I had heard this phrase many times before through the ghost box over the years, but it never failed to touch me.

My next question was directed at little John. "John Matthew DeFeo, are you still here with me?" After a few seconds, I received the answer, "Yes," in the familiar childlike voice he had been using. "Hi, John, are you ok?" He answered, "Yes." I knew I had to try to help this lost and frightened young spirit, help him to understand his situation, attempt to help him leave this house and move on to the spirit realm to be reunited with his family, and most of all help him escape the oppression of the evil spirit John Ketchum.

I asked little John, "John, do you know where you are?" It took a few seconds for him to respond. I received the answer, "Yes, home." I then asked, "John, is there anyone else here in the house with you?" With this question, I was hoping to receive an answer that would help guide my queries in the direction of finding out how many entities were present in the Amityville house and who they were. I waited for little John's response, and he said, "Yes, bad man." All the communications I had received from little John up to this point had a fearful air about them; however, these last few communications I received since the negative entity John had apparently left my location were somber yet sounded a bit more at ease and not so panicky, as if the spirit entity who obviously kept him in a state of fear and confusion was gone. When I say gone, I mean gone for the moment. I had no doubt that the evil spirit of John Ketchum would return with renewed energy and spoiling for confrontation. I did not know how long it would take for negative John to recharge and return, so I had to try to continue my communication with little John in the hopes of getting more information and helping him take his first steps to escape 112 Ocean Avenue.

I continued, "John, does the bad man hurt you?" To this question, I received the answer, "No, scared," immediately followed by, "I want Mommy." I was able to hear these communications live. Little John's shaky words tugged on my heart. I felt for him and felt a need to protect him, but my ability to do so was bound by the constraints of only being capable of helping little John through the communication of the ghost box. It wasn't like little John was a physical boy I could just pick up and carry from the house where evil dwelled, nor could I physically protect him from John Ketchum or elicit the help of law enforcement in the salvation of the situation. I was determined to help little John no matter the cost to me mentally, emotionally, or physically. To me, little John Matthew DeFeo was a child in trouble; his being a spirit was of no consequence.

I focused my attention on little John and said, "John, don't worry, I will do whatever I can to help you, but you have to promise to listen to me and pay attention, ok?" To this statement, I received the answer, "Yes, ok." Before I could continue, a voice I recognized as my spirit technician Mike came through. "Bruce." I replied, "Yes, I hear you; go ahead." The next words from Mike were all too clear. "He's coming back." When I heard Mike's communication, I felt a cold chill fill the room; my pulse quickened. I took a deep breath and let out a sigh of anxiety peppered with a bit of anger. I was not ready to lose communication with little John, and too mentally weary at this point to stand toe-to-toe with the freshly charged spirit of John Ketchum.

I heard mixed into the ghost box sweep the sound of a frightened child, accompanied by the now familiar guttural grumblings of the negative entity John. At that moment I decided I needed to recharge my energy supply, so I would end this session, which had already run too long, and pick up the fight at a later time, knowing that my next live ghost box session encounter with the spirit of John Ketchum would not find me alone but would be a session conducted with all of my team members present, lending all our combined positive physical energy to the encounter as well as that of my spirit technicians Mike and Lisa. I stated out loud that I was ending the live ghost box session and thanked Mike and Lisa for their assistance and protection. I turned off the ghost box and the voice recorder.

I stood up, picked up my ghost box, and headed for the target objects, which I intended to gather up and return to the operations room. As I reached the target objects, I bent over to retrieve them. When I looked down at the wooden children's blocks that were lying on the floor, they were placed in a straight line and spelled out the words "YOU DIE" in different colored letters. I glanced up at the running video camera and realized it should have captured the blocks being moved, but was not able to view the words that were spelled out due to the distance of the camera and the low-light conditions. I pulled my small digital camera from my equipment pouch and snapped a few pics of the ominous words constructed using the wooden blocks. It was ironic that a child's toy, so innocent and meant for fun, could be the catalyst for such an evil message. I gathered up the objects, flicked on my flashlight, and made my way over to the lantern that had helped illuminate the dark basement room. I switched it off and headed up the basement stairs.

I reached the operations room with my ghost box in one hand and an arm full of target objects. I placed the ghost box on the table and placed the bunch of target objects on the floor next to an equipment case. I sat down at the head of the operations table just as Tom was walking in. He said, "Hey, Bruce, you made it here before me."

I nodded and looked down at my watch; it was 1:19 a.m. I had told everyone to return to the operations room at around 1:30 a.m., so while Tom and I waited for Bill and Sue's return, Tom checked the video feeds and the video recorders to make sure there had been no glitches during our previous investigation; all were working well. I took ten or so minutes to shut my eyes and contemplate all I had experienced up to this point. As the events of the live ghost box session I had just performed ran through my mind, I could feel myself slipping in an out of a light sleep state. It was dark and quiet, and because I was relatively relaxed, my mind took these conditions as an opportunity to initiate sleep. I sat straight up in my chair, rubbed my eyes, and said, "Hey, Tom, you sleepy?"

Tom replied, "Yeah, I'm getting there." I decided that once Bill and Sue arrived at the operations room, barring any spectacular tales of paranormal experience, I would, before taking an account of their investigations, call for a four-hour sleep break. It had been a long day so far, and everyone had been emotionally and physically taxed, so a break and forty winks were in order. Normally on an investigation of this type, the team would sleep in shifts, two members investigating while the other two slept; however, in this instance I decided the best course would be for all of us to get some rest and recharge. Also, I intended to have a group live spirit ghost box session in the next stage of the investigation, which included all members of the team.

At 1:30 a.m. on the button Sue and Bill entered the operations room. Both of them looked tired and ready for a break. I told everyone, "Before we debrief, I want us all to get some sleep. It's 1:30 a.m. We will rest until 5:30 a.m., after which we can discuss the latest investigations and plan for the next phase."

All agreed. Tom set his cell phone alarm for 5:30 a.m. We all picked a spot, got comfortable, and shut our eyes.

I no sooner shut my eyes than I felt myself drifting off to sleep. I suddenly found myself walking slowly down the aisle of a big movie theater. It was an old-fashioned theater with big ornate chandeliers and long heavy curtains draping either side of a tremendous movie screen. The walls were red with gaudy gold molding, and the seats were covered in red velvet material. I could hear people talking but could not understand what they were saying. I reached the end of the aisle and turned to look for a seat. The theater was completely empty except for a single man sitting in the middle seat of the third row. I made my way into the row were the man was sitting, walked up to the seat next to him, and asked, "Is this seat taken?" The man was dressed in vintage clothing and wore a long black coat and a wide-brimmed black hat. As he turned his head to address me, I never got the chance to see his face. I immediately found myself back in the basement of the Amityville house, the very basement I had just left.

I was sitting on the floor in the middle of the basement, it was dimly lit, I did not have any equipment with me, and I had no awareness of being on a paranormal investigation. I looked down and noticed I was barefoot. When I looked up, I noticed there were three people standing quietly at the far end of the room; their details were obscured by shadow. I did, however, notice that the tallest of the figures was a male; the other two I instinctively knew to be women. Although I could make out very little detail about the three people, I did notice that the tall male figure had what looked like three long, thick bird feathers hanging down alongside his head and face. I tried to stand up, but it felt like I had lead weights tied to me. I could not get to my feet. I called out to the three figures, "Hey, can you help me? I can't get up." As I called out, the figure of the male turned to face me. He had what I could only explain as a look of chaos on his face, and his eyes were wild and crazy, darting back and forth. He opened his mouth widely to speak, but no sound came out. The next thing I knew, I was awakened by the loud beeping of Tom's cell phone alarm.

With somewhat blurry vision, I saw Tom reach for the cell phone and stop the alarm. He then asked, "Is everybody awake?" as he sat up straight and stretched.

We all took a few moments to rub the sleep out of our eyes and get our bearings. Sue was the first to her feet. "I'm getting a water; would anyone else like anything?" I declined. Tom was at the video monitors already and said, "No, thanks." Bill replied, "I'll take a water if you don't mind."

I got to my feet, feeling a slight twinge of pain shoot through my lower back. I guessed I was getting a little old for sleeping in chairs. I walked over to Tom, who was focused on what he was doing. I asked, "Is everything good?"

Tom replied, "Yeah, everything's working perfectly," followed by, "I had the weirdest dream."

"Really? I had an odd dream also."

"What was your dream about?" Tom asked.

I told him I had dreamt I was in the basement of the house, and there were three shadowy figures there with me. Now that I was awake and could contemplate the dream, my first impression was that the three figures were Native American.

Tom immediately responded, "Holy crap, me too," and went on to say, "Only in my dream there were two figures, a woman and a boy, and I was in the living room on this floor of the house. I couldn't make them out clearly but felt the impression that they were Indians."

Knowing Tom to be the joker of the team, I asked, "You're not just messing with me, are you?"

He answered quickly and firmly, "No way, man, that was my dream."

I walked over to a small folding table we had set up in the operations room that held water bottles, some basic snacks, and a large thermos of black coffee. I filled one of the small Styrofoam coffee cups that were sitting next to the thermos and walked back to my chair. As I sat there sipping the now lukewarm and bitter coffee, I thought to myself, *The two dreams Tom and I had could not be a coincidence. I mean, what are the odds of both of us having similar dreams, with similar figures, and a similar interpretation? I wouldn't want to bet anything valuable on the odds of it being a coincidence. It has to be something here in the house, a presence that infiltrated both our dreams, but who, what, and why?*

I was so deep in thought at this moment that I didn't hear Sue when she first called my name. She managed to snap me out of it when she called in a louder than normal voice, "Bruce!"

I looked at her and answered, "Yeah, what's up?"

She said, "I called you three times. Are you ok?"

I answered, "Yeah, yes, sorry, deep in thought."

Sue nodded understandingly. "What's the plan?" she asked.

I took a few seconds to gather my thoughts and stated, "Ok, everybody, I would like to do a group ghost box session." With the attention of my team, I went on to explain, "I would like to do a group box session in the living room area. I will conduct the ghost box session. Bill, I would like you to set up two additional video cameras at opposite ends of the room and take temperature readings and EMF levels during the session. Tom, you can have a digital voice recorder running to get a secondary session recording and capture any traditional EVP." It was always a good idea when feasible to run a second recorder, which could corroborate any live spirit communication received by the main voice recorder. "Sue, I want you to place some target objects and a K2 meter, monitor them, and keep your camera ready. Of course, we will observe the group ghost box session protocol. Ok, let's do what we have to do and meet in the living room in fifteen minutes."

CHAPTER FIVE

DEFEATING THE EVIL JOHN KETCHUM AND MEETING THE SHINNECOCK INDIAN SPIRITS

I grabbed my ghost box and digital voice recorder and headed to the living room to get a feel for the general atmosphere. As I left the operations room/dining room, I headed across the hall toward the living room. This extremely short walk took me past the first-floor staircase. As I was passing the staircase, I detected movement on the stairs out of the corner of my eye. I snapped my head to the right to look at the stairs, and as I did, I could see the figure of a child walking up the stairs toward the second floor. My first instinct was to grab my still camera; however, when I reached for my equipment pack, I realized I had left it in the operations room. I was not in the habit of removing my equipment pack from around my waist on an investigation, but we had been on a couple of hours' sleep break, and I had taken off the pack in order to be more comfortable. I turned and dashed back into the operations room to grab my camera. When I got back to the staircase, the figure, of course, was gone. I quickly made my way up the stairs to the second-floor landing and began to snap still photos of the second floor. After taking a couple of dozen photos, I made my way back down to the first floor and into the living room. I was disappointed in myself for forgetting my equipment pack, but I knew a missed opportunity of this measure would stay in my mind and help me not to make the same mistake again.

I entered the living room to find Bill setting up the extra video cameras and Sue placing various target objects around the room. I got their attention and told them about what I had just experienced.

Bill said, "Oh, I thought I heard running up the stairs."

I replied, "Yeah, that was me."

There was a small table and two chairs against the southeast wall of the living room, opposite the big fireplace. I decided to use this to perform the live ghost box session. I walked over and placed my ghost box on the table and plugged it into the electrical outlet that held the plug for a lamp that sat on the table. I took out my voice recorder and placed it on the table next to the ghost box. I decided to turn on the ghost box and check the signal reception in the spot I had chosen; in the event of poor reception, I would need to choose another spot. I sat down and flicked the ghost box power switch on. The box came to life. It had a strong and relatively clear sweep with an abundance of sweep sound fragments; the spot was ideal for the live ghost box session. I reached for the power switch to turn off the ghost box until we officially began the session. Before I could flick the switch, a loud and clear child's voice emanated from the ghost box speaker. "HELP!" was the only word delivered.

Both Bill and Sue immediately turned their attention in my direction. Bill stated, "Wow, I heard that loud and clear."

Sue jumped in with, "Yeah, a child asking for help."

I replied, "Yeah, that was pretty clear." I went on to say that I believed that was the spirit of the DeFeo boy John Matthew. I told them I had chosen to refer to this child entity as "little John" so as not to confuse things in the ghost box session recordings, being that the aggressive male entity's name was John also. We all agreed that the upcoming group ghost box session would be a very interesting and hopefully fruitful part of the investigation. With all the equipment and target objects set, we were ready to begin.

The way a group live ghost box session is performed is that one individual, the session operator, in this case me, controls the session by asking the majority of the questions and controlling the direction of the session. All other participants, in this case my three team members, will listen for any live spirit communication that is delivered and will ask questions and give responses only when asked to do so by the session operator. This protocol eliminates the possibility of group session members shouting out alleged spirit communication they believe they heard in a random and chaotic manner. Doing so would only serve to create confusion and add unnecessary verbal content to the session recording, which could be mistaken for spirit communication and pollute any live spirit communication that might have been in the process of being delivered by having their voice step on said communication.

I asked, "Is everyone ready?" I received three positive replies from my team members. I started my digital recorder and announced the live ghost box session information. I placed the recorder next to the ghost box and turned on the ghost box power. The ghost box crackled and began to emit a strong and steady sweep of broken-down radio broadcast sound fragments. I glanced at my watch; it was 5:51 a.m.

With the group's attention focused on their individual tasks as well as the live ghost box session, I asked my first question, which was always to confirm the presence of my spirit technicians Mike and Lisa. "Mike, Lisa, are you guys there and ready to assist with this session?" A couple of seconds passed, and the response of, "Yes, here," was delivered in a male voice through the ghost box. I heard this live and received a nod from all three team members, indicating they had also heard the response. It was very common for my spirit tech Mike to answer first. I never actually asked, but

I had the idea that Mike was the senior spirit technician; however, I never forgot to make sure I addressed Lisa as well after Mike's initial communication. "Lisa, are you there also?" I received the answer, "Yes, Bruce," in a female, but somewhat low-toned voice. I acknowledged both my techs and proceeded to ask my first session question. I had not prepared a special plan for this group session. So far in this investigation, the two sessions I had done could not have adhered to a session plan, so I decided to do this group session in a manner that I called a "freestyle session."

As the ghost box sweep sound filled the room, I asked my first session question. "Are there any spirit entities here or on the other side who would like to communicate?" I could hear the faint attempts of spirit communication intermingled with the sound of the ghost box sweep, my instinct, years of listening to a ghost box sweep and live spirit communication told me that those faint unintelligible voices were emanating from spirit entities on the other side trying to get their communication through. I could make out a word here and there but nothing understandable. I attributed this to the suppressive energy that must be coming from the negative entity John Ketchum. His influence in the house was obviously strong. It had been a few hours since my last encounter with John, quite enough time for him to recharge his energy supply while my team and I slept and recharged ours. I asked my spirit technicians Mike and Lisa to do the best they could to counteract the negative energy of John, and to try to protect myself, my team, and the child entity little John. I knew I would need all my concentration and all the positive energy of myself and my team to combat the negative energy of John.

I wanted my interaction with John in this session to be singular, so I asked my spirit techs to please block any outside communication from any entities who were attempting it, except, of course, any and all attempts by little John to communicate. My plan was to, one, get as much information as I could from the evil spirit John, and two, once again attempt to have him drain enough of his energy so that his stifling grip over this house and the spirit of little John could be eliminated, if only for a short time. This, if successful again, would allow me and my team the opportunity to communicate with little John. I apprised the team of my intentions for this session; they all nodded in acknowledgment.

I fired my first question to the evil spirit John. "John Ketchum, are you here in this room with us now?" A few seconds went by, and I heard an all-too-familiar-sounding response. "Yes, here," came through in the similar low gravelly voice John had employed in our previous ghost box sessions. I responded, "Hello, John, can we communicate with you?" We all listened for an answer; it came in the form of, "Yes, fools." I looked at my team members, who up until this point had not experienced actual live interaction with the malevolent entity John through the ghost box. They could now put a real and tangible voice to the spirit entity who had perpetrated most of the paranormal activity they had experienced so far. Being seasoned paranormal investigators, they were able to disguise their concern, but I noticed their facial expressions change from calm enthusiasm to stoic attention. I didn't believe they were prepared for the strength and forcefulness of the live spirit communication they just heard.

I replied to John's comment with, "John, come on, we all know there is only one fool here." My statement was an attempt to antagonize John; this hopefully would amp up his energy use. After my provocative statement, the response, "Not again," was followed by a sinister-sounding, "Ha, ha." I was afraid this would happen. John was a spirit but not a gullible one, he had figured out what I had perpetrated in my last ghost box session with him, and he let me know I would not trick him again. I was not about to change my plan. I knew through experience and gathered information from my years of live spirit ghost box communication that spirits can and do retain the feelings and emotions they carried while in their physical life. I also knew John was an angry, evil, and quick-tempered entity. Given enough prodding and poking, no matter what John knew about our tactics, he would let that anger and frustration explode, hence depleting his energy supply.

My next question to John was, "John, what do you mean 'not again'?" We waited a few seconds and received the response, "I'm not foolish." This comment from John came in a more forceful and aggressive tone. I realized John had a very short fuse, and it would not be long before he would lose control of his temper and lash out in anger. I gestured to Bill, letting him know that I wanted him to make a statement or ask a question. Bill nodded; as he poised to speak, a loud and growling voice came through the ghost box, "GET OUT!" Not only did we all hear this loud and clear, but I thought the neighbors did too.

Bill took a breath and fired the statement, "Who do you think you are ordering us to get out? We'll leave when we are good and ready." As we all awaited a response to Bill's arrogant statement, a glass vase that was sitting atop the fireplace mantel aggressively flew off its perch in Bill's direction and smashed on the floor only a couple of feet away.

We all jumped in our seats. Tom looked at Bill and said, "Whoa, that was close."

Sue followed by saying, "Yeah, too close." I nodded in agreement.

We all knew at that point we would have to ramp down our antagonistic attack on John and opt for a more lengthy and less aggressive campaign. It would take longer to accomplish our goal, but it might serve to prevent any further violent paranormal attacks and keep any further property damage to a minimum. We all realized this, but we also did not want John to think he had frightened us to the point where we were backing off. This would give John the upper hand and only accomplish the opposite of what we were trying to do. It would serve to strengthen John's energy as opposed to weakening it.

I gave Sue the nod to continue. I wanted to see how John would react to a woman attempting to interact. Sue nodded in understanding, took a moment to gather her thoughts, and then asked, "John, why are you so angry with us?" followed by, "We haven't done anything wrong," and then, "You're not a bully, are you?" As we listened intently for John's next response, we kept a close eye out for flying objects. About fifteen seconds had passed with no response from John heard through the ghost box and no poltergeist response either. Sue asked her next question. "John, do you not want to talk to me because I am a woman. Are you afraid of women?" John's response came almost immediately, "You're nothing," came across the ghost box speaker, almost in a low dismissing tone of voice.

I thought to myself at that moment that it was a good thing John was delivering his communication in two- and three-word answers as opposed to trying to deliver five -or six-word phrases or sentences, which would make the communication much more difficult to hear live as John delivered it. Lengthy communication that was not heard live in its entirety would serve to slow down the ghost box session and possibly have us misinterpret any part of a communication we were able to hear, thinking at the moment that it was the entire content of the communication.

This response by the entity John was obviously directed at Sue in response to her question. This answer by the spirit John Ketchum to Sue did not surprise me. Not only was this spirit entity mean and aggressive, but also lived in an era of time when women were considered inferior to men and merely dismissed as servants and objects of male pleasure, not like the present day where all people are considered equal, male and female alike.

Sue immediately fired back a response to John's comment. "I'm nothing? You're nothing, a sad rejected soul that needs to try to intimidate the living and the dead just to feel like a man." As soon as Sue's retort left her mouth, I, as well as my team members, knew it would be met with a forceful response, either verbal or physical. We all braced for John's response. A minute or so passed; we had not heard any verbal response come through the ghost box. I knew the entity John would not take that insulting comment by Sue lightly. My first thought was that John might be trying to exercise restraint in order to conserve his energy and quell our attempt to drain it, or maybe it would take a couple of minutes for the hammer to fall.

I had decided we had waited long enough. I was about to ask my next question when from the other room, the operations room, came a loud crashing sound that caused us all to stiffen up from the shock of it. We all jumped from our seats and ran to the operations room. I was the first to enter the operations room. As I did, I could see two of the four video monitors lying on the floor next to the table. One of them was still operating, and the other had a black screen. There did not seem to be anything else affected. Bill went over to the fallen monitors, picked them up, and placed them back on the table. The monitor that remained running was undamaged except for a small crack to its plastic housing. Bill concentrated on the one that had stopped functioning.

"Looks like this one is fried," said Bill. "Nothing we can do about it now."

I told everyone to return to the living room, and we would continue with the group session. As we were walking from the operations room back to the living room, I realized I had left my ghost box there unattended and running. I pushed past Tom and Sue, who were in front of me, and rushed into the living room. As I entered, I could see my ghost box was sitting right where I had left it and still running perfectly. I breathed a big sigh of relief. If the entity John had seen fit to take advantage of the situation and do harm to the ghost box, it would have been a great loss to me. It would not be just losing a piece of investigative equipment, it would have been the loss of a personal device that I had worked with, imprinted with my energy, and that had served me well for many years. Each ghost box is unique, there are no two exactly alike, and it takes a long time to learn its nuances, and quirks. Losing this ghost box, although it may sound strange, would have been like losing a friend, not to mention the blow to my research in general. Ghost boxes like this one were not easily come by.

I sat back down next to my box; the rest took their prior seats. I checked the recorder to make sure it was still operating normally;

it was fine. At that moment the thought crossed my mind, *Did John deliver communication through the ghost box while we all attended the calamity in the operations room?* I could not wait to review the recording of that time. *Ok, back to work.* I focused my attention back on the session. I knew the entity John must have expended a good amount of his energy to throw those two bulky video monitors from the table, but I also knew this was not the time to back off. If his energy supply was depleted, it would be like a boxer having his opponent weak and on the ropes; I couldn't let up. It was time to deliver the knockout punch that would basically eliminate any useful energy John might have had left, and in doing so, give us the opportunity to communicate with my spirit technicians Mike and Lisa and the child spirit John Matthew DeFeo or any other entities wishing to communicate.

My next comment to the entity John was meant to elicit another poltergeist-type response. I knew any physical effort on John's part would serve to better deplete his remaining effective energy as opposed to a strong verbal response through the ghost box. What I didn't factor into the equation was the type of physical response he was capable of. I told my team members to expect a strong response; they nodded in agreement.

I fired my comment into the still air of the room. "John, your little fit of rage didn't do much, only a minor inconvenience." I went on to say, "You're sort of like a small child having a tantrum when mommy scolds him." We all braced for John's response. It came through the ghost box in the form of a surprisingly calm response. His voice was still dark and agitated but much less aggressive than I would have expected. "Can't fool John." His communication through the box was relatively easy to hear and understand live. I attributed this to his being here in the house, his being in direct proximity to the ghost box, and to his apparent control over his surroundings. However, from the subdued response he'd just delivered, I could tell his batteries were in the red.

I didn't hesitate. I immediately followed his response with,

"No one is trying to fool you, John." I allowed a couple of seconds to pass and then said, "John, I have a question for you. When you were in the physical body, is it true that you liked to sexually abuse your victims, especially young children?" This question, I knew, was the match that would light the fuse, and since this evil entity had a very short fuse, it should not take long for him to explode. We all tightened up a bit more in anticipation of the inevitable response that my scathing question would bring, as I thought we would not have to wait very long. As I sat there waiting for some object to go crashing to the floor, I put a sturdy hand on the top of my ghost box to make sure it was not that object. No sooner did I raise my head from looking at my ghost box than I felt a sharp sting across my left cheek, and my head snapped to one side. It took a split second to register, but I realized I had just been slapped across the face, not a love tap but a smack that you would expect coming from an angry full-grown man. I paused for a second to wrap my mind around what had just happened.

As I looked at my team members, who had been alert for any movement, they all had a look of shock on their faces. Bill asked, "Did you just get hit?"

I replied, "Yes, I think so."

Sue responded with major concern in her voice, "This is getting serious. Maybe we should—" Before she could finish her sentence, the digital camera she was holding in her right hand was forcefully removed from her hand and thrown to the floor. Sue gasped and jumped up and back from her seat, knocking her chair over in the process. "Oh my god, this is crazy!" she shouted.

I knew Tom and Bill were solid experienced paranormal investigators and not given to losing their cool no matter what took place, but Sue was relatively new to this with only one and a half years of experience in the field under her belt. I had complete confidence in her, but I also knew she had never experienced the physical interaction we had experienced here in the Amityville house. I told Sue to stay calm and go to the operations room and take a few minutes to regain her composure. She agreed, picked up the fallen chair, and headed to the operations room.

I looked at Tom and Bill; both gave a thumbs-up. I didn't let on to my team, but I was a bit shaken myself. I had been the subject of spirit activity before in the form of a touch and even a shove but never anything as severe as the slap I'd received. It was time to exercise a higher level of caution. I was contemplating ending the session at this point to regroup, but knew that if I did, it would only serve to allow the entity John Ketchum to regain some of the strength we had managed to rob from him. I decided to continue with the ghost box session.

As I prepared for my next interaction with John, Sue walked back into the room and over to her previous position. I looked at her; she smiled and mouthed the words, "I'm good." I nodded, and she took her seat. The mark of a good paranormal investigator was being able to conquer their fear and go on with the task at hand. I knew I had made the right decision when I chose her to join our team.

I realized the negative entity John Ketchum would have fed on the negative energy emitted by the fear and anxiety we'd all felt during the previous interactions, and I hoped it was not enough to significantly raise his energy store. I addressed John with, "John, I hope you are over your little display and can speak with us like a man." I knew this would evoke a strong response but didn't believe John had enough energy to do any real damage at this point. We awaited a response from John through the ghost box. We didn't have to wait long; an aggressive but low-toned response came through the box's speaker. "Fools, strumpet." I managed to catch John's two-word response live and asked the others if they had heard it.

Tom shook his head. Bill answered, "I think I heard 'fools,'" and Sue replied, "Yes, I heard 'fools' and another word I didn't quite understand."

Because of the low tone of the live spirit communication, it was much harder to hear and understand than John's previous comments; however, I knew it would be apparent in the session recording. Strumpet, I knew the word, and I knew it was an antiquated derogatory term used to describe a woman of ill repute. I also knew the term was not commonly used in the modern day, indicating that the entity John was not from this century.

I delivered my next statement to John. "John, if you are going to insult us, at least have the decency to deliver your insults higher than a whisper." I began to hear what sounded like low muttering coming from the ghost box. It was apparent that it was not part of the ghost box sweep but buried in it. I knew the entity John Ketchum was once again on the ropes energy-wise; this was my opportunity to attempt communication with the spirit of little John DeFeo, my spirit techs Mike and Lisa, and any other entities who had been blocked from communicating.

I looked at my team and said, "Ok, we did it; we drained his energy. We can all take a breath and relax for now." This lull from having to deal with the entity John Ketchum and his aggressive and violent reactions would serve to alleviate some of the negative energy derived from our anxiety and fear, depriving the entity John of a source to recharge his energy supply. I called out to my spirit technicians, "Mike, Lisa, are you guys able to get through and communicate?"

Almost immediately a familiar-sounding voice came through the ghost box. "Yes, Bruce, here." A warm feeling ran through me as I said, "Hey, Mike, is that you?" The reply came, "Yes, Bruce, Mike." Before I could address Mike further, a female voice came through the speaker. "Bruce, careful, danger." I knew this was my other spirit tech Lisa. "Hi, Lisa, thank you. We will be careful." I noticed for the first time since this group session began, a small smile came across Sue's lips, and I could see that her tense nervous expression had relaxed. This was good, we all felt relieved at the evil entity John's retreat, and hearing the live spirit communication we attributed to our trusted spirit technicians would create an air of positive energy that would be to the evil spirit John Ketchum like garlic is to a vampire.

I asked Mike and Lisa to help any other spirit entities who wished to communicate to form and send their communication, and then asked, "Are there any entities here who would like to communicate with us?" I fully intended to hear from the spirit of little John in a similar child's voice to the one he had used previously. As we waited for any response, we could hear only the ghost box sweep sound. I did, however, hear what sounded like a distinct word of live spirit communication; it stood out from the rest of the ghost box sweep in clarity and loudness. I asked, "Did someone just try to communicate? Can you say your message again?" I listened intently, focusing on every aspect of the rapidly moving ghost box sweep. I heard the same-sounding word come through the speaker of the box, this time repeated twice, "*Hakame, Hakame.*" I committed the word to memory even though I fully expected it to be just ghost-box-sweep gibberish. I had a strong urge to ask for the spirit of little John, but I did not want to devote the rest of the session to him alone. I wanted to give any other entities present an opportunity to deliver their messages.

Because we were in a relatively calm state at the moment and directing our attempts at communication with any willing entity, I turned the questioning over to my team. Sue asked the first question, "Are there any spirits here in this room with us now?" The answer, "Yes," came through in a female voice, followed by, "Lisa." We all heard the responses live. Sue then asked, "Lisa the tech, is that you?" Another quick response of, "Yes," came through the ghost box. Sue thanked Lisa for her reply and nodded to Bill, indicating that he should ask the next question.

Bill, being a seasoned live spirit ghost box communication researcher himself, did not skip a beat. He asked, "Lisa, if there are other spirits here in this room with us, can they communicate?" A two-word answer was delivered within seconds of Bill's question, "Yes, hard," which was heard live as it was delivered. Bill followed with, "Hard, why is it hard?" A few seconds passed, and the response, "No English," came through the ghost box. I asked if everyone heard the communication.

Tom answered and repeated it aloud, "I heard 'No English.'" We all nodded in agreement. What did Lisa mean by this statement? Were there entities here in the Amityville house who could not speak English?

I put a hand up, gesturing for Bill to hold his next question or statement. I jumped in, "Lisa, are the entities here from a different country?" A response of, "No," came through, which only served to confuse me a bit. I followed it with, "Lisa, if they are from the United States, why can they not speak English?" Lisa's next response was heard loudly and clearly by all of us: "Indian." I immediately asked, "Lisa, did you say Indian?" A resounding, "Yes," came through the ghost box speaker. Indian, did Lisa mean the spirit entity of a person from India, or was she referring to an American Indian? No sooner did that thought cross my mind than I remembered the dreams both Tom and I had; both of us had dreamed of shadowy figures who reminded us of American Indians.

My next questions to Lisa had to be posed in a way that would allow Lisa to deliver the most accurate answer possible in relatively few words. The longer the communication from a spirit entity was, the more difficult it was for them to form and deliver it, and for us to hear it live as it came through the ghost box. "Lisa, are the spirits here American Indians, or are they from India?" I asked. After a few seconds, Lisa answered, "American," followed immediately by the word "Indian." Lisa was the spirit version of a well-seasoned and experienced live spirit ghost box communication practitioner; she knew that the shorter the answers and responses she gave were, the better opportunity we would have to hear and understand them live. Now that Lisa my spirit technician had confirmed that the other entities present were the spirits of American Indians, I remembered that there were reports of American Indians of the Shinnecock tribe who were native to this part of Long Island, New York, and had reportedly occupied the land that the Amityville house stood on.

I quickly returned my attention to the ghost box session.

Knowing that the spirit John Ketchum was undoubtedly recharging for another assault, time was of the essence. I asked, "Lisa, are the Indian spirits who are here from the Shinnecock tribe?" Lisa answered, "Yes." I then asked, "Is it possible for us to communicate with them?" Again an answer of, "Yes," was sent through the ghost box. "Ok, Lisa," I replied, followed by, "Lisa, is it possible for you to translate their communication so we can understand it?" We received the answer, "Yes, I can," from Lisa.

As Lisa and I exchanged communication in an attempt to establish a suitable way for us to communicate with the non-English-speaking Shinnecock Indians, I could hear the faint sound of sobbing in the background of the sweep. I immediately felt a wave of sadness and despair come over me. I had experienced this type of feeling a couple of times before during a live ghost box session. In those instances the connection and communication was with lost, very sad, and confused spirit entities who had suffered tragic and / or unexpected deaths and did not realize they were no longer physical living beings. A live spirit ghost box communication session opens a portal between our physical world and the spirit realm. This portal allows for the exchange of energy between the ghost box operator and the communicating spirit entities. This would help explain the sudden experience of emotion felt by the ghost box operator during a live ghost box session. Since energy is mutually exchanged, it is theoretically possible for the operator to feel the emotions being radiated from the communicating entity through the energy exchange, be they good or bad.

I posed my next question directly to the Indian spirits. "Can the Indian spirits here please tell me your name?" After a few seconds, I could hear a male voice mixed in the ghost box sweep that I recognized as an attempt to send communication. Lisa came through and replied, "Red Cloud." I didn't catch the whole response, only the word *cloud*, which I immediately repeated aloud. Tom spoke out and said, "I think I heard Red Cloud." I asked, "Lisa, did you say Red Cloud?" The response of, "Yes," came through. I replied, "Ok, great, Red Cloud," followed by, "Red Cloud, are you a Shinnecock Indian?" Again Lisa said "Yes," translating for the spirit Red Cloud.

I had an idea. I asked Lisa, "Lisa, can you tell me the Shinnecock words for yes and no?" My idea was that if I could recognize the native Shinnecock words for yes and no, I could ask questions of Red Cloud that would only warrant a yes or no answer, and thereby have my spirit tech Lisa only translate the more detailed answers. A response of, "Wait," came through the ghost box speaker. I responded, "Ok, I'll wait." A few seconds passed, and Lisa came through, "Ok, now." I heard Lisa's response and knew it to mean that she was ready to communicate the answers to my previous request for the yes and no Shinnecock Indian words. I stated, "Ok, Lisa, what is the Indian word for yes?" I listened intently, and Lisa delivered a word that sounded like "nook." I asked, "Lisa, did you say nook?" Lisa immediately replied, "*Nuks* (yes)," and then repeated it, "*Nuks* (yes)." I asked intently, "Did you say *nuks* (yes)?" She replied, "Yes." I replied, "Great, ok," and then asked, "Can you tell me the word for no?" We waited a few seconds, and Lisa replied with what sounded like the words "me too." I again asked, "Did you say me too?" Lisa immediately replied, "No," sounding a tad bit frustrated, and understandably so. She then repeated the word, which came through as "*Mutu* (no)." I asked Lisa for confirmation of the word, and she repeated, "*Mutu* (no)," twice. I thanked her and apologized for my lack of understanding, and asked for her patience during this interaction between myself and the Shinnecock Indian Red Cloud.

The process of obtaining these two simple words had taken quite a few minutes, and my anxiety was on the rise. I knew that every moment spent in communication with the Shinnecock Indians would be a moment for the evil entity John Ketchum to build his energy. At the risk of missing live spirit communication from the Indian spirit, I knew I had to pick up the pace of the session, so without hesitation, I asked my next question, directed to Red Cloud, remembering to ask questions that would entail a basic yes or no answer. "Red Cloud, do you know you are dead?" I was relying on the belief that Lisa had been able to explain our process to Red Cloud and that he understood. A few seconds passed, and from the ghost box sweep came the response of, "*Nuks* (yes)." I was able to hear Red Cloud's response clearly. It stood out above the sound of the ghost box sweep; undoubtedly Lisa and Mike were assisting Red Cloud in his efforts to communicate.

I looked up at my team members, who had been uncharacteristically quiet during this later part of the session. I must have had an inquisitive look on my face because Bill said in a low voice, "We're with you, this is important, so we are just being quiet and letting you do your thing." I nodded in agreement and appreciation.

My next question to Red Cloud was, "Are you the only Shinnecock Indian spirit here in this house?" Red Cloud returned the answer, "*Mutu* (no)," which I understood as a no. "How many Indian spirits are here with you in this house?" I asked, and the response of what I heard as "nice" or "niece" came through. I asked, "Did you say nice?" The reply that came through was from Lisa; she responded, "Two," and then, "*Nis, nis.*" I asked, "Lisa, does *nis* mean the number two?" A resounding, "Yes," came through the box's speaker. I told Lisa that I understood and asked Red Cloud, "Are there two other Indian spirits here with you?" Red Cloud responded, "*Nuks* (yes)."

As I poised to ask my next question, I heard the dreaded sound that I was becoming very familiar with, the low guttural voice of spirit John Ketchum that had heralded his return in the previous ghost box sessions. With that, I asked, "Lisa, is the spirit John Ketchum here?" Lisa immediately answered, "Close." I realized this meant I had only minutes to get as much communication from the Indian spirit Red Cloud as I could before the negative entity John returned and overpowered the ghost box session.

I asked quickly, "Red Cloud, can you leave this house and go on to the spirit world?" The next response came from Lisa answering for Red Cloud; "Need help," was her response. I knew that by this answer Lisa was telling us that the grounded Shinnecock Indians would need our help to cross over into the spirit world. I also knew that with the evil spirit John lurking on the fringe of the session, waiting to interfere, there would be no time to attempt a crossover assistance session for the wayward Shinnecock Indians. At this point, we could hear the guttural growls of the fast-approaching spirit John Ketchum getting louder and stronger, and knew it was only a matter of a couple of minutes before he aggressively burst onto the scene.

I looked at my team and suggested we end the live ghost box session before the spirit John had the opportunity to do it; they all nodded in agreement. I made my last statement to Lisa and Red Cloud. "Ok, Lisa, Red Cloud, I know you are aware of the approaching evil spirit John, so I will end this session for now." I followed it by saying, "Red Cloud, we will not abandon you or your people. We will help you in every way we can. Please have hope." With that, I thanked Mike and Lisa for their unyielding assistance and devotion to me and to live spirit ghost box communication, and said goodbye. Before I flicked the ghost box switch off, my spirit technician Mike came through and said, "Bye, Bruce, love you." We all heard this loud and clear.

With Mike's last message ringing in my ears, I turned off the ghost box to end the group session. We all rose to our feet, stretched, gathered our equipment, and headed for the operations room across the hall. I glanced at my watch; the time read 7:36 a.m. I had not realized the group ghost box session had taken an hour and forty-five minutes. I did not usually like to run a live ghost box session for much more than half an hour, but given the situation and the events of the session, it was far from usual.

I entered the operations room, placed my ghost box on the table, and sat down. This ghost box session had drained all of us emotionally and physically, with the amount of physical, emotional, and spiritual energy given and taken during that session, it was no wonder we were spent. I looked at my team members, all of whom looked like they had just run a marathon. I asked, "Is everyone ok?"

Tom answered, "Yes." Bill and Sue nodded.

"Boy, that was some session," Bill said.

Sue added, "You can say that again."

I agreed and asked for my team members' assessment of the group ghost box session.

Tom was the first to speak up. "That ghost box session had to be one of the top three live ghost box sessions I have ever been involved in." He went on to say, "The box was receiving a really good radio signal; given that, the live spirit communication was unbelievable even with such a great signal." Tom went on to say, "I can't believe we actually received communication from the spirit of a Shinnecock Indian. I had heard the reports of there being some kind of Indian burial ground or something on the property, but it didn't occur to me that we would actually get live spirit communication from one of the Indian spirits."

Sue interjected, "I believe the reports were of a special structure on the spot where this house sits now, and that it was used by the Indian tribe to house their old, sick, and mentally ill people. Pretty much they would be put there waiting to die."

Bill added his comment to the topic. "Which would explain why the Indian spirits are grounded here; their last days were probably not very good."

When Bill finished his statement, I said, "I believe Tom and I mentioned that during our sleep break last night, we both had dreams where we saw shadow people who were reminiscent of Native Americans. Some would explain that away as just coincidence, but for the two of us to have dreamt of the same type of figures at the same time would be a very far stretch to explain away as coincidence. I believe the figures Tom and I saw in our dreams were those of the Indian spirits grounded here." Everyone agreed.

I turned the discussion to the evil entity John Ketchum. "Any thoughts on the entity John and the activity we experienced from him?" Of course, I knew everyone would be chomping at the bit to voice their opinions on the subject of John Ketchum. "Sue, why don't you start us off?"

Sue began by saying, "I know I haven't been doing this as long as the rest of you, and I haven't experienced a tenth of what you guys have, but I consider myself to be a solid paranormal investigator who could deal calmly and objectively with any situation that arose, that is, until last night. I have experienced quite a few terrifying things since I joined the team. What happened last night during the session with the physical attacks and the aggressive poltergeist activity, that was a first for me, and I'm a little embarrassed about the way I reacted."

I wanted to jump in at that point and tell Sue that we had all reacted that way to something at one time or another in our paranormal careers, but I kept silent for the moment and allowed Sue to continue.

Sue paused for a second and then went on, "This spirit John, he's very strong out of the gate. Once the interaction with him starts, it seems that he can't hold that energy level for very long though. Don't get me wrong, initially, he can be very dangerous, but it seems like with enough antagonistic prodding, he can be made to expend most of his energy, which forces him to retreat to lick his wounds, giving us enough time to contact and interact with the other spirit entities present in this house. I think if we stay extra cautious and aware of his potential, we could continue to disarm him energy-wise, and that will allow us to try to help the other entities who are stuck here. That's pretty much my take on it."

When Sue finished, I rendered my consolation statement. "Sue, firstly, don't ever be embarrassed about displaying emotion, even if that emotion is fear. We have all been there and done that; think of it as baptism by paranormal activity. That being said, I think Sue is right on the money. There are spirit entities here in this house who need our help, little John DeFeo and the Shinnecock

Indian spirits. If we can continue to weather the evil entity John's aggressive assaults and bleed his energy store in our encounters with him, we can use the time when he is disabled to try to help the others."

Bill and Tom both agreed. Tom added, "We all have to be extra careful; we don't know just how harmful he can get physically. Bruce, remember the Walden investigation where I received those three deep scratches on my back?"

I did remember; how could I forget? The team had been investigating an old house in rural Pennsylvania that had belonged to the town butcher back in the late 1800s, early 1900s. The reported story was that this town butcher, James Walden, had abducted and killed a number of women, whom he proceeded to butcher in the basement of his home and sell in his butcher shop to the local townspeople, claiming it was pork. The Walden house has had several owners over the years, almost all of whom have reported paranormal activity in the home, with the last residents fleeing the house due to violent poltergeist activity and leaving it abandoned.

During our investigation of the Walden house, we'd encountered what we believed to be the spirit of James Walden as well as two other spirit entities we believed were those of his victims. At one point during the investigation, Tom had received three deep and bloody scratches across his lower back, which he still carries faint scars from to this day. We were able to deal with the evil spirit James Walden and help those two trapped spirits to cross over to the other side, with the help of our spirit technicians Mike and Lisa, of course. Although these types of encounters were few and far between, and the incidents themselves were alarming, they did serve to give us the experience, knowledge, and a sense of awareness needed to continue our work no matter what the situation.

With all in complete agreement on continuing the investigation to its end, no matter what was encountered, we set about the task of formulating a game plan for the next leg of the investigation. I checked the time; it was 8:41 a.m. on Saturday morning.

Since we had primarily covered most of the house in our individual investigations, we could concentrate on a plan that would allow us to attempt, with the help of our spirit techs, to assist in the crossing over of the innocent spirit entities we believed were being trapped here by the evil entity John Ketchum.

CHAPTER SIX

TRAPPED SPIRITS GO HOME TO THE SPIRIT WORLD

I suggested we do another group live spirit ghost box communication session in the living room where we had performed the last one. I told Bill to place the video monitors on the floor prior to the session to help guard against their being forcefully knocked off the table, and to retrieve and set up two extra video cameras in the living room. Bill nodded. I told Tom and Sue that I wanted them to each run a digital voice recorder for the entire session, and that we could dispense with the target objects and any other equipment that was designed to alert us to the presence of a spirit entity; we would definitely know when they were there.

I explained that our goal was simple. We would definitely encounter the evil spirit John Ketchum, and he would have his renewed energy at full at the onset of the session. That was when we needed to be the most alert and prepared for forceful activity. We would follow the same game plan as before, try our best to have John deplete his energy store, and then use the time that came after to work with our spirit techs Mike and Lisa to try to get the spirit of little John, and the Shinnecock Indian spirits to cross over to safety in the spirit realm. I believed that with our combined positive energy and that of our spirit counterparts Mike and Lisa, we had a good chance of accomplishing our objective.

I asked the group if there were any questions, and Sue spoke out. "What if one of us gets hurt like the scratches Tom received?" She added, "What should we do?"

I explained that if any of us during the course of the live ghost box session were to be physically injured by the evil spirit John Ketchum, the individual, accompanied by another team member, should go immediately to the operations room and deal with the situation. The remaining two of us would continue with the session. All nodded in agreement.

"Ok, gang, let's make this happen. we will all meet in the living room in twenty minutes."

We all stood up. Bill went to retrieve the two extra video cameras, and Tom proceeded to place the video monitors on the floor, while Sue replaced all the voice recorder batteries with fresh ones. I grabbed my lead ghost box, placed new batteries in my own voice recorder, made sure both were in working order, and started toward the living room. I entered the living room as Bill was setting up the two extra video cameras. I suggested the two extra cameras be placed so that they could capture a wide view of the whole room from both sides. Bill agreed, placed the cameras in position, and started them running. I walked over to the spot I had occupied in the prior group ghost box session, placed my ghost box on the table along with my voice recorder, and sat down. Sue entered the room.

I asked, "Are you ready for this? It could get hairy."

Sue looked at me with a slight grin and answered, "I'm a little nervous but ready to rock and roll."

I smiled back at her and nodded. "Bill, are the cameras ready?" I asked.

"Yeah, up and running," he replied.

Tom walked into the room and stated, "Ok, guys, let's do this."

Everyone took their seats and braced for whatever was to

come. I switched on my voice recorder and then turned on the ghost box. The ghost box began sweeping the radio broadcast band. The signal was strong and clear; a cacophony of broken-down radio broadcast gibberish filled the room. Again I would conduct this session on the fly without a set agenda, allowing me to adapt the session to whatever the situation called for.

I was about to address my spirit technicians Mike and Lisa to establish their presence. As I attempted to speak, a loud angry voice came booming through the ghost box speaker. "GET OUT OF MY HOUSE," came through in the gruff, aggressive, and threatening tone I had come to recognize as communication from the evil spirit entity John Ketchum. From the forcefulness of his initial communication, I could tell he was at full strength and spoiling for a fight. Everyone heard John's demand loud and clear. I could feel an air of tension move through the room as we all braced for the upcoming encounter.

I told my team, "Stay calm, focus, and try to keep a positive energy flow; we don't want to fuel his negativity." All nodded to confirm they understood.

As I started to address John's comment, a large mirror that hung above the fireplace started to shake and vibrate. Sue was seated just to the left of the fireplace. I shouted, "Sue, move!"

Sue jumped to her feet and quickly crossed the room toward where Tom was seated. As she turned to face the position she had just left, the large, gaudy mirror fell, hitting the fireplace mantel, shattering it into a thousand shards of glass that shot out across half the room. Thankfully we were all positioned on the outer perimeter of the room, and the glass had not reached any of us; however, the giant ornate gold mirror frame took out one of our video cameras.

Bill started to get up and check the damage to the camera. I stopped him and asked, "Is everybody ok?" Everyone acknowledged that they were not physically hurt. I knew, however, the fear level just went up exponentially, mine included. I told Bill to leave the camera for now, and we would just continue with the session. I reminded everyone that we expected some violent activity from John during this session, and we needed to stay calm and positive, even in the face of what had just happened. All agreed.

I knew from experience that John's initial assaults cost him a decent amount of his energy, and making that big heavy mirror fall from the wall must have depleted a good portion of his energy reserve. Now was not the time for us to err on the side of caution and back off. We needed to keep up the pressure and bait John into expending the remainder of his energy, which would loosen his grip on the other spirit entities trapped here in this house by him, giving us and my spirit techs the opportunity to help them leave here and cross to the spirit world.

I rendered my next comment to the evil spirit John Ketchum. "Wow, John, impressive, but not very effective. You broke a mirror, big deal; now you're going to have seven years of bad luck." I ended the comment to John with a loud laugh. Now I awaited a response, a few seconds passed, and a male voice came through the ghost box, "Not," followed a second or two later by, "Amused." We all heard this clearly, the voice we knew was John, but it did not have the punch of his usual communication; his delivery had lost its sting. Had the destruction of the mirror cost him more energy than I thought?

I immediately followed his comment with, "What's wrong, John? You sound tired." A response of, "Go to blazes," was delivered through the ghost box immediately following my comment, and we all heard it clearly. John's communication had become benign and weak; could he actually be nearing the end of his energy supply so soon? I looked up at my team members, an air of optimism showing on their faces. "Ok, guys, John is fading; let's keep it up."

Tom spoke out. "Hey, John, what's wrong, old man? Moving that mirror was too much for you? I think I saw a rocking chair upstairs; you'd better go take a rest." After a few long seconds the response, "All—will—be—dead—soon," came from the ghost box. It was so faint we almost didn't catch it. I looked at Tom, and he gave a thumbs-up. We all knew that this comment would be John's last for a while; he would have to retreat as before to try to rejuvenate his energy supply. It was a stroke of luck for us, but bad luck for the evil spirit John, that he had decided to make his initial attack so costly to his energy supply. This entire encounter with John from beginning to end took only about twenty minutes, far less than we all expected.

I spoke to the group. "Ok, I'm pretty sure we have seen the last of John for now, but who knows for how long. Let's get started on the crossing attempt." I wanted to start with bringing forward and communicating with the child spirit little John DeFeo; everyone agreed.

The first thing I did was to call for my spirit techs, Mike and Lisa. "Mike, Lisa, are you there? Can you communicate with us?" From the ghost box came the answer, "Yes," and then, "Yes, here," first in a male voice and then in a female voice. I responded to the communication with, "Hi, Mike. Hi, Lisa, thank you for your assistance." In Mike's familiar way he replied, "No problem." Hearing my spirit technicians reply strongly and clearly gave me a feeling of reassurance and calm; it confirmed the evil entity John had made his retreat, and now my techs and the other spirits in this house were free to communicate.

I spoke to my spirit techs. "Mike, Lisa, please help the spirit of little John DeFeo come forward to speak with us." A few seconds passed, and Mike responded, "Wait." This was a common response whenever I asked my technicians to locate a spirit entity and bring them forward to communicate. After waiting ten or fifteen seconds for a confirmation from Mike or Lisa that little John was there and ready to communicate, I asked, "Mike, Lisa, is little John there? Can he communicate?" The sound of a childlike voice emanated from the ghost box. "I'm here." The voice was low and timid in tone but able to be heard by all of us. "Little John, was that you who said I'm here?" The response of, "Yes," now in a bit stronger voice, came through. "Hello, John," I said, followed by, "How are you?" About ten seconds passed and the answer, "Hi, I'm ok," was delivered through the ghost box speaker.

As I poised for my next question to little John, I became aware of the sweep of the ghost box becoming less clear, the sweeping sound had become more staticky with white noise, and the radio broadcast signal reception had become weaker. This could have been due to a number of things, EMF (electromagnetic frequency) interference, a change in the weather conditions, or battery power, which could not be the case since the ghost box was plugged directly into the electrical outlet. These were just a few of the things that could wreak havoc on a live spirit ghost box communication session. Conditions during a live ghost box session were always in a continuous state of fluctuation, so this was not an uncommon occurrence; however, it was odd because we had enjoyed such a powerful and clear radio broadcast signal in this room.

The noticeable degradation of the ghost box sweep would not cause us to abandon the session, but it would make hearing and understanding the spirit communication that was delivered more difficult. I asked my spirit techs to aid any communicating entities in their delivery of the communication, and if need be, please relay any communication that a communicating entity was not able to deliver on their own. We received the response, "Yes, Bruce, we know." I, of course, knew Mike and Lisa were seasoned spirit technicians and would know what to do without being told, but for the sake of my peace of mind, I needed to reiterate it and receive their confirmation.

I directed my next question to little John. "Little John, do you want us to help you cross over to the spirit world so that you can be with your mother, father, brother, and sisters?" A few seconds passed, and I heard a, "Yes," come through the static of the ghost box sweep. Due to the spirit of little John being here in this room, in direct proximity to the running ghost box, it allowed his communication to be delivered as part of, but separate from the actual ghost box sweep. This allowed us to hear his communication clearly in spite of the extra static interference now plaguing the ghost box. This was very beneficial in our attempt to help little John cross over; we would have to be able to hear his communication in order to give him direction on what to do in order to successfully cross.

As I prepared my next question, we heard a very childlike, timid voice come through the ghost box. "I'm scared," the little voice said. I called out to Mike and Lisa, "Mike, Lisa, please comfort little John and help him to understand what we are trying to do, and not to be afraid." A response of, "Yes, Bruce," came through. "Little John, I want you to look around; do you see a bright light?" The response, "Don't know," came from the ghost box. "Little John, look carefully and tell me if you can see a really bright light, like the sun." After about ten seconds the response, "I see now," came through the ghost box; we all heard it clearly.

Sue moved forward in her seat. She quietly said to me, "Do you want me to take over? Maybe a woman's voice will be more reassuring for him?" I nodded in agreement. Sue spoke. "Hi, little John, my name is Sue. I'm going to help you, ok?" The response, "Yes," came through. As it did, Sue jumped back in her seat; she gasped.

I asked Sue, "What's wrong?"

Sue told us that as little John answered her, she could feel what felt like a small child's hand brush across her cheek. She said it didn't scare her, just startled her. She asked the spirit little John, "John, did you just touch my cheek?" The answer, "Yes," came through loud and clear. This was a very positive sign on the part of little John; it showed a connection with Sue and a certain amount of trust. Sue then asked, "John, can you walk to the bright light?" We waited for his answer for the next fifteen seconds, but none was delivered. Sue repeated her question. It was common to repeat a question or statement a number of times in an attempt to garner a response. Sometimes the communicating entity could not capture the sound fragments it needed at that particular moment to form a relevant communication and deliver it; the repetitive questioning would afford the spirit entity more than just a single opportunity to deliver a relevant answer or statement. After Sue repeated her question, a response of, "Yes," came through the ghost box speaker. We all breathed a small sigh of relief that little John was still there and able to continue his communication.

The ever-present threat of the evil entity John Ketchum returning at any moment had lent a certain urgency to our situation. If he were to return, he would assuredly stop any and all communication and contact with little John, and our efforts to successfully cross him over would be fruitless. We also knew that if we moved too quickly, the already apprehensive spirit of little John DeFeo could retreat from confusion and fear. We did not want to make a mistake, this was an extraordinary situation, we had to proceed with care, but we also had to move things along.

As Sue prepared to make her next statement to little John, I heard a dreaded sound that was faint and buried in the ghost box sweep, faraway-sounding growls and a muffled aggressive male voice. The evil entity John was not far away; the growls we heard were always a preamble for his returning. We had maybe ten minutes at the most, if that long. I asked my team, "Did you guys hear that growling sound?" Everyone nodded. I told Sue I would take it from here, and she acknowledged by nodding and sitting back in her seat.

I spoke firmly. "Little John, I want you to go to the bright light. Your mommy and daddy are waiting there for you." A small voice came through and said, "Ok, I will." I now addressed Mike and Lisa. "Mike, Lisa, please help little John to reach the light any way you can." An answer of, "Yes, Bruce," came through. I waited a few seconds and then asked, "Little John, are you near the bright light?" The answer we received came in a male voice. "Yes, he is," was the response sent by Mike. "Ok, good. John, I want you to walk into that bright light. Don't be afraid; your family is in there waiting for you." No sooner did that statement leave my lips than a pretty loud child's voice came across the ghost box speaker. "Mommy, Mommy." It was heard clearly by all. Sue put her hands to her lips in a compassionate gesture. Since these words had been delivered through the ghost box and made up of random sound fragments that were pieced together, it was not easy to tell if little John's cries of mommy were out of fear or from happiness in recognition of his seeing his mother waiting for him in the light.

With a somewhat shaky voice, I asked Mike and Lisa, "Mike, Lisa, did little John go into the light?" We all tensely waited for a reply. It seemed like forever; then a loud and clear female voice came through with the distinct sound of happiness and accomplishment, "Yes, John crossed," immediately followed by "With family." All of us collapsed in our chairs; we had literally been sitting on the edge of them. I spoke to my team. "Congratulations, guys, thank God, it sounds like little John DeFeo has made it home."

Tom and Bill had big grins on their faces, and Sue proceeded to wipe away a tear. I myself could not feel better; however, our elation at what we'd just helped to accomplish, guiding little John to the spirit world and the arms of his loved ones, was to be very short-lived. I asked Mike and Lisa for an ending confirmation that little John was in fact on the other side and safe. The response of, "Yes, Bruce, here, safe," came through in Mike's telltale tone of voice.

As we sat there, engrossed in the moment, there came a booming and unmistakable evil voice through the ghost box, "BASTARDS!" followed by, "I will send your souls to Hell." What a moment ago was joy and happiness, knowing we helped little John DeFeo cross to the spirit world, now turned to tension with a side order of fear. The evil entity John Ketchum was back, and he was pissed! We all knew the evil spirit John had renewed his energy and was back among us now with a vengeance. He had lost one of his spirit prisoners when little John DeFeo crossed over, and I was sure he was hell-bent on exacting his revenge on us for our participation in this act.

Before the spirit John Ketchum could speak, I switched off the ghost box. I did this to eliminate at least one of the venues he had for his negative attack, the only one I had control over. I knew, however, this would only serve to infuriate him more; it was like someone yelling at you over the phone and, in midsentence, hanging up on them. I told everyone to hold their seats; we would be in a more secure position staying put rather than moving around through the house. I also told them that whatever activity was forthcoming by the entity John would be better weathered by us having to monitor only this room. I explained that I believed John was as infuriated as he could be, and he would inevitably attempt some kind of destructive act. Barring any physical injury to us, we would stay here and let him punch himself out. In other words, if he went into a fit of rage, which I believed he would, that would take a good amount of energy on his part, hopefully enough to weaken him into another retreat. This would allow us the opportunity to reestablish the ghost box session and try to help the spirits of the Shinnecock Indians trapped here.

We all sat there in rigid anticipation, wondering what was to come. It was like watching the timer on a bomb count down, just waiting for the explosion. As we sat quietly braced in our chairs, I happened to glance down at the floor. It was covered in pieces of the broken mirror from the evil entity John's previous attack. As my eyes focused on the shards of the mirror, I saw a dark figure reflected in them. It moved across them from one piece of mirror to the next. I snapped my head up in anticipation of seeing the dark figure moving across the room, the one that was reflected in the scattered shards of mirror. I saw nothing; the room was clear. I asked my team members, "Did anyone see anything, a dark figure, anything at all?" They all responded with a no; hopefully one or all of the running video cameras had captured whatever it was I saw reflected in the pieces of the mirror.

Bill did, however, point out that there was a substantial drop in the temperature of the room. I had not noticed it until he mentioned it, but now that he did, wow, it was really chilly. Theoretically, a sudden drop in temperature in association with an alleged paranormal situation was believed to indicate a spirit entity was present. The theory was that the spirit entity would absorb the thermoelectric energy from its surroundings, thus initiating a noticeable drop in ambient temperature. I happened to subscribe to this theory. I have experienced this phenomenon on countless occasions, having it coincide with other data that indicated a spirit presence. As a matter of fact, we had all encountered this phenomenon in this house multiple times during this investigation. The temperature drop also indicated to me that the evil entity John was gathering as much energy as he possibly could, no doubt in preparation for a strong and aggressive assault.

About twenty minutes had passed since I'd switched off the ghost box, and all remained quiet. I could actually feel the anxiety level in my team members rising with each passing minute. Why wasn't the entity John commencing his attack? What was he up to? Why didn't he do something? I caught myself; I too was becoming the victim of anxiety, waiting for the other shoe to drop. I could feel my pulse pounding in my neck. I had to calm down, and so did my team members. Our anxiety levels would surely be producing negative energy from us. As that thought went through my mind, I realized we were unconsciously being manipulated by the evil entity John; he was more cunning than I gave him credit for. By having us wait in nervous anticipation of an aggressive assault by him, John was creating anxiety, stress, and fear within us. This resulted in our emitting negative energy that could be absorbed by him, giving John even more strength.

I immediately spoke up. "Everyone take a deep breath and try to calm yourselves. John is using the negative energy we are producing from our anxiety and fear to strengthen himself even more. We need to calm down and try to establish a positive aura in the room." All agreed. I knew this was exponentially easier said than done, but now that we were aware of the evil entity John's intention in making us wait, hopefully, we could rationalize the situation, which would help to alleviate the anxiety and eliminate the negative energy we were surely emitting. Now that John's little plot had been uncovered, I was sure it would not be long before we experienced some sort of reprisal from him.

We went back to waiting. Just as I thought, we didn't wait very long. We began to hear a faint rattling sound. Everyone looked around, trying to pinpoint where the sound was coming from.

Bill said, "Tom, it's the window behind you."

Tom turned quickly to look at the window, and it began to shake more.

"Tom, get up!"

Tom jumped to his feet and scrambled away from the window. As he reached the middle of the room, the window began to shake violently. The window was large and heavy, just what you would expect in a home of this age. We all ducked down, fully expecting a shower of glass at any moment. To all our surprise, the violent shaking started to subside, it became less and less until it stopped completely, and the room once again fell silent and calm. We all looked at each other with confused looks on our faces. What had happened? Did John decide not to complete his attempt at shattering the window, or was he simply not strong enough to accomplish the task?

Bill asked aloud, "What the hell just happened? I thought for sure that window was going to shatter."

Sue responded to Bill's question, "Maybe the evil old bastard was too weak to make it happen."

My three team members turned to me for my thoughts. "Hard to say. Maybe he was not strong enough. Maybe he decided to back off because it was costing him too much energy. Can't say for sure." We all took a breath and returned to our vigil.

I decided to turn on the ghost box and possibly get an answer from John Ketchum as to why he did not follow through with the destruction of the window. I flicked the power switch, and the ghost box came back to life. The sweep was strong and clear, just as it had been in the earlier session. I asked my question. "John, what happened? Were you not able to finish the job on the window?" We all focused on the ghost box, waiting for John's reply. After a few seconds the response of, "Damn you all," came across the ghost box speaker. John's comment seemed surprisingly passive. I fully expected a loud aggressive reply at the very least, if not another attempt at a poltergeist attack. Could it be possible? Was the evil entity John Ketchum low on energy so soon? Did his attempt at destroying the window take that much out of him?

I gestured to Sue, signaling her to pick up the questioning. I knew that out of all of us, John wanted to deal with Sue the least. His antiquated disdain for women would serve to further infuriate him, resulting in a more aggressive reply, thus expending a greater amount of whatever energy he had left. I realized that over the course of my interactions with the spirit of John Ketchum, his energy level waned faster and easier with each encounter. It was possible that over the span of time that John Ketchum's spirit had occupied this house, he'd had the opportunity to develop and keep his energy at an optimal level, given that he had gone unchallenged for all that time. Now that we were taxing his energy with every encounter, it was becoming harder for him to restore and maintain enough energy to be a threat for more than a few minutes. It was apparent that the control over his energy level was weak, and he could, with a little prodding, be manipulated into expending the energy he had stored quickly. This was a major plus for us and for the remaining spirit entities of the Shinnecock Indians.

Sue was aware of John's weakening condition and took the opportunity to capitalize on it. "Hi, John, I know how much you love talking to me. It must be very hard for you to realize that a woman is your equal." This comment to John from a woman would be like poking an angry dog with a stick, but Sue knew that. It was meant to infuriate him and possibly elicit a response that would make him expend whatever energy he had left, and send him into another retreat. Over the sweeping sound of the ghost box came the angry but faint response, "Weak female," followed by, "You are nothing." A few seconds passed, and before

Sue could respond, the last comment from the evil spirit John Ketchum in this ghost box session came. It was delivered in a low weak tone. "WOMAN, you will di..." As the comment from John came through the speaker of the ghost box, it was apparent to all of us that his energy was spent; he did not even have enough energy to complete his last comment.

I looked at my watch; it was 10:45 a.m. We were a little under one hour and forty-five minutes into the session.

I called out to my spirit technicians Mike and Lisa. "Mike, Lisa, are you guys still with us?" A familiar and comforting response of, "Yes, Bruce, here," came through the ghost box. "Great, glad to hear your voice," I said in a reassured tone. An air of calm and anticipation filled the room; with the evil spirit John Ketchum off licking his wounds, we were free to try to help the grounded spirits of the Shinnecock Indians cross over to the spirit realm. I continued, "Mike, Lisa, are the spirits of the Shinnecock Indians in this house here with us now?" A response of, "Yes, here," came through the box. I knew I would not have to remind Mike and Lisa to render any and all assistance needed in my communication with the Indian spirits.

I directed my next question to the Indian spirit Red Cloud. "Red Cloud, if you are here, can you let us know you are here and can communicate?" The response, "*Nuks* (yes)," came through the ghost box. "Very good, nice to hear from you again, Red Cloud." Once again the response, "*Nuks* (yes)," came through. I knew our attempt at crossing the Indian spirits would not be as easy as it was for us to accomplish the crossing over of the child spirit of little John DeFeo. The Shinnecock Indian spirits were strongly attached to this land and had stayed here in spirit form for over a century. For that reason they might be reluctant to leave; however, I knew they had been under the oppression of the evil entity John Ketchum for almost as long and would be eager to escape his torment. "Red Cloud, it is possible now for you and your people to cross over to the spirit world. There you will be reunited with the spirits of your family and ancestors. Are you willing to cross to the spirit world?"

We waited for Red Cloud's reply, about ten seconds passed, and we heard no distinctive reply. I was able to discern among the ghost box sweep a sound I recognized, the sound of spirit entities interacting with each other, speaking to each other. This type of sound mixed in with the sound of the ghost box sweep was very subtle; normally only a very experienced ghost box practitioner would be able to detect it and know what it was. It sounded like the din of conversation you would hear at, say, a party or in a restaurant. You would know that people were talking around you, but their speech was muffled and part of the background noise. I asked, "Red Cloud, are you still with me?" The response, "*Nuks* (yes)," came through, followed by the word, "Wait," in a female voice sent by my spirit tech Lisa. "Ok, we'll wait," I replied.

About another ten or fifteen seconds passed, and the communication, "Ready, Bruce," was delivered by Mike. I reiterated my previous question, "Red Cloud, are you and your people willing to cross over to the spirit world?" Almost immediately the answer, "*Nuks* (yes)," came through the ghost box. With a sense of relief, I responded, "Red Cloud, that's very good. We, along with Mike and Lisa, will help you to make the crossing, ok." Again the response, "*Nuks* (yes)," was delivered. My next question would serve to begin the crossover process. "Red Cloud, can you see a bright light anywhere around you?" A few seconds later the answer, "*Mutu* (no)," came through the box. We all heard this. I then asked, "Red Cloud, look carefully; are you sure you do not see a very bright light, maybe far away?" The response, "*Mutu* (no)," was followed by, "*Kisusq* (sun)." I didn't understand the last word but knew it was Red Cloud speaking. I asked, "Red Cloud, I did not understand; can you repeat your last word?" My tech Lisa came through with the answer "*Kisusq* is sun." I replied, "Oh, ok, the word means the sun." Lisa replied, "Yes." I realized Red Cloud was saying "no sun," which I understood was his way of telling us that he did not see a bright light.

I paused for a moment, deciding what to do next. Apparently the bright light that always indicated the point where a spirit could cross from the physical world to the spirit world was not present. I asked my spirit technicians, "Mike, Lisa, is there no crossing light to guide Red Cloud and his people to the other side?" After a few seconds, the response of, "No light," came through the box in Lisa's telltale voice. I had only encountered this maybe two times in all my years as a live spirit ghost box communication researcher and investigator. I thought for another minute; then I remembered, the last time I encountered this situation was in the crossing-over attempt of an accident victim who could not accept that she was dead. I remembered that with the help of my spirit technicians, the wayward spirit was able to use the open portal that the live ghost box created between the physical and spiritual realms to cross to the other side.

Before I could speak, Tom asked, "Bruce, the open portal of the ghost box, remember?"

I smiled and told Tom I had just thought of it. He smiled and nodded. I spoke to my spirit technicians. "Mike, Lisa, can the Indian spirits use the open portal to cross to the spirit world?" A few seconds passed, and I received a response from Mike, "Yes," and then one from Lisa, "Yes, Bruce." I felt a twinge of excitement. All was not lost; the crossing over of the Shinnecock Indian spirits was still possible.

I spoke to Red Cloud. "Red Cloud, for you and your people to cross to the spirit world and reunite with your loved ones, you must do as our spirit friends Mike and Lisa instruct you to do. Do you understand?" The response, *"Nuks* (yes)," came through clearly. "Good. Mike, Lisa, please take the Indian spirits to the portal." I followed it with, "Red Cloud, you and your people follow Mike and Lisa." As I finished my statement, Mike's voice came through the ghost box. "Bruce, danger near." We all heard this loud and clear. It could only mean one thing; the evil spirit John Ketchum was close and making his way back. This was not good; it meant we only had a short time to get Red Cloud and his people to cross through the open portal to safety in the spirit world. If the evil spirit John made it back before the Indians had a chance to go through the portal, there was a good chance John could block their escape.

I shouted, "Mike, Lisa, HURRY!" We all waited with bated breath for a response through the ghost box. After about a minute, which to us seemed like an hour passed, we heard the next comment from the ghost box, "Bruce, portal here." I didn't think, I just reacted. "Ok, don't stop; send them through the portal," I said excitedly. I waited a few seconds and asked, "Mike, Lisa, did they make it through?" About ten nail-biting seconds passed, and the answer, "Yes, here," came booming through the ghost box speaker. We needed confirmation. "Yes, here, does that mean they made it through to the other side?" The answer, "Yes, Bruce, here," came through loud and clear. We did it, the spirits of the Shinnecock Indians were safely in the spirit realm.

I looked at my team; all had an ear-to-ear smile. "Mike, Lisa, thank you. We could not have done any of this without you." The response, "Love you," came across the ghost box speaker, and I replied, "Love you too." As we all breathed a collective sigh of relief, the voice we had come to know as Red Cloud came through. "*Pomshawok wikun.*" I knew this to be Red Cloud and replied, "Mike, Lisa, I don't understand; can you translate?" A male voice answered, "Good journey." We all heard this clearly. Before I could comment, the message, "*Pumotamsh wuyohtiyokanuk*," came through; again I asked Mike and Lisa to translate Red Cloud's words, and Lisa replied, "Live in peace." I thanked Red Cloud and wished him and his people happiness in the afterlife. The final message from Red Cloud came through the ghost box. "*Nahunshash nimat.*" Before I could ask for a translation, the response, "Goodbye, brother," was delivered by my spirit tech Mike.

We had accomplished something extraordinary here. Not only did we manage to fend off the aggressive and violent attacks from the evil spirit John Ketchum, but we were able to be instrumental in helping the spirits of little John DeFeo and the Shinnecock Indians cross over safely to the spirit realm and be reunited with their family and loved ones. I would be saving a place in my prayers for all of them, the spirit of John Ketchum included.

I stood up from my chair and glanced at my watch; the time was 11:51 a.m. All in all, the entire group ghost box session had taken almost three hours up until this point. I told the team I was ending this session, and we would all meet up in the operations room. I again thanked my spirit technicians for their invaluable help, their undying loyalty and friendship, and I said my good-bye. The last voice to come through the ghost box before I flicked the power switch off was Lisa. She said, "Bye, Bruce."

I turned off the ghost box and my voice recorder. I picked them both up and headed toward the living room exit. As I walked from my chair to the door, Bill was checking the video camera that had been knocked over for damage. Sue was just sitting quietly in her seat, no doubt running the events of the last few hours quickly through her mind, and Tom had already left the room and was probably checking the equipment in the operations room and the other floors of the house.

I walked across the hall to the operations room and placed my ghost box and recorder on the table. I made my way over to the cooler we had there containing water bottles and a few cans of soda. I intended to get a bottle of water, but when I saw those frosty cans of cola, I couldn't resist. I grabbed a soda and went back to my chair to sit down. Just as I began to sit, I heard Tom's voice yell out from the second floor. "Oh shit," I heard him cry. I left the can of soda unopened on the table and hurried to the second-floor staircase. I yelled up, "Tom, are you ok?"

Tom replied, "Yeah, be down in a minute."

I turned and made my way back to my chair in the operations room and the cold soda that was there waiting for me. As I entered the operations room, I could see that the can of soda I had left unopened on the table was now on the floor and had been crushed to the point that it burst open, spewing cola all over the dining room rug. I looked to my left at the adjoining opening that led to the living room. Bill and Sue were standing there casually talking. I called to them, and they came into the operations room.

Sue asked, "What happened, Bruce, have a little accident?"

I shook my head and told them I had left the soda on the operations table and went to check on Tom. When I returned, this was how I found it.

Bill exclaimed, "Seriously?"

Sue added, "Wow," and went to the kitchen to get some paper towels to clean up the mess.

Bill offered, "Our old friend John, no doubt."

I nodded in agreement.

Just then Tom came walking into the room. "What happened here?" he asked.

I told him what had taken place, and he shook his head and added, "I guess we're not done with that cranky bastard." We all agreed.

Sue came back with the paper towels and proceeded to kneel down over the spilled soda. I stopped her, saying, "Thanks, Sue. It's my mess, I'll clean it up."

She smiled and handed me the paper towels. Before I could act, Bill came over with a digital camera and snapped a couple of pics of the crushed can and spilled soda. I mopped up as much of the spilled cola as I could and discarded the crushed soda can and sopping wet paper towels. I went over to my chair and sat down, without thinking I was still thirsty. Before I could get up to get another can of cola, Sue's arm reached out in front of me, holding one. "Thanks, Sue."

She smiled and sat down.

"Ok, guys, let's review. I'll start. That group session, in my opinion, was the most active and most productive I have ever done or even been a part of. The amount of live spirit communication and physical poltergeist activity was unprecedented, not to mention the successful crossing over of the spirit entities who were trapped in this house. Two successful crossovers in one live ghost box session, that's got to be one for the books. I want to say thank you all for your courage, stamina, and expertise. This would never have been possible without you."

The group nodded in humble acceptance of my remark. I went on to say, "This whole investigation has been extraordinary from beginning to end. We have gathered more outstanding evidence and data in the last twenty-four hours than our last ten investigations combined, and we're going to have a ton of audio, video, and still images to go over, which will be another daunting task in and of itself. I have no doubt that you guys will be up to the task.

"All that being said, I don't believe we are finished with the Amityville house just yet. I'm sure the evil entity John Ketchum still has a few tricks up his sleeve; he's down but not out. My thoughts are that for many, many years, the spirit of John Ketchum fed off the negative energy that was emitted by the sad, lost, and desperate spirits of the Shinnecock Indians and then later the poor spirit of little John DeFeo. I also believe that in life John Ketchum was an evil and sadistic tormenter of people and a practicing Satan worshiper who carried these negative traits and emotions with him when he left his physical life. My thinking is, hear me out now, since the innocent spirits Ketchum held trapped here are gone, so is his source of energy regeneration. When he returned after little John DeFeo had crossed over, he was weaker initially than in previous encounters. I'm sure that now after the successful crossing of the Shinnecock Indian spirits, he will remain weak with no real source of energy to draw from. Actually, his only source of negative energy would be us; let's all do our best to stay positive and not give him an opportunity to use our energy to recharge his own."

Bill, Sue, and Tom all nodded in agreement.

"Ok, this is my plan. I think that given John's new situation, and the reality that his sources of negative energy and sadistic amusement are gone, it may be possible that he will listen to reason and leave this house; however, the spirit John Ketchum is evil for sure, but he's not stupid. He knows the only place he could possibly go beyond this physical world will be a dark and evil place. I'm sure he is aware that the only place for him other than here is HELL. Given that, I don't believe it will be an easy task to try to convince him to move on. I mean, he has to believe that an unending existence of loneliness here in this house is far more appealing than an eternity of torment and pain at the hands of the demons he pledged his loyalty and devotion to in his physical life. Then again, on the other hand, he may possibly believe he will be accepted in the dark realm as one of their own, due to his heinous acts in his physical life and his spiritual life. He may just believe he will go on to a place of honor in Satan's kingdom. Whatever the case may be, I would like to do one last group ghost box session to try to persuade the spirit of John Ketchum to leave this house. It won't be easy, and it most likely will be fruitless, but I think we should try."

With that, I finished my dissertation. I asked my team for their thoughts.

Tom was the first to speak. "I agree with everything you just said, but I'm going to play devil's advocate. What happens if we do attempt another session to get John to leave this house and go wherever he is going? Are we all willing to chance another violent encounter with him, at the risk of one of us being physically injured? Or do we just call it a day, be satisfied with what we were able to accomplish here, and move on ourselves? I can't speak for anyone else, but, for me, I'm willing to give it a shot. Yeah, there are risks, but I think the risks were much higher in our last sessions. I believe the entity John Ketchum is much weaker than he was, and the risks involved in another encounter with him are acceptable when you weigh them against the reward of cleansing this house of the plague it has endured since it was built. That's pretty much all I have to say."

I thanked Tom for his input and turned to Sue. "Sue, your turn; what are your thoughts?"

Sue paused for a second to gather her thoughts. "Well," she said, "in my opinion, and I know it's not based on the knowledge and experience the rest of you have, but I think we should do the session. I mean, sure, I'm scared of what might happen, but hey, what are we here for, why are we even in the paranormal research and investigation field if not to push the envelope and to go places and do things not many other people would do? If we can manage to have this bitter evil spirit leave this house and not be around to torment anyone else who lives here or will live here, then I'm all for it. Let risk be damned."

"Thanks, Sue, I admire your guts," I said with a smile. Sue smiled back. "Ok, Bill, you're up."

Bill grinned and let out a faint chuckle. "You know, you guys just never cease to amaze me. I agree with everything that was said here. Heck yeah, the spirit of John Ketchum is evil and dangerous, but he has never run into our team before. Let's do it; let's get his cranky ass out of this house and on a one-way trip to Hell."

With that, we all enjoyed a momentary round of applause for ourselves. I was glad everyone agreed to stay and do the final group ghost box session and that all had a high spirit of comradery, friendship, and loyalty to each other and our work. I told everyone, "Like before, the plan is simple. We will go back to the living room, take our previous positions, and initiate the ghost box session."

We would have to play it by ear, take each moment as it came, and deal with any activity and/or incidents as they arose. The video cameras were still in place and running, the other equipment had been untouched during our last session, so everything was ready to go. There was no time limit set for the upcoming session. I suggested we take a half-hour break, have something to eat and drink, and use the bathroom. All agreed.

I looked at my watch; it was 1:00 p.m. I told the team, "Let's all stay as positive as possible," and we would gather in the living room at 1:30 p.m.

I got up and made my way to the first-floor bathroom. I flicked on the bathroom light, as there were no windows, unbuckled my pants, and sat down. At this moment I had time to fully relax, the events of the entire investigation began to race through my mind. As I concentrated on those thoughts, the light in the bathroom started to flicker, and I felt a cold chill run across my bare legs. I was snapped back to reality. My first thought was, *Great, the spirit John Ketchum would have to pick this very minute to make his presence known*. My second thought was, *He has chosen the perfect time for him; my being caught in this compromising position would undoubtedly cause me uncontrollable stress and anxiety, which would lead to my exuding negative thoughts and energy, thereby allowing John to absorb some negative energy to charge his batteries.* As these thoughts crossed my mind, the light in the bathroom went out, leaving me in complete darkness.

I fumbled in the dark to finish the immediate task at hand. I stood up, pulled up my pants, and proceeded to feel my way to the door. As I groped in the darkness, my hand crossed the bathroom light switch; it was in the off position. I flicked it on, and the lights went on. I turned and looked at the bathroom. All was as it should be; nothing else was disturbed. I took a breath and let out a small sigh. I walked over to the sink and began to wash my hands. As I did, I looked down into the sink and noticed the water that was running clear from the faucet was turning a dark brown, almost black, as it hit the sink and went down the drain. I pulled my hands from under the running water and took a step back for a second. I then reached over and shut the water off. I thought at that moment, *Never go anywhere or do anything on an investigation without a camera handy.* I dried my hands and left the bathroom.

CHAPTER SEVEN

A FITTING END FOR THE EVIL SPIRIT JOHN KETCHUM

I walked back into the operations room. Tom was at the table, looking at the monitors. Sue and Bill both were enjoying a sandwich and a drink. I sat down and proceeded to tell them what had just happened. As I spoke, I noticed all three were trying to hold back their laughter, but it didn't work, and they all burst out into a chorus of belly laughs. I exclaimed, "What are you laughing at? That incident was not funny." As the words left my mouth, I felt myself wanting to laugh. It started as a slight snicker, and then I broke into a full laugh, making the trio into a quartet. After a few moments, the laughter started to subside.

Tom offered, still with a slight snicker, "Gee, Bruce, we're sorry that happened to you." With that, we all broke out into another round of laughter.

I caught my breath, as did the others. "Ok, everybody, let's get serious. We have a tough and potentially dangerous job to do, and we need to be focused. Let's finish up here and get to it." I looked at my watch; the time was 1:35 p.m. I stood up, grabbed my ghost box and digital recorder, and headed out of the operations room. "See you all inside," I said as I walked toward the living room.

I entered the living room and made my way over to what had

become my spot. I set the ghost box and recorder down and took my seat. I sat there quietly contemplating the live group ghost box session to come and awaiting the arrival of my team.

As I was thinking about how I would like to begin the session, I began to feel a light burning sensation on my left forearm. I instinctively reached down to touch my arm, and when I did, the burning feeling intensified, not to the point where I would jump, but it was tender to the touch, like having a sunburn. I rolled up my sleeve to find four raised red welts, all about three inches long, running one next to the other; it looked like I had been scratched. There was no blood; the scratches had not broken the skin; they were just raised welts. Still and all, I wanted to put something on it. I knew there was a first aid kit in the operations room that had some antibacterial spray. I stood up to make my way back to the operations room just as Bill and Sue were coming into the living room.

"Hey, where are you going?" asked Sue.

I showed them both the inexplicable scratch marks on my left forearm.

Sue said, "Oh my God, what happened?"

I told them, "I was just sitting here, waiting for you guys, and I felt my arm burning. When I looked, there were these scratch marks. I was just heading to operations to put something on them."

Bill asked, "Are you ok? Do you want us to come with you?"

"No," I answered. "I'm fine. I'll be back in a few."

Sue and Bill nodded and went into the living room. I found the first aid kit in the operations room and proceeded to spray my arm with the antiseptic spray. The scratches were too big for Band-Aids, so I left them uncovered and rolled down my sleeve. I noticed Tom was not in the operations room, and I had not passed him on my way here, which was odd. Where could he have gone? I stowed away the first aid kit and made my way back to the living room. When I walked in, Tom was there.

"Hey, Bruce, Bill and Sue told me about your arm. You ok?" Tom asked.

"Yeah, fine." I asked Tom, "Where were you? I didn't pass you in the hall."

Tom explained that one of the second-floor video cameras was acting up, and he had gone to check it.

I nodded and asked, "Did you get it fixed?"

Tom replied, "Yeah, no worries," and then asked, "Your arm, you think that was the work of John Ketchum?"

I answered, "Of course, who else?" I told the team we could talk about the arm later. I wanted to get this session going; the longer we waited, the more potential the evil entity John had to renew his energy. Everyone agreed.

Sue stood up and said, "Before we get started, I want to take a couple of pics of those scratches."

I nodded and rolled up my sleeve again. Sue snapped a couple of pictures of the scratches on my left forearm and then returned to her seat. "Ok, guys, let's begin." We all brought our focus back to the task at hand.

"Everyone turn on your voice recorders. Sue, keep that digital camera handy." I checked my watch; it was 1:50 p.m. I reached for my recorder and turned it on, then flicked the ghost box power switch on. The ghost box started sweeping. I was relieved to hear that we still had the optimal reception of the radio broadcast signal we had experienced in the previous group ghost box sessions.

I let a minute pass before delivering my first question. Previously when I'd initiated the ghost box session, the evil spirit John would deliver a comment within seconds, or there would at least be an indication of his presence, a growl, a muffled gravelly voice, something. The ghost box sweep continued without any sign of the evil entity John Ketchum.

I decided to call for my spirit technicians Mike and Lisa. If Ketchum was here, he would surely block them from responding.

"Mike, Lisa, are you around? Can you assist with this session?" A few seconds later Mike's familiar tone came through. "Yes, Bruce, here," followed by a, "Yes," from Lisa. I responded, "Hey, guys, great. How are you?" The answer, "Good," was delivered. "Good, good," I replied.

"Mike, Lisa, is the spirit John Ketchum here with us now?" A "no" came across the ghost box speaker. I responded, "No? Can you tell where he is?" After a few seconds the answer, "Near," came through. I asked for confirmation, "Did you say near?" Lisa answered, "Yes, Bruce, close." I thanked Mike and Lisa and then directed my next comment to Ketchum. I raised the tone of my voice. "John Ketchum, if you're here, let us know you're here." After about ten seconds the response, "You know," came through the box. The communication was uncharacteristically subdued for John; usually, he sent his responses in an aggressive and/or threatening manner. John's passive response was surprising and a bit unnerving. What was he up to? This was the first live spirit communication from John Ketchum that did not have murderous undertones. I had to admit I was a bit confused, as I was sure everyone else was.

I decided to ask a passive question after John's passive reply. "John, how are you?" About fifteen seconds passed with no response. I reiterated, "John, I asked you how you are." A few seconds went by, and, "Don't care," came through the ghost box in a monotone male voice. I asked, "John, what does don't care mean? Is it you who doesn't care?" The answer, "No," came across, followed by, "You," and then, "Don't care." Was it me, or did John sound almost sad and dismayed? I looked at my team members. Bill and Sue just looked back at me, and Tom shrugged his shoulders. I had to admit, this took us all off guard. How should I continue? Did the evil spirit John have an ulterior motive for his now benign demeanor, or was he actually weakened to the point of submission?

As I pondered this new turn of events, a twinge from my forearm reminded me that only a short time before, I had received scratches that I believed had been perpetrated by John Ketchum. I spoke out to John. "John, you seem different, almost scared. Was it you who scratched my arm a little while ago?" I not only wanted an answer to confirm the scratches, but I threw in the scared comment to see if it would get a rise out of John. We waited for John's reply. After about twenty seconds, I asked, "John, what's wrong? Don't you want to answer me?" The reply of, "Yes, me," came through the box, even more timid than before. "John, I have to ask, why are you being so nice? That's not what we would expect from you." After a few seconds, the response, "Tired," came through.

I decided to consult my spirit techs, who had been silent during the communication with John. "Mike, Lisa, are you guys still there and able to communicate?" "Yes, Bruce," came through in a female voice. "Great, do you know what is happening with the spirit John Ketchum?" The answer came through, "No energy," followed by, "Spirits gone." I acknowledged hearing my technician's reply. I paused for a minute to think. Oh yes, the spirit entities John Ketchum had trapped in this house had served as a source of negative energy for him. Their despair, sadness, desperation, and fear were a continuous source of energy renewal for John's rage and power. Now that they were gone, and because my team and I did our best to keep a positive attitude, the evil entity John had virtually no way to gather enough energy to be any kind of threat. Sort of like a boxer in the late rounds of a fight, legs are gone, energy spent, been knocked down a couple of times—he just had nothing left to fight with and no way to regain his strength; now on the canvas he was being counted out. I decided to get my team members' input before proceeding.

I told everyone my thoughts and asked, "Ok, guys, what do you think?"

Tom was first to offer his thoughts. "I don't really know what to think, you could be right, maybe he is spent and is just giving up, but maybe he is playing us. I can't tell for sure."

Bill went next. "I agree with Tom's feelings; this could be a trick. I'm sort of leaning toward the down-and-out theory."

Sue delivered the most coherent opinion. "My thoughts, so far John Ketchum has been an evil, arrogant, and violent bastard. It would be a far stretch to think he would or could give up so easily; however, I don't think he actually has the intelligence or emotional control to put on the act of being beaten for long." Sue went on to say, "I think if we give it more time and continue to prod him, if he is acting, he will eventually lose it and act out according to his nature."

I agreed with all my team's assessments. I thought for a minute and decided to go with Sue's idea. We would prod the spirit John just enough to get him to reveal his true intentions; of course, if he was beaten and weak, we did not want to take advantage of that by assaulting him verbally. I was not one to kick a man when he is down, even if he is an evil entity. The back-and-forth with my team had taken around ten minutes. During that time, not a word of spirit communication had been delivered through the ghost box.

I spoke to John. "John Ketchum, I don't think you are being totally honest with us. I think you're lying about your condition, and I think you are trying to trick us into a false sense of security only to deliver whatever assault you have planned." Quite a few seconds passed, and the reply of, "No trick," came through the box. Of course, if John was lying, that was exactly the response I would expect. I replied, "John, that's exactly what I expected you to say; that's what a liar would say." An aggressive but still pathetically sad response of, "Not lying," came through the box's speaker. "Well, John, that's another thing a liar would say; that's two for two." After about ten or fifteen seconds the response, "So tired," came through the box. That was two antagonistic comments from me, and John did not show any change in his submissive demeanor.

I had to amp up the next comment a bit, something that, if he was lying to trick us, would surely bring his aggression to light and expose his real intentions. "Wow, John, I have to tell you, you sound like a weak, fragile woman." I looked at Sue and winked; she smiled in an understanding way, knowing full well why I made that type of comment. Some seconds later the response of, "No, not a woman," followed by, "Just tired," came across the ghost box speaker in the same subdued tone as all the preceding comments so far.

I decided it was time to deliver to John the most important communication from me up until this time. "John, if you are truly tired, you should think about leaving this house, there is nothing left here for you, and you will continue to be weak and tired as long as you stay here." I followed it with, "John Ketchum, are you willing to leave this house and move on to the spirit realm?" We all waited anxiously for John Ketchum's reply.

The box continued its sweep of the radio broadcast band, delivering its continuous stream of gibberish sounds. It occurred to me for a second that there was no indication of attempts by any other entities to send communication; the ghost box sweep was completely devoid of any spirit chatter. I attributed this to my spirit techs, Mike and Lisa. Realizing the importance of this ghost box session, they were undoubtedly blocking any attempts from spirits on the other side to use the ghost box to send communication; they were real professionals.

After about thirty seconds, I called out to the spirit John, "John, did you hear and understand my last question?" The answer, "Yes," came through the box. I went on to ask, "Well, are you willing to leave here and cross over?" An answer came through the ghost box; it was delivered in a shaky, timid manner. "Scared," was all the evil entity John Ketchum said. I knew then that the entity John Ketchum was defeated. If he were in his true form and disguising his intent, knowing his aggressive nature and arrogant ego, he would never admit to being scared; he would have sent some other benign response to try to keep us on the hook. I looked at my team members, they knew what I was thinking and acknowledged it with nods of approval. I spoke to

BRUCE HALLIDAY

John. "John, don't be afraid. I know you have never been anywhere but this house, and leaving it is scary. We are going to help you to go to a better place where you won't be weak and tired." A few seconds passed, and the response of, "Yes, help," was heard through the ghost box.

Now I was really sure about the spirit John Ketchum. A wave of inner excitement ran through me. Could this be happening? Would we be able to cleanse the Amityville house for good? I took a calming breath and said to John, "John, do you see a bright light anywhere?" The answer, "No," followed by, "Light," came through. I called on my techs. "Mike, Lisa, is there a crossing light anywhere that John can see?" The response, "No white light," was delivered by Mike. "No white light, what does that mean?" I asked, and the response of, "Orange light," came through. This was brand new to me. In the many crossover ghost box sessions I had performed in the last eighteen years, I had never heard the description of an orange light; it had always been described as a bright white light.

I glanced at my watch; it was 2:47 p.m. We had been at this now for about an hour, and we were not finished yet. I asked Mike and Lisa to confirm the last answer. They responded with, "Yes, orange light." My next question to Mike and Lisa was, "Can the spirit John Ketchum use the orange light to cross the same way an entity would use the white light?" The answer, "Don't know, Bruce," came through. This was unprecedented. I decided to follow the accepted crossing-over protocol I had developed many years ago in the fledgling days of live spirit ghost box communication; since I had never experienced this orange light before, I decided to go with the tried and true.

I spoke out to John Ketchum. "John, can you see an orange light where you are?" The answer, "Yes," came through the box. "Good, John. I want you to go to that orange light." The response, "No," came through the ghost box. "John, if you want to leave this lonely house, you will need to go to that orange light." Again the response, "No," came through, followed by, "Scared." It was hard

120

for me to fathom that the spirit John Ketchum, who only hours before had dislodged a hundred-pound mirror from the wall and smashed it, was now cowering like a frightened child. It reminded me of something my father told me when I was a child, "All bullies are really cowards at heart." That statement surely rang true in this instance.

I spoke to my spirit technicians, "Mike, Lisa, can you help John go to the orange light? Can you reassure him that it's ok?" The response of, "Will try," came through the ghost box. "John, there are spirits there who can help you go to the orange light; are you aware of them?" The answer, "Yes," came through. "John, good. Their names are Mike and Lisa; they will help you go to the orange light, ok?" Once again we received the answer, "Yes."

I waited about thirty seconds and then asked, "Mike, Lisa, is John going to the light?" The answer, "Yes, Bruce," came through. I waited another few seconds and asked, "John, are you near the orange light?" Lisa answered for him. "Yes, here," was her response. "Great. Ok, John, walk into the orange light; it will lead you to the spirit realm." As the words left my mouth, the sound of screaming came across the ghost box speaker, in both male and female voices. "Mike, Lisa, we hear screaming; what is that?" About fifteen or twenty seconds passed; at this point, only the sound of a single male voice could be heard screaming; its sound seemed to fade gradually until it could not be heard at all. I called out, "Mike, Lisa, are you there?" We received no response. I waited a moment and asked again, "Mike, Lisa, John, are any of you there?" I began to become very concerned, and I could see my team members were also. It had been about two minutes since the screaming that we heard stopped.

As I was about to ask for my spirit techs again, a voice came through the ghost box; it was Lisa, "Bruce." I replied, "Yes, Lisa, I'm here; go ahead." A few seconds later the message, "John gone," came through. "John gone. What does that mean? Did he cross over?" A few seconds passed, and Mike's voice came through. "John, demons, bad." We all heard this clearly. I replied,

"Demons bad, what do you mean?" We waited a bit for our tech's next reply.

Explaining a specific situation was not easy to do, especially when a spirit had to choose the correct words to express what they needed us to understand. It was not as if they were simply speaking into a microphone or telephone; the communication had to be built from the small bits of sound fragments produced by the ghost box sweep. This made live spirit communication often cryptic, like a jigsaw puzzle that was missing pieces. The delivering entity needed to choose the correct words in order to deliver an abridged version of what they actually wanted to say.

After a few more seconds, the response of, "John grabbed," and then the words, "Pulled in," came across the ghost box speaker. "What do you mean, grabbed, pulled?" Lisa followed with, "John pulled in." I contemplated the preceding messages for a second or two and asked, "John pulled in where, into the orange light?" The response, "Yes," came through. "Ok, who pulled him into the orange light?" What Mike conveyed next confirmed what we had suspected. "Demons took him!" Mike said. We now all understood the evil spirit John Ketchum's fate; everything fell into place: the orange light instead of a white light, the screaming when John and my techs approached the orange light, and the fading sound of a single male voice into nothing. The evil entity John's spirit had been dragged by demons to Hell. I sat back in my chair and thought to myself, *I suppose that is a fitting fate for such a poison-filled spirit who committed horrible and violent atrocities in both his physical and spiritual life.*

I looked at my team. Everyone had a stoic look on their face. There was no happiness, no joy at what had just been accomplished; it is a very sad and unfortunate thing when one of God's souls is lost to eternal damnation. This was the end of what was one of the most monumental live spirit ghost box communication sessions ever performed, by me or any other living individual.

Before ending the session and turning off the ghost box, I thanked my spirit technicians Mike and Lisa for their invaluable help and protection, and for placing themselves in harm's way to help cleanse the Amityville house of an evil presence. Mike and Lisa responded with the familiar closing message, "Love you all." This was the last live spirit communication of the session. I turned off the ghost box and my digital recorder and got up from my chair.

CHAPTER EIGHT

THE INVESTIGATION ENDS & THE AMITYVILLE HOUSE IS CLEAN

I looked at my watch; it was just about to turn 4:00 p.m. The whole session had taken just over two hours; it felt like it lasted for a week. As we all entered the operations room, I could tell my team, as well as I, were all mentally, emotionally, and physically exhausted. We all fell into a chair.

Sue asked, "I'm getting something to drink; anyone else want anything?"

We all asked for a bottle of water, and Bill asked, "I could use a couple of aspirin; do we have any?"

Sue answered, "I think so," handed us all a water bottle, retrieved the aspirin from the first aid kit, and handed them to Bill.

Tom asked, "Bruce, how's your arm?"

I had forgotten about the injury to my arm. I touched it and brought on a slight twinge of soreness. "It's fine," I told Tom. "I guess my arm, the broken mirror, the broken video monitor, and the messy bathroom sink are all that's left of John Ketchum." I knew everyone was eager to discuss the events of the group session, but I suggested we postpone the debriefing until after we'd all had some rest.

"Good idea," offered Bill. "My head is pounding."

I told everyone to make themselves comfortable, and since we had only grabbed about two hours of sleep in the last thirty hours, if anyone wanted to catch a nap, feel free. I went on to say, "We'll take a two-hour break and then discuss the session." All more than willingly agreed. It was 4:20 p.m. "We will resume at 6:30 p.m." Everyone nodded in agreement. We all found a comfortable spot and settled in for a much-needed, and well-deserved rest.

My cell phone alarm rang at 6:15 p.m. I opened my eyes and reached over to silence it. I sat up from the reclining position I was in and felt a twinge of pain in my lower back. I was getting way too old to be napping in a chair. I looked around. Tom was reclined in his chair with his eyes closed, and Bill sat curled up on the floor against the wall, rubbing his eyes.

Sue walked into the room and exclaimed, "Good evening, boys, time to wake up." Sue carried a small tray with four Styrofoam cups filled with coffee.

"Oh, you're a lifesaver." Tom sat up in his chair and said, "That cannot have been two hours. I'm more tired than when I fell asleep."

"Me too," Bill said.

Sue said, "Aww, come on, you guys are lightweights," as she handed out the cups of coffee. We all gathered groggily at the table, sipping the hot coffee.

"Ok, is everybody coherent enough to discuss the last session?" I asked.

Bill offered, "Almost there, one more sip."

I told Sue since she was so chipper, she could speak first.

Sue put down her coffee and paused for a second to gather her thoughts. "Ok, so I can sum up this whole investigation in one short phrase, 'un-freaking-believable!' I experienced more paranormal activity in one hour of this investigation than I have in my whole life all put together. I mean, just the fact that we were able to help cross over four trapped spirits was over the top, but then to be able to help defeat and remove the evil spirit entity John Ketchum, who has plagued this house since the day it was built. I mean, that has to be the greatest accomplishment in paranormal research and investigation history. When the results of our data and evidence come out, it's going to be huge." Sue went on to say, "I just want to add that even in the face of violent paranormal attacks and physical injury, we were all able to hold it together and do something here that is unprecedented. I am so proud to work with you guys and to be a member of this team. That's about all I have to say for now."

I thanked Sue and turned the floor over to Bill.

Bill scratched his head and said, "I can echo what Sue just said; however, my brain is still trying to process everything that happened here in the last two days. There is just so much we all experienced that needs to be contemplated that right now my mind is reeling. Thank God we have the technology that allowed us to document all that occurred, audio, video, and data collection. Without that, nobody would ever believe what happened here. Unless you want me to elaborate on one specific incident, that's pretty much all for the moment." Bill scratched his head one more time and went back to sipping his coffee.

"Ok, Tom, your turn," I said.

Tom was sitting at the table behind the video monitors and laptop computer. The first thing he said was, "Oh my God, you're not gonna believe the shit ton of audio and video we have to review and document; this will take months easily." Evidence and data review and documentation was a double-edged sword. On the one side, it was exciting to discover audio and video evidence that was not heard or seen live by the investigators; on the other side, audio, video, and data review was an extremely tedious and painstaking process that took an extraordinary amount of time to sift through and decipher. Tom was right; it would take literally months to go over all the data we'd collected on this investigation.

Tom continued his thoughts, "Well, I think Bill and Sue pretty much said it all. Bruce, you and I have been working together now for about fifteen years. I don't know about you, but this investigation has to be in the top two of all time for quantity and

quality of paranormal activity. I mean, just the ghost box communication alone was the best I can ever remember, plus what we
captured on video, not to mention what we missed hearing live
during the ghost box sessions, and the video that was captured
that we weren't aware of. The review is gonna be grueling, but
I'm sure there will be quite a few surprises yet to come. As far as
the investigation itself, everybody was super professional and
super brave, especially you, Sue, for a novice investigator with
only, what, a year and a half experience. Great job."

Sue looked at Tom and smiled. "Thanks, big brother," she said.

Tom finished with, "I'm not really a sentimental guy, but there
are no other people in the world I would want to go through an
experience like this one with than you guys." With that, Tom was
finished.

"Ok, guys, there's not much more I can add to what has
already been said. I mirror those feelings exactly. I would just like
to add that I am proud of you all, and proud to have and work
with such a great team of paranormal investigators." I raised my
coffee cup and said, "Here's to a great team, good friends, and a
super-successful investigation."

Everyone raised their cups. "Hear, hear," "Absolutely," "To
us," were the team's responses.

"Ok, everyone, I think we have pretty much run the gamut for
this investigation. I know we still have another night remaining;
however, I don't believe there are any more entities here in the
Amityville house. I believe we have done all we can do here. I
suggest we tie up any loose ends, clean up, pack up, and head
home." All agreed.

"There is one more thing we need to do before we wrap it up. I
want to turn on the ghost box and have our spirit technicians
Mike and Lisa confirm that the house is clear." I reached for my
ghost box and digital voice recorder. I started the recorder and
switched on the ghost box. As the ghost box started its sweep, I
asked for my spirit techs. "Mike, Lisa, you guys around?" The
response, "Yes, Bruce," came through. "Hi, Mike, hi, Lisa, can you

tell me is this house clean? Are there any other entities here in this house?" About thirty seconds passed, and the response "Yes, clear," came through the ghost box. I replied, "Great, thanks, guys." As I was about to shut off the ghost box, a male voice came through and said, "Wait." I asked, "Mike, did you say wait?" The response, "Yes, wait," came through. "Ok, I'll wait," I answered.

A few seconds later a child's voice came through the box. "Hi." We heard it clearly. "Hi, who is that?" I asked. The response, "John," came across the box's speaker. "John, is that little John DeFeo?" The reply "Yes, John," came back. "John, how are you?" Little John answered, "Good," and then, "Now." A warm feeling came over all of us knowing that little John DeFeo was in the spirit world and happy. "John, we are glad you are ok. Be happy, and please communicate with us whenever you can." A few seconds later the response, "Thank you," came through in the innocent tone of a child's voice. "You're welcome, John," I answered. I thanked my spirit technicians Mike and Lisa and shut down the ghost box and turned off the recorder. We were all happy, proud, and a bit emotional after hearing from a happy little John DeFeo.

I looked at my watch; it was 7:15 p.m. Saturday evening. We had officially begun the investigation of the Amityville house at approximately 3:00 p.m. on Friday afternoon, and officially ended the investigation on Saturday evening at 7:15 p.m. The entire investigation had taken approximately thirty hours. My team and I had initially planned to spend forty-eight hours conducting our investigation; however, events occurring as they did, we had wrapped it up around eighteen hours ahead of schedule.

I told the team we needed to clean up as best we could. Bill and Sue volunteered to clean up the living room, the broken glass from the mirror still lay strewn across the living room floor, and the room needed general straightening out, chairs, tables, and so forth. I asked Tom if he would start to break down and retrieve all the equipment that had been placed around the house.

"Of course," Tom replied.

I told the team I would contact our Amityville house liaison, Sarah, and inform her that we had completed our investigation, and then I would proceed to start getting the operations room in order. Everyone nodded in approval and left for their designated tasks.

I sat down and dialed Sarah's number, the phone rang a few times, and Sarah picked up. "Hello."

I answered, "Hi, Sarah, it's Bruce Halliday."

"Oh, yes," she replied.

I went on to tell her, "We have completed our investigation."

She replied, "Oh really, I thought you would be there until sometime tomorrow."

"Yes, that was the plan, but circumstances have led to our finishing the investigation ahead of time."

Sarah replied, "That's fine. I will try to be there in about an hour or so."

"Ok, great," I said, followed by, "Goodbye, Sarah."

"Goodbye," she replied.

I ended the call and began to assess what needed to be done to get the operations room ready to be packed out.

I had just about finished disconnecting and packing the video monitors in their cases when Tom came in carrying an armload of wires and two video cameras. "Got everything disconnected and am just carrying it down now," said Tom.

"Good, I'm squaring away this room," I replied.

Tom put the cables and the cameras in their respective cases and headed back upstairs for another load.

With that, Bill walked in from the opposite side of the room, carrying a large cardboard box filled with shards from the broken mirror. "Sue found a vacuum cleaner in the hall closet. She is vacuuming the rugs in the living room," Bill announced.

"Is that what I hear? I couldn't figure out what that was," I replied.

"We are going to finish up in the living room and then head up to give Tom a hand."

"Ok," I told Bill, "sounds good."

"Hey, Bruce, is it ok if I keep a piece of this broken mirror for a souvenir?" Bill asked.

"I don't see why not. Be careful; don't get cut," I answered.

Bill set the box down, removed a piece of the broken mirror, and wrapped it in a piece of old cloth. Bill went back to finish up in the living room, and I resumed opening the remaining hard cases for the rest of the equipment to be stored.

Tom came back with another load of cables, extension cords, and two more video cameras, placed them in their respective cases, and said, "Only the tripods and one more camera and the upper floors are clear."

"Great," I replied. "I'm pretty much done here. Do you need a hand?" I asked.

"Well, yeah, if you're not busy; it will save me another trip."

"Ok, lead the way."

Tom and I proceeded to the third floor to retrieve the last of the equipment. As we walked up the stairs, I remembered that we needed to clean up the bathroom sink where the dark brown water had backed up earlier. Tom and I gathered up the remaining equipment and started to make our way down to the operations room. As we walked, Tom said, "Wow, can you feel the difference in this house, it feels cozy and inviting now, sort of a warm feeling?"

I replied, "Yes, it does; nice feeling, isn't it?"

"Uh-huh," Tom exclaimed.

We reached the operations room to find Bill and Sue waiting there. We stowed the remainder of the equipment and closed all the equipment cases.

"Ok, everybody, let's make one more sweep of the house and make sure we didn't miss anything. Also, the bathroom sink on this floor may need to be cleaned; any volunteers?"

"I'll do it," said Sue.

"Ok, thanks. Ok, guys, let's do a sweep and meet back here in a few minutes."

All of us headed off in different directions. About ten or fifteen minutes later everyone made their way back to the operations room. Bill was carrying a K2 meter. "Found it in the basement," he said and put it in one of the cases.

"Great job, guys," I said. "That went pretty smoothly. Sue, is the bathroom sink good?"

Sue nodded and smiled.

"Ok, let's take a break. The woman, Sarah, should be here shortly." As we all sat down, I heard the sound of the front door opening and closing. A few seconds later Sarah walked into the room.

"Hello, everyone," she said. "Is it me, or does it feel different in here?" she asked.

"Yes, it does; it's that noticeable, huh?" I asked.

"Yes, that feeling of heaviness and chill is gone." Sarah then asked, "Did everything go alright; any problems?"

I asked her to take a seat, and she did. "There were a couple of incidents. The large mirror over the fireplace in the living room was pulled from the wall and shattered—"

Sarah cut me off. "WHAT? How was that big heavy mirror pulled from the wall? It was there in the same spot for over fifty years," she exclaimed.

"Would you like an explanation of the investigation, which will cover the mirror?"

"Wait, you said there were a couple of incidents. What else happened? Was there more damage?" she asked.

I told her about the light and the sink in the bathroom, not damage per se, but an incident concerning objects in the house.

"Ok, so the mirror was the only thing damaged?" she asked.

"Yes," I replied.

"Ok, Mr. Halliday, I will make an inspection of the house and meet you back here in a bit."

I replied, "Ok, fine. Please call me Bruce."

Sarah managed a small smile and left the room.

Tom suggested that we start to carry the equipment out to the vehicle while we waited for Sarah to complete her inspection, and I agreed. We all stood up, and Tom said, "Bruce, why don't you stay here in case miss congeniality needs anything."

I chuckled and nodded. Tom, Bill, and Sue started to carry the equipment outside. I fanatically went and checked my two equipment cases to make sure my ghost boxes and personal equipment were safe and secure. About a half hour passed, and I could see Sarah enter the living room from where I was seated. Just then Sue came in and sat down while Tom and Bill took the last of the equipment cases out to the vehicle. As Sarah reentered the operations room, so did Tom and Bill.

"Ok, Bruce," Sarah said, "everything seems to be ok. Is there anything else you need to tell me?"

I paused for a quick second and answered, "No, that's about it, unless you would like to hear how the investigation went."

Sarah replied, "No, no, that's for you to report to the owners."

I told her, "Well, it will be some time before we have had a chance to review all the evidence and data we collected, but you can tell the owners that their house is clean, free of any paranormal entities."

Sarah replied, "That's great to hear. I will pass that along," followed by, "I will tell them also that you will contact them at some point to schedule a meeting for your report of the investigation."

I thanked Sarah. Sarah then asked if we were just about ready to leave. I told her that everything except the mirror was as we found it, and that we were ready to go. We all got up, Sarah shook everyone's hand and thanked us again, and we all headed for the front door. We all exited the famed Amityville house carrying what would surely be a lifelong memory. Sarah followed us out, turned, and locked the front door. She smiled as she walked to her car. We proceeded to our vehicle, made one more visual scan of the area to make sure we were not leaving anything behind, and then got in.

I was driving. As we made our way down the long driveway

to the main road, I glanced into the rearview mirror and watched as the renowned Amityville house faded from view, forever etched in our memories. I could not help but feel a proud sense of accomplishment for myself and my paranormal investigating team.

CHAPTER NINE

THE CONJURING HOUSE INVESTIGATION

I n January 1971, the Perron family—Roger, Carolyn, and their five daughters, Andrea, Nancy, Christine, Cindy, and April—occupied a large rural home in Harrisville, Rhode Island, at 1667 Roundtop Road.

Almost immediately upon moving in, the Perron family started to experience odd occurrences in the home. Carolyn

Perron began to notice small things either missing or moved, strange noises around the house, and small things appearing out of nowhere. Carolyn decided to investigate the history of the house. It had been in the same family for eight generations; she also discovered that a number of people had died there under suspicious and heinous circumstances. A number of children had drowned, one individual was murdered, and a number of people committed suicide by hanging themselves.

| The Perron Family

As time went on, the Perrons reported incidents with a malevolent entity that called itself Bathsheba. Carolyn, during her investigation of the dark past of the house, discovered that there was actually a woman named Bathsheba Sherman who occupied the property around the middle 1800s. The woman Bathsheba was reported to have practiced satanism, and had been reported to have been responsible for the death of a neighbor's child. She was never formally charged with the murder, and no trial took place. Upon the death of Bathsheba Sherman, who died from an unexplained paralysis that could not be explained by doctors, her remains were interred in a nearby cemetery in Harrisville, Rhode Island.

| The Actual Headstone of Bathsheba Sherman

The Perron family believed it was the evil spirit of Bathsheba that was the cause of the negative activity they were experiencing. Andrea, one of the Perron children, said the family experienced other spirit activity and entities that carried the stench of rotten flesh. She reported that there were incidents of beds rising up off the floor, and that her father, Roger, would experience unusually cold temperatures when entering the basement of the home, and also feel a foul-smelling presence following him. The home's heating system would often stop working mysteriously, causing Roger's trips to the basement. Over the course of the Perron family's ten-year residence in the house, the paranormal investigating team of Ed and Lorraine Warren were called upon to investigate and had visited the home on multiple occasions.

Ed and Lorraine Warren

During one of the Warrens' visits, Lorraine Warren performed a séance, during which Carolyn Perron was reported to have begun speaking in tongues in a voice not her own; the entity believed to be speaking through Carolyn was that of Bathsheba Sherman. At one point during the séance, Carolyn was said to have, while sitting in her chair, risen above the floor and been thrown across the room. These reports were corroborated by Andrea, one of the Perron children, who had secretly witnessed the events. It was reported that following the events of the séance, Roger Perron asked the Warrens to leave the home, as he was in fear for his wife's mental state.

Ed and Lorraine Warren, after their investigations of the home, declared there was a demonic entity occupying the house. Carolyn had also reported to the Warrens that she had experienced severe pain in her calf; upon inspection she discovered a bloody puncture wound that could not be explained. Andrea Perron reported that the family continued to live in the home due to their financial situation, but were finally able to leave the home in 1980. After the Perron family left the home, there continued to be further reports of paranormal activity made by subsequent residents. There have been many reports of strange and paranormal activity in the Harrisville house and surrounding property over the years that continue to this day.

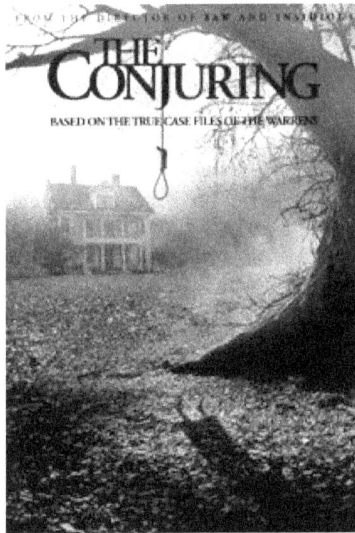

| The Motion Picture *The Conjuring*

On July 19, 2013, the motion picture titled *The Conjuring* was released by Warner Bros. Pictures. The film was written by Chad Hayes and Carey W. Hayes and directed by James Wan. The movie starred Patrick Wilson and Vera Farmiga as Ed and Lorraine Warren, the renowned paranormal investigators, and was said to be based on their experiences in the home of the Perron family in Harrisville, Rhode Island. Following the major success of the film, the alleged haunted house in Rhode Island would be referred to as "the Conjuring house." The popularity of the film, which grossed a whopping $319 million worldwide, gave birth to a film franchise known as the "Conjuring" films, which were loosely based on the case files of Ed and Lorraine Warren. The subsequent films depicted various other hauntings and possessions investigated by the Warrens, including the famed "Amityville Horror" case.

As I did with the other case depicted in this book, I will give my interpretation of how a paranormal investigation of the Conjuring house could have gone if I and my paranormal investigating team conducted the investigation with the main investigative tool being a "ghost box." I will once again attempt to give an account of the interaction that might have occurred between myself, my team members, and any spirit entities that were found to be in residence at the infamous Conjuring house, which will include audible, visual, and physical experiences of any and all paranormal activity experienced by myself and my team members.

CHAPTER TEN
BEGINNING THE CONJURING HOUSE INVESTIGATION

My paranormal investigating team and I were driving down Route 98 in Rhode Island, headed for one of the biggest paranormal investigations we had ever done. We saw the sign for Harrisville, Rhode Island. We exited onto Route 96, which would lead us directly to our destination. We had been driving for about four hours; it was around noon on Friday. We were contracted to do an in-depth paranormal investigation of one of the most famed hauntings in history, "the Conjuring house." Along with our investigation of the Amityville house, this would be the second-most-popularized alleged haunted location we had ever had the opportunity to investigate. If the Conjuring house turned out to be half as active as the Amityville house, we were in for quite an investigation.

As we entered the drive at 1677 Roundtop Road, we saw the ominous-looking Conjuring house. I had never had the opportunity to see it in person, only in pictures; it was much bigger than I expected. We pulled up to the house and could see a man coming out the front door. He was an older gentleman dressed in rural clothes, jeans, boots, and a thick woolen coat. We all exited the car as the man walked up.

"Hello, I'm Bruce Halliday of Halliday Paranormal." I

extended my hand, and he shook it. "This is my investigating team, Tom, Bill, and Sue."

The man introduced himself with a slight New England accent. "Hello, I'm John," he said. "Pleased to meet you all." John had a very nice demeanor, sort of jolly, and he wore a welcoming smile. As he turned toward the house, he waved us on and said, "Come on in. I'm sure you're eager to see the old place."

As we walked to the front door, I couldn't help but notice that the house was oddly structured. It looked as if there was a smaller house attached to a larger two-story house. It was very rural in appearance; the whole house was covered in dark wooden planks and had what looked like a makeshift door with a circular viewing portal in it. It reminded me of a big glorified log cabin. John pulled open the front door, and we all walked inside. The interior of the house was not what I expected. By the way the outside looked, I was expecting a floor made of wooden boards, rustic furnishings, and a potbellied stove. The interior of the Conjuring house was unexpectedly modern. It was clean and inviting, the décor was relatively modern, and the walls were brightly painted. The house did not seem ominous at all, but looks were deceiving, which I had learned all too well on many a paranormal investigation.

John asked if we would like a tour of the house. I thanked him and told him we preferred to explore on our own. Still smiling, John nodded in understanding. "Ok, then, I'll leave you to it," John said. He extended his hand; in it was a piece of paper. "Here's my phone number. Give me a call about half an hour before you're ready to leave." We both smiled, I thanked John, and we all said goodbye. As he walked out the front door, he turned and said, "Oh yeah, try not to break anything, and have fun. See you tomorrow." John left, shutting the front door behind him.

The house was chilled, which was to be expected; after all, it was late fall. There were multiple fireplaces located throughout the house; however, it was a standing rule, we never utilized a fireplace during an investigation. The house was heated. I assumed John had only turned on the heat shortly before we arrived, and it would take some time for the big spacious house to arrive at a comfortable temperature. I told the team to get started unloading the vehicle while I got a general feel for the place. They agreed and headed outside.

I made my way from the initial living area on the main floor to the dining room, passing through a small hallway with a staircase leading to the second floor. The dining room was where the Warrens had performed the infamous séance in which all present claimed to have experienced Carolyn Perron speaking in tongues with a voice that was not her own, and being levitated in a chair, only to then be violently thrown across the room.

As I walked into the dining room, I saw a large wooden dining room table with eight chairs, a fairly large fireplace, and a break-front that held some dishes and various knickknacks. An eerie feeling came over me. I began to feel queasy and a bit dizzy. I did not know whether to attribute this to a paranormal presence or the power of suggestion, thinking about the events that were reported to have taken place on the spot where I was standing.

I made my way out of the dining room and into the adjoining room, which was the kitchen. The sick feeling that had come over me in the dining room was starting to subside. I took a deep breath and shook off the remainder of the feeling. I paused for a moment to assess any feelings I might have concerning the nature of the room. With the heat running, I noticed the room was quite comfortable, and the entire house should be warming up to an acceptable temperature. The kitchen was brightly lit and contained everything one would expect a kitchen to have, a stove, refrigerator, cabinets, etc.

I left the kitchen and walked back through the living room; to the left side of the living room was a small library. I walked into the library. There were a number of chairs with small end tables next to them; the walls were covered with bookshelves from floor to ceiling, containing hundreds of books. The entrance from the living room into this library had two separate doors that abutted each other, which struck me as odd.

As I made my way to the staircase leading to the second floor, I thought to myself that the whole layout of this house was odd; anyone could tell that this house was very old and not designed for modern living. I climbed the short staircase leading up to the second floor. I entered the second floor into a small bedroom. There was a bed to my right; the room also contained a dresser, a rocking chair, and a fireplace. To my left was a door leading through a small space used as a clothes closet and into the next room, which was also a bedroom. This room was also sparsely decorated, with a bed, chair, dresser, and a small writing desk. I walked straight through this bedroom and entered another bedroom. This small bedroom had a pitched ceiling and contained two small single beds facing each other end to end against the wall, two night tables, a dresser, and a large round cushion-covered chair. At the far end of the room, there was an entrance leading to a small attic space used for storage. It was dimly lit and dusty, just what you would expect an attic storage room to look like. The bedroom also had access to a staircase leading back down to the main floor.

I made my way back downstairs and exited the staircase. I found myself on a small landing that led to a relatively empty room with a few boxes and a clothes rack; at the far end of the room was a doorway that led to yet another living room area. As I crossed the threshold into this third living room, I immediately felt a blast of cold air and began to feel the hair on the back of my neck stand on end. Standing in this room, I had the distinct feeling of being watched. I turned and looked around me. I was alone in the room. The room contained a couch, a leather office-type chair, and a makeshift desk. It also contained a red door, which for the moment I did not open to see where it led; I assumed it led outside the house.

I had only one more area to check out, the basement. I searched for a staircase that would lead me down. I found the basement stairs in the front room where we had entered the house. I walked down the basement staircase. As I entered the basement, I could see the walls consisted of big stones held together by mortar, the floor had been covered in sheets of plywood, and there was the typical musty damp smell that was commonly found in a basement. To my left was a small room that oddly enough contained a table, with four chairs set around it, and a couple of old beat-up cabinets. The basement ran the whole length of the house. As I walked through, it became apparent that the whole basement was under construction. There were a couple of small rooms being constructed on the left side of the basement, and there were building equipment and supplies in various spots throughout. Other than the usual creepiness of a basement, especially in an old house, I could not sense anything that seemed to be paranormal. I had no odd feelings or emotions.

I made my way back up to the area where we entered the house to find my team bringing in the last of the equipment cases. "Hey, guys," I said, "got everything in ok?"

Tom answered, "Yeah, no problem."

Sue asked, "How does the place look? Did you sense anything?"

I answered by suggesting we choose a spot for the operations room, and I would go over my walkthrough once we were settled; all agreed. I told the team that, in my opinion, this front living room would be the best spot to set up operations; it was just as good as any other room and would save us the trouble of lugging the equipment cases farther into the house.

Bill asked, "Why not use the dining room?"

I told Bill that I believed we would be getting a lot of activity in the dining room, and I wanted to use that room for the group ghost box sessions I had planned for the investigation. Bill nodded understandingly. I asked Tom to retrieve the folding table we had stored in the vehicle so it could be used to set up the video monitors. Tom left to get the folding table. I asked Bill and Sue to gather a few random chairs for us all that we could place here in the operations room. As Bill and Sue went in search of the chairs, I began to open and unpack the equipment cases.

Tom came in carrying the folding table.

"Let's move this couch back, Tom, and we can set up the table in its place." Tom and I pushed the couch back to one side of the room and proceeded to open up the folding table. Bill and Sue entered the room, both carrying two chairs.

"How are these?" asked Sue.

"Great," I replied. Tom and I turned the folding table right side up and placed it down. Bill placed one chair behind the table, facing the middle of the room. Sue and I placed the other three chairs at either end of the table. "Ok, guys, let's take a seat. I'll tell you about my walkthrough before we get started setting up." Everyone took a seat and listened intently. I took a breath and began, "First off, let me say that this is the most oddly situated house I have ever been in. When they built this house, it is obvious they built it for utility and not comfort or aesthetics. The house is a maze. You go into one room that leads to another, and then you turn, and there is another unexpected room. It's crazy, but I guess it served the purposes of the original owners. There are three living rooms and only one and a half bathrooms. Why anyone would need three living rooms on the same floor escapes me."

I went on to explain the layout of the house and the different rooms it contained. I also explained the cold spots and ill feelings I had experienced in certain rooms. Everyone, including myself, was eager to get started, we were only given twenty-four-hour access to the Conjuring house for this investigation, and we didn't want to waste a minute of it. I told the team to start going about the task of setting up and placing the equipment and, while doing so, to choose the locations they wanted for their initial individual investigations. I told everyone I would be conducting my first live spirit ghost box communication session in the library room here on the main floor, and we should all meet back here in forty-five minutes. Everyone nodded, got up, and got busy. I looked at my watch; it was 1:45 p.m. on Friday.

I stood up and went over to my personal equipment case, opened it, and removed my #1 ghost box, digital voice recorder, and equipment pouch. Since I had chosen to perform my first live ghost box session in the library, I decided to go and make sure there were electrical outlets for me to plug my ghost box into. I had formed the habit of using the power cord to run my ghost box as opposed to using battery power. There was always the chance that an entity could drain the power from the batteries in any device, and I did not want to have to interrupt my live ghost box session to either change the ghost box batteries or utilize the power cord after the fact.

As I walked to the library to check for outlets, I heard the distinct but faint voice of a woman. I could not understand what was said, but I did not immediately assume it was paranormal in nature. I called out to Sue, "Sue, are you around?"

A reply to my shout came from the other room. Bill answered, "Bruce, Sue is upstairs helping Tom set up the video cameras."

I answered Bill with a, "Thanks."

Bill responded, "Is there something you need help with?"

"No," I answered, "I'm good."

Bill came back with, "Ok."

I knew I had heard a distinctly female voice, and thinking about it, the voice sounded nothing like Sue. I committed the incident to memory and proceeded to check the library for electrical outlets. I found three outlets in the library that I could use to run my ghost box, and returned to the operations room. I entered the operations room to find Tom and Sue sitting there. "Where's Bill?" I asked.

"He's setting up two cameras in the dining room, should be here in a few minutes."

"Ok, great, as soon as he gets here, we will go over the plan for the initial investigation." We sat around chitchatting for a few minutes, and Bill walked in.

"Sorry if I kept you guys waiting," he said.

"No problem. Now that we are all here, I want to go over the plan for the first phase of the investigation. Since we only have twenty-four hours for the whole investigation, I want to make sure we use every minute of it wisely." All three nodded. I started by asking Sue which section of the house she picked and what she would be doing.

Sue explained that she had chosen the living room at the far end of the house for her first investigation. She added that she would be doing an EVP session and taking still photographs, as well as taking temperature and energy readings.

Bill went next. "I picked one of the upstairs bedrooms. I want to take a handheld video camera and place some target objects. I also want to do an EVP session and monitor a K2 meter."

"Good," I said. "Tom, what about you?"

Tom said he chose the basement for his initial investigation, and he would be doing an EVP session as well as taking IR (infrared spectrum) video with the new IR video camera the team had just acquired.

"Ok, great, sounds good. I will be doing a live ghost box session in the library here on the main floor." I glanced at my watch and said, "All right, everybody, it's 2:15 p.m. Let's get to it, be careful, and we will meet back here around 3:45 p.m. Good luck, and happy hunting."

Everyone rose from their seats, grabbed the equipment they needed, and headed out of the operations room.

CHAPTER ELEVEN
THE INITIAL INVESTIGATION

I picked up my ghost box and digital recorder and attached my equipment pouch around my waist. I walked to my left into the second living room and walked through the entrance of the library. I placed my ghost box on a small round table and plugged the power cord into the electrical outlet underneath it and sat in a big Victorian-style chair next to it. I placed my digital recorder next to the ghost box and retrieved my temperature gun and EMF detector from my equipment pouch.

I turned on the temp gun and aimed the red laser at the wall of books facing me; the temperature read 68 degrees Fahrenheit. This was understandable, the house was large, and the heating system was probably not as big as it should be for a house this size, explaining the cooler temperature. I made it a point never to seek out and mess with the thermostat settings in any location we investigated, the homeowner set the temperature at their desired level, and that was where it would remain. It was always more advantageous for our investigation if the ambient temperature of a location was higher than it should be, a higher ambient temperature would make any cold spots experienced in the house more easily felt and detected. I was sure the temperature would fluctuate throughout the house, so it might be warmer than 68 degrees in other sections of the house.

I put away the temp gun and took out my EMF (electromagnetic field) detector, turned it on, and held it out in front of me; the reading was fluctuating between zero and three, which indicated there was a very low EMF field in this room. I attributed this to there being no electrical devices running in the immediate area of the library. It also indicated to me that there was most likely no paranormal presence in attendance at the moment. Instead of putting the EMF detector away, I kept it handy. I wanted to take a quick EMF reading after I turned on the ghost box to see how much the running ghost box would affect the EMF level.

I did not prepare a predetermined set of questions for this ghost box session. I would conduct a general question session and adapt the session to whatever circumstances arose. I reached for my digital voice recorder and turned it on and stated the information of the location and session date, and time. I then flicked the power switch on the ghost box to the on position. The familiar sound of gibberish produced by the ghost box sweeps breaking down the radio broadcast of human speech, music, singing, and white static noise that comes between the radio stations came through the ghost box speaker. The sweep contained a bit more static noise than I would have liked, which I attributed to the home's rural location and its distant proximity to a broadcasting radio station.

I asked the first question I always asked at the onset of a live spirit ghost box communication session. "Mike, Lisa, are you there? Can you assist me in this session?" Even though I asked this same question at the beginning of every ghost box session, I knew the answer; my spirit technicians Mike and Lisa have never failed to be in attendance and render their help and protection in every live ghost box session I have ever done. I waited a few seconds, and a familiar-sounding male voice came through the ghost box speaker, delivered above the sound of the ghost box sweep. "Yes, Bruce, here." Although I knew already without asking that it was my tech Mike, I always verified the communicated answer. "Mike, was that you?" The answer, "Yes," came through. "Hi, Mike, how are you, buddy?" I asked. Mike replied, "Good." I acknowledged his communication by saying, "Great, Mike, nice to hear you."

I then asked, "Lisa, are you there also?" After a few seconds the answer, "Here, Bruce," came through the box. It was funny, Lisa's two-word answer was delivered in both a male and female voice. Because the live spirit communication that is delivered through a ghost box is constructed by the communicating entity from random sound fragments produced by the ghost box sweep, it is not uncommon for the words of communication from a female entity to be sent in a male voice, or a combination of male and female voices; the same rings true for a male entity that builds and delivers live spirit communication. I acknowledged Lisa and asked how she was. I received the reply, "Fine, Bruce." I thanked both my spirit technicians for being in attendance, and prepared to deliver my first session question.

As I was poised to ask my question, I felt the temperature in the room drop. What had been a cool but comfortable temperature of 68 degrees had suddenly turned to a feeling of bitter cold. I could feel the cold actually nipping at my exposed face and hands. I took out my temp gun and took a reading: 47 degrees, the temperature had dropped 21 degrees in a matter of seconds.

I put away the temperature gun and turned my head to look at the still operating EMF meter. As I did, I noticed I could actually see my breath as I exhaled. I looked at the EMF detector; the indicator needle was pinned beyond the meter's highest reading. This was not due to any electrical device in operation or a power surge; this dramatic EMF reading, and the drastic reduction in temperature, could only mean one thing, there was an entity in this room with me, and a powerful one at that.

I turned my attention back to the ghost box. I immediately

asked, "Are there any spirit entities here with me?" I waited for a response from the ghost box, but none was forthcoming. I repeated my question in a slightly higher tone of voice; after about fifteen seconds, still no response. I called out to my spirit technicians, "Mike, Lisa, if there is an entity here with me, please help them to use the ghost box to communicate." I followed that request with, "The entity here with me now, you can use the sound coming from this device (I pointed to the ghost box) to communicate with me. I will be able to hear everything you say." After a few seconds, I heard a loud and clear female voice that was low and almost masculine in tone. "My house," came across the ghost box speaker, followed immediately by, "Leave now." The communication was surprisingly clear and concise given that I believed this entity was not at all familiar with communicating through a ghost box, not to mention the less than pristine ghost box reception and sweep conditions.

The ice was broken. I had made initial contact with a spirit entity I believed was here in this house and in the room with me at this very moment. I asked my spirit technicians, "Mike, Lisa, is the entity here with me now negative in nature?" I waited for an answer from my spirit techs. As I did, I could hear, buried in the sound of the ghost box sweep, low muffled voices making an attempt to communicate. I then asked, "Mike, Lisa, are you guys still there? Can you still communicate?" I waited about twenty or thirty seconds for a reply from my techs, but received none. At this point, I realized my spirit techs Mike and Lisa could no longer deliver their communication. This could only mean one thing, the entity in attendance here was strong enough to block any and all attempts by my technicians or any other entities to deliver communication. This had now become a one-on-one interaction.

I took a second to gather my thoughts and formulate my next question to this seemingly disgruntled female entity. I took a breath and asked, "The spirit entity here with me now, can you tell me your name?" After quite a few seconds the response, "All leave now, NOW!" came through the ghost box. I heard the demand loud and clear. I knew now that we would not be dealing with a benign spirit entity, but a malevolent one that clearly did not want us here in the Conjuring house. I decided to be respectful in my approach to this obviously angered entity in an attempt to find out who she was and what she was doing here.

My next question was, "The spirit that is here with me now, can you please tell me your name so I can properly address you?" Before long, the response of, "Mistress," came through, followed by a definite attempt at further communication that I was not able to understand. I replied, "Mistress, ok, can you tell me your name, Mistress?" The redundant question of her name seemed to anger her more; the response, "Told you," came through the ghost box in a more aggressive tone. "I apologize, I did not understand the communication. Can you please say your name again?" I asked. After a few seconds the answer, "Bathsheba, mistress, house," came booming through the ghost box speaker in a very impatient-sounding tone of voice.

Bathsheba, I didn't know why this was not already foremost in my mind. The Perron family reports described a dominant female spirit named Bathsheba; she was allegedly the dominant entity plaguing the Conjuring house during the time they resided here, and was reportedly responsible for all the torturous incidents perpetrated on the Perron family members.

At the risk of annoying this already disgruntled entity further, I asked, "Did you say your name is Bathsheba?" I listened closely for a response. After a few seconds the answer, "YES, FOOL," came through the ghost box in a very loud angry tone. I continued my docile interaction with the angry spirit entity who now claimed to be that of Bathsheba Sherman, the purportedly evil Satan-worshiping murderer of children who presided over this home over a century and a half ago, and who evidently believed she still did. "Are you Bathsheba Sherman, the woman who once lived in this house?" The entity Bathsheba responded with, "Who else," followed by, "Fool." Before I could ask my next question, "All leave now!" came through the box. I responded with the question, "Bathsheba, why are you so angry?" I waited for a response, but the entity did not answer. I asked the question again and still no response.

I was about to ask if the entity Bathsheba was still willing and able to communicate when a voice came through the ghost box. "Bruce, she not with you." I recognized this communication to be from my spirit technician Lisa. I replied, "Lisa, was that you?" The answer, "Yes," came through. I asked, "Lisa, where did she go?" I received the response, "Away." This was confusing; why would the entity Bathsheba just abruptly leave in the middle of our interaction?

As I pondered Bathsheba's hasty departure, I heard a loud scream come from the far end of the house. I knew it was Sue. I jumped to my feet and ran in the direction of the living room at the other end of the main floor, where I knew Sue was conducting her investigation. As I entered the room, I saw Sue sitting in a chair, obviously shaken. I asked, "Sue, what happened? Are you ok?"

Sue looked at me. "Yeah, I'm ok, just a bit startled is all," she said.

"What happened? Why did you scream?"

Sue explained, "I was just sitting here conducting an EVP session. I took all my readings and a few still pics with zero results. Frankly, I was getting a bit bored, so I decided to do an EVP session. I turned on the recorder and asked a couple of questions. About five minutes into the session, I felt like a blast of cold air rushed in from the doorway. It was weird because it kind of felt like someone turned on a fan, and the burst of cold air hit me right in the face." Sue went on to explain, "I asked out loud, 'It just got very cold; is there a spirit here with me?' I subconsciously knew I would not hear a response live with EVP, so I put the recorder down next to me and started to reach for my temperature gun to take a reading. Just then someone or something forcefully pulled my hair from behind, yanking my head back."

As Sue told me what had happened, I noticed she was rubbing the back of her neck. "Sue, is your neck hurt?" I asked.

"Not really, when my head got yanked back, I got, like, a sharp pain in my neck; it's just a fading ache now."

I asked her if she needed to go for medical attention, and she said with a small chuckle, "No, I'll be fine."

I told Sue to go back to the operations area and take a break.

Trooper that she was, Sue said, "No, I'm fine. I want to finish my investigation."

I looked at my watch; it was almost 3:00 p.m. I told Sue we still had about forty-five minutes before we ended the initial investigation, and if she did not feel well, to go back to the operations room and call me. Sue agreed, and I left to return to the library.

As I walked back to the library, I realized I had left my ghost box there and running. I quickened my pace; hopefully, nothing nefarious had happened to my prized ghost box. I reentered the library to see that all was well; my ghost box and digital recorder were still running smoothly. I took my seat and immediately addressed my spirit technicians Mike and Lisa. "Mike, Lisa, sorry for leaving the box running and the session unattended." The response, "Ok, Bruce," came through immediately. I then asked my spirit techs, "Mike, Lisa, is the entity Bathsheba here with me now?" I waited about twenty seconds with no response.

I repeated my question, and this time I received a response but not from my technicians. A male voice came across the ghost box speaker. "I am here." The voice was monotone and not aggressive or passive; it sounded devoid of any emotion or intent. I responded, "Who just said I am here? Who are you?" A few seconds passed, and I received the answer, "Adam." Although the communication was a bit low in tone, it came through clearly. I responded, "Hello, Adam, can you tell me who you are?" The next response was a direct result of my asking Adam to tell me who he was immediately after he had just told me his name. He responded, "I am Adam," now delivered in a more intentional tone of voice. I smirked, knowing I should have posed the question to discover what Adam had to do with the Conjuring house and why he was there. My next question was, "Adam, why are you here in this house?" I received the answer, "My home."

Before I could pose my next question to Adam, a booming and aggressive gravelly female voice came across the ghost box. "ENOUGH, ALL LEAVE!" The evil spirit Bathsheba was back with me and angrier than before. Now that I had reestablished contact with Bathsheba, I asked about the hair-pulling incident Sue had just experienced. "Bathsheba, were you the one who attacked Sue in the far living room?" The loud and clear answer, "Yes, me," came through. "Why did you attack Sue?" I asked, and the malevolent spirit replied, "My house, leave now." I was now convinced that the angry female entity I was communicating with and who had physically assaulted Sue was the same dark entity that the Perron family and subsequent residents of the Conjuring house had reported contact with, the evil spirit of Bathsheba Sherman.

I paused for a moment, contemplating how I would proceed with this session. Should I continue to try to reason with this angry dark spirit, or should I attempt to gauge her strength and energy level by antagonizing her into a verbal and/or physical reaction? It was apparent that the dark entity Bathsheba was not a conversationalist and was not at all interested in an exchange of information. She was angry, obstinate, and seemed bent on only one thing: having us leave what she still believed to be her house. I decided to prod her a bit to try to gauge what she was capable of and how far she would go.

Before I attempted this, I wanted to see if she would answer one more direct question. I asked, "Bathsheba, I know who you are. Do you know that you are dead and do not belong in this house anymore? Why are you still here?" I waited for a response. As I sat there awaiting Bathsheba's answer, a bloodcurdling scream came booming through the ghost box speaker. I did not expect this, and it actually made me jump. Immediately following the scream came the response, "THIS IS MY HOUSE," followed by the ultimatum, "LEAVE OR DIE." The evil Bathsheba was now screaming her communications through the ghost box; it was starkly apparent that she was not going to participate in any rational exchange of information or interaction. That would be my last attempt at dealing with Bathsheba in a considerate and passive manner. I would now begin to try to get even more of a rise out of her so that I could assess her limitations.

I took a calming breath, keeping in mind her physical attack on Sue, and knowing she was to some extent capable of inflicting physical harm on us, I fired my next statement fully intending to infuriate her more. "Bathsheba, I can see you are not very intelligent. Just remember, you may have been able to hurt little children, but we are not little children, and we will stay here as long as we wish." As I anticipated Bathsheba's response, be it verbal or tangible in nature, my muscles tensed a bit in expectation of a possible physical attack, and I waited. A moment passed with no retaliation in any form. The ghost box was running and spewing its usual plethora of gibberish.

I asked, "Bathsheba, are you still here, or did you run away?" As I finished my question, the books that lined the library walls began to fly violently from their resting places on the bookshelves and came directly at me. I crouched forward in my chair, covering my face and head with my left arm; with my right arm I reached for my ghost box and quickly shoved it under my chair. I would rather take a book to the head than have my ghost box knocked to the floor. The flying book assault lasted only a few seconds. I managed to weather Bathsheba's attack without injury to myself or my ghost box; however, the lamp that had been sitting on the table next to me did not fare as well. One of the books hit the lampshade and knocked the lamp to the floor. I composed myself and grabbed my ghost box from under the chair. As I was placing the ghost box back on the table, a voice came through in a direct and authoritative tone. "Just beginning." The comment from the evil entity Bathsheba was chillingly monotone and carried an air of accomplishment along with its ominous connotation.

Knowing Bathsheba would not render any information and having basically accomplished my goal of finding out how much she was capable of, I decided to end this live spirit ghost box communication session. I glanced at my watch; it was 3:35 p.m. It was just about time to conclude the initial investigations and meet the team in the operations area anyway. I instinctively offered my thanks and said goodbye to my spirit technicians Mike and Lisa. "Mike, Lisa, thank you for your assistance. I will do another session soon. Goodbye." Unconsciously expecting to hear Mike and Lisa acknowledge my statement and say goodbye, I listened for their reply. A gravelly female voice came through in place of the voice of my spirit techs. "Can't help now." I knew the meaning of Bathsheba's comment; she was able to use the energy she had to block communication and assistance from my spirit technicians, which was a matter for concern.

I reached for the ghost box power switch and turned it off, along with my voice recorder. I unplugged the ghost box power cord from the wall outlet. I got up and started to make my way across the next room back to the operations area. As I did, my mind raced with the events of this initial investigation session, my verbal and physical experience with the dark entity Bathsheba, and the physical assault on Sue. I could not wait to hear what Tom and Bill had experienced, and to explain what I believed we were up against.

I was the first to arrive in the operations area. I placed my ghost box in its protective case as opposed to just placing it on the table. I was aware of what the entity Bathsheba was capable of and did not want any harm to come to my favorite ghost box. I walked behind the operations table and looked at the video monitors; there were live video feeds being recorded from select rooms and areas of the house. I noticed Sue was still seated in the far living room. I could not see Tom in the basement; he was either on his way here or in a blind spot hidden from the view of the camera. I saw Bill in the upstairs bedroom, collecting the target objects he utilized in his investigation in preparation to make his way down to the operations area. I took a seat at the table and waited for the others to arrive. A few minutes passed, and Tom came into the operations room.

"Hey, buddy, where are the others?" Tom asked.

"They should be here in a minute," I answered. Not even a minute later, Bill came walking in with an armload of target objects and placed them down.

"Hey, guys, where's Sue?" Bill asked.

"Yes, where is Sue? She was only a few rooms away, and I'm sure she could have heard us moving around and talking, alerting her to the fact that it was time to end her investigation and join us."

Tom was behind the table; he said, "I see her here on the video monitor; she is still sitting in the room she's investigating."

"Something is not right," I said. We all quickly headed to the far living room where Sue was. As we entered the room, we could see Sue seated in a chair at the far end of the room. She did not move; she did not even turn her head to acknowledge our presence. As I walked over to her, I called her name, "SUE." She rendered no response; she just stared straight ahead as if she were in a trance. I looked at Sue; her eyes were glassy and staring into the distance as if she were looking straight through me. I reached out and grabbed her by the shoulders and shook her gently. "Sue, Sue, come on, snap out of it."

As I shook her, she opened her mouth widely, but no sound came out. I let her go and gave her a quick slap across the face, attempting to wake her from whatever catatonic state she was in. After the slap, she again opened her mouth and moved it as if trying to speak; again only silence.

Bill asked, "Should I call an ambulance?"

I replied, "Hold on a second." I immediately remembered there had been reports made by members of the Perron family that the wife, Carolyn Perron, had at one point been possessed by the evil spirit of Bathsheba Sherman and had begun speaking in tongues; however, Sue was not speaking in tongues, she was not speaking at all. She made gestures as if she wanted to speak, but nothing came out. I was starting to believe Sue was not experiencing a physical malady but had been overtaken by the dark entity Bathsheba.

I had an idea. I asked Bill to go to the operations room and retrieve my ghost box and a digital recorder; no sooner did the request leave my lips than Bill was on his way. Bill returned in a flash with my ghost box and voice recorder. I plugged the ghost box into the nearest outlet and switched on the voice recorder and the ghost box. Because Sue was attempting to speak, or the entity Bathsheba was attempting to speak through her, my intention was to give Bathsheba a means of speaking using the ghost box. At the very least, we would be able to hear her and possibly find out what she wanted, but hopefully, her attention would be focused on us and the ghost box, which might cause her to relinquish her hold on Sue.

I dispensed with any ghost box session formalities and directly asked my first question; because this situation and the use of a ghost box in this manner was unprecedented, I did not know what to expect or frankly if it would even work. "Bathsheba, are you in control of Sue?" The ghost box emitted the typical sweep sound of broken-down radio broadcast fragments. Tom was running a handheld video camera focused on Sue's face, while Bill initiated a second voice recorder. We waited anxiously for any response from the ghost box. About twenty or thirty seconds passed, and Sue opened her mouth as if to speak. We focused on any sound that might come from Sue. As we focused on Sue and her attempt to speak, we heard a female voice come through the speaker of the ghost box. "Yes, she is mine," was the message.

We all heard this communication clearly. Bill, who was taking the video footage, said, "Oh my God, when the words came through the ghost box, Sue mouthed the exact words as they were delivered from the box." We were stunned. In all my years of working with the ghost box, and in the paranormal research and investigation field for that matter, I have never experienced this type of phenomenon. I told Bill to keep the video camera focused on Sue no matter what happened.

I quickly asked my next question. "Bathsheba, was that you who said she's mine?" The response of, "Yes," came through, immediately followed by, "Leave now." Every response through the ghost box from the dark spirit Bathsheba was mouthed by Sue in concert with the delivered communication. I had to think; how could I get Bathsheba to relinquish her hold on Sue? Then it dawned on me; if I could bait the entity Bathsheba into a physical reaction, she might have to leave Sue in order to accomplish it.

I made my next comment to Bathsheba. "Bathsheba, so far I have seen you throw a few books and use an unsuspecting girl as a puppet. I have to say that your actions are very unimpressive. It will take a far sight more to make us leave this house; as a matter of fact, we may stay indefinitely." Not even a minute passed when we heard a crash in the adjoining room; we learned later on that the loud crashing sound was a heavy metal light fixture that had been pulled from the ceiling and sent crashing to the floor. We all turned to our left in the direction of the loud sound, and before we could act, Tom yelled, "Sue, are you ok?"

I looked back at Sue. She was sitting forward in her chair and rubbing her eyes. "Sue, are you all right?" I asked.

"Yeah, I think so. What happened?" Sue replied.

I immediately told Sue, "Come on, let's get some fresh air, and I'll explain."

Sue agreed, and we all walked back to the front door and made our way out into the front yard. Bill was the last one out the front door. He had no sooner stepped across the threshold when the heavy wooden door violently slammed shut behind him. Bill almost jumped out of his skin. "Holy crap," he exclaimed.

We were all a bit shaken by the events that just took place. We stood in a circle with our arms folded against the chilled air outside the house. Truthfully, it felt good; the air was fresh and crisp.

Sue asked straight away, "What's going on? What happened in there?" She went on to ask, "One minute I was finishing up my EVP session, ready to wrap up the investigation, and the next minute I felt like I had just woken up from a night's sleep and had you guys standing there wide eyed and asking if I was ok. Somebody want to tell me what happened?"

I explained to Sue that we believed she had been possessed by the dark spirit of Bathsheba Sherman, the woman who resided in this house in the 1800s and whose spirit was the one believed responsible for all the negative activity here over the years. Sue listened intently to my explanation of the events that had unfolded.

When I finished, Sue just stood there silently looking at the ground. After a minute or so she said, "So, you're telling me I was possessed by an evil spirit and she spoke through me, and you heard it through the ghost box. I don't remember any of that happening."

"That's exactly what took place," I answered.

Bill spoke up and said, "I even got it all on video."

Sue exclaimed, "No way, I gotta see that right now."

We lingered outside for a few more minutes, and I suggested we go back in the house, as it was starting to get colder. All agreed. Before we went in, I asked Sue, "Are you ok? Are you ready to go back in there?"

Sue nodded reluctantly. I could see she was shaken by what had just happened and what I'd just told her, but Sue was a pro. She did not want to show any cowardice or fear. She knew if she wanted to continue to be an effective paranormal investigator, she would have to face and conquer the fear and apprehension of any and all paranormal experiences she was or possibly could be subjected to.

We all reentered the Conjuring house, fully knowing what might lay in store beyond the front door. We took our seats around the operations table, and Bill proceeded to plug the video camera into the laptop computer. Sue wanted to see the footage of her possession. Sue watched the computer screen intently; her face was expressionless. After the video clip ended, Sue walked back to her seat and sat down without saying a word.

I waited a moment and then told Sue, "That was the second physical attack on you by the dark spirit Bathsheba in less than two hours; evidently this entity is singling you out as prey for her attacks." I went on to say, "With that in mind, none of us would think any less of you if you wanted to forego the remainder of this investigation. Tom can run you over to the motel we passed on the way here, and you could stay there and get some rest until we finished the investigation, maybe review some of the EVP recordings to pass the time."

Sue looked at Tom and Bill and then turned to me and said, "What kind of investigator would I be if every time I took the brunt of some sort of paranormal activity, I turned tail and ran away? If that's the case, then I might as well quit the paranormal and take up knitting." She continued, "If it were any of you who was the recipient of those incidents, would any of you quit and run away? I don't think so; stop treating me like a little girl." Sue ended her statement with, "I'm a professional paranormal investigator. I fully know the risks involved in every investigation and am prepared to face them regardless of what they are. At the end of this investigation, Bathsheba or no Bathsheba, we will all leave the Conjuring house together."

When Sue finished, there was nothing more to be said on the subject. I addressed everyone, "Ok, gang, with that, let's discuss our individual initial investigations." All nodded in agreement. "Tom, why don't you start," I said.

Tom began to explain his initial investigation. "I investigated the basement, just let me say creeeeepy. It's like walking down there and suddenly being back in the 1800s when this place was first built. The walls are stone, the floors are dirt covered with sheets of plywood, the entire basement seems to be undergoing some sort of renovation, and there is that old musty, mildewy smell, just creepy. As soon as I got down there, I felt like I was not alone. Oddly enough there is a room at the bottom of the stairs that is sort of finished. It has a table and chairs and was lit up. I decided to do my main investigation from that room. I sat at the table, started the voice recorder, and fired up the IR camera. I figured I would ask questions while I scanned the area with the IR camera. I started to ask my first question when I felt a really cold blast of air on the back of my neck. I whipped the IR camera around and just caught a figure leaving the room I was sitting in. The figure was dark blue set against the light blue background produced by the IR camera. I had the camera recording, so hopefully, I captured it. I haven't checked yet, but I'm sure I did."

Tom went on to say, "One more odd thing, when I felt the cold air hit my neck, I also smelled a really bad odor like rotting meat or rotten eggs, it was only for a second, and then it disappeared." Tom finished with, "That was the only activity I experienced, not even an EVP."

I turned to Bill. "Ok, Bill, you're up."

Bill started with, "Ok, I was in the upstairs bedrooms. The three rooms up there are a little cramped. I don't believe they were designed to be bedrooms. I think at some point they finished the attic of the house and made the three bedrooms up there. It was warmer up there than in the rest of the house, a typical attic, the heat rises, so the top floor of a house is usually warmer than the lower floors. I brought some target objects with me, a rag doll, a rubber ball, and ten wooden blocks with letters on them. I also took a K2 meter, plus my digital camera and voice recorder. I settled in the middle bedroom, it was the most spacious, and I could see both the other bedrooms to my left and right. Plus it was the room the video camera was set up in, so it was the best place if I were to experience any physical activity. I placed the doll and the running K2 meter on the bed in front of me, and the ball and wooden blocks on the floor to my left. I sat in a chair in the center of the room, facing the bed. The first thing I did was take some pics, about a dozen or so. I then turned on my voice recorder and started an EVP session.

"I started the EVP session by asking if there were any spirit entities present who would like to communicate. I stated out loud that any spirit willing to talk could direct their message to the small device in my hand, and I would be able to hear what they had to say. I continued the EVP session for the next few minutes, asking all the generic questions, 'If there are spirits here, can you tell me how many?' 'Can you tell me your name?' etc.

"About four or five minutes into the EVP session, I felt a cool breeze pass by me, coming from the far bedroom on my right. It felt like someone opened a window, and the rush of cool air from outside made its way from one side of the third floor to the other. At that moment I realized I should have taken a temperature gun with me, and remembered mine was sitting in my equipment case downstairs. As I chastised myself for forgetting the temp gun, I caught the K2 meter out of the corner of my eye. The colored lights on the meter were fluctuating back and forth from one end to the other.

"With the voice recorder still running, I asked, 'Is there a spirit here with me now?' I gave a few seconds for any response made to be left on the recorder. I then asked, 'If you are here in this room with me, can you move one of the objects I have here, the doll or the ball?' I put the running voice recorder in my lap and started to snap pics around the room. As I turned to snap a pic of the target objects on the floor, the rubber ball began to roll slowly in the direction of the other bedroom to my left. I instinctively turned my head to see if the running video camera was able to pick up the movement of the ball; thankfully it was. The ball stopped just short of crossing from the room I was in, to the next bedroom. I immediately snapped several still pics of the ball and the area where it settled. While I had my attention trained on the ball and taking the pictures, I did not notice that the doll I placed on the bed had moved. I'd placed the doll at the foot of the bed facing me; it was now at the head of the bed facing away from me.

I had missed it being moved, but I'm sure the video camera didn't. The flurry of paranormal activity stopped as abruptly as it started. The rest of my time on the third floor was uneventful, but I know the video picked it all up, and I can bet I got some really good EVPs."

I thanked Bill and turned to Sue. She seemed to be recovering from her experience. I asked her, "Sue, do you feel up to an explanation of your investigation, I mean the parts we don't know already?"

"Yeah, absolutely," Sue answered.

"Ok, Sue, go ahead."

Sue started the account of her initial investigation by saying, "You all have to bear with me; there are parts I don't remember."

"Of course," we all said.

Sue started her explanation. "I got to the far living room just after leaving you guys here in the operations room. There is a long L-shaped sectional couch against the far wall. I went to the end and sat down facing the room. I started by taking a temperature reading. I think it was around 72 degrees. I took out my EMF meter and got a reading of 0.5 or 0.6; nothing to write home about. I put away the temp gun and EMF meter and started taking some still digital pics of the whole room. There is a small half bathroom directly across from where I was sitting, and I snapped a couple of pics of it.

"After the pictures, I started an EVP session. I had just gotten going and had asked a couple of general questions when it got very cold. I put my running recorder down and reached for my temp gun. All of a sudden something grabbed a handful of the hair on the back of my head and yanked my head back; my neck is still a little sore. When my head got yanked back, I screamed and jumped to my feet. I looked around, but of course, I was alone. The digital voice recorder was still running; too bad there was not a running video camera in the room. I sat back down and was going to take a few more pics. Bruce, that's when you ran in. I explained to Bruce what had just happened. After I assured him I was ok and wanted to continue, he left and went back to the library.

"I rubbed the back of my neck and went back to my EVP session. Obviously, my first question was, 'Who the hell just pulled my hair?' I can't wait to review the recording to see if I got an answer. I continued the EVP session.

"After a little while, I started to feel cold. There was no breeze or drastic drop in temperature; it came on kind of gradually. I turned off the recorder and took out the temp gun, 56 degrees, a 16-degree drop in temperature from my first reading. I grabbed the EMF meter and turned it on; the needle was pinned past the red. Just at that minute I remember feeling a tingling sensation go from my feet to my head in kind of a wave. I started to feel short of breath. I remember thinking, *Am I having some sort of panic attack?* That's the last thing I remember; the next thing I knew all of you were shouting my name and asking me if I was ok. It was super weird, it felt like I had fallen asleep, but it didn't. I don't know how to explain it. Anyway, that was the extent of my initial investigation."

I thanked Sue for her explanation and her bravery. "Ok, guys, that leaves me. I had quite an eventful initial investigation and ghost box session. Firstly, Sue, after I left you when your hair was pulled, I went back to my ghost box session and asked if it was in fact Bathsheba who attacked you, and she answered loudly and clearly, 'Yes, me,' so we can pretty much assert that it was her who possessed you also." I went on to explain my initial investigation, detailing the live spirit ghost box communication I had received and the incident of the flying books. I wrapped up my explanation by saying, "I'm sure we can all agree that even though we all experienced some paranormal activity in our initial investigations, Sue experienced the most intense and unsettling experiences. Of course, none of us wants to be the recipient of a physical spiritual attack; in my opinion, Sue handled herself courageously and professionally and really earned her paranormal investigator wings today."

Everyone agreed, "Yes," and, "Absolutely." We all gave Sue a quick round of applause. With this, we wrapped up our initial paranormal investigation of the Conjuring house. Given the amount and extent of the activity we all experienced, the rest of the investigation should prove to be very interesting, and with the Lord's help, not dangerous.

CHAPTER TWELVE

THE FIRST GROUP GHOST BOX SESSION

We wrapped up the briefing of the initial investigation and took a quick bathroom and refreshment break. When everyone returned to the operations room, I asked, "Is everybody good?"

All responded positively.

"Ok, great, then let's move on to the next phase of the investigation."

Everyone nodded in approval.

"I would like to do a group live ghost box session in the dining room. I'm sure you are all familiar with this story. Back when the Perron family resided here, and Ed and Lorraine Warren did their initial investigation of this house, there was a report of major paranormal incidents in the dining room. It was documented by the Warrens and corroborated by the eldest Perron daughter that Carolyn Perron, while taking part in a séance led by Lorraine Warren, was allegedly possessed by the spirit of Bathsheba Sherman, the former mistress of this house, who I believe possessed Sue in our initial investigation. The report stated that Carolyn Perron began to speak in tongues and act abnormally; it was further stated that Carolyn Perron, while seated in her chair, was lifted off the ground and thrown across the dining room. These reports were deemed controversial; many believed the reports were highly embellished. Given the events of today, I believe those reports to be accurate. That is why I would like the next phase of our investigation to be a group ghost box session in that very dining room.

"The goal is to make contact with the dark entity Bathsheba and to try to determine how powerful she is, how strong her hold on this house is, and what, if anything, she wants or needs. I also believe there are other spirit entities present in this house. How many, we don't know, but I would like to find out how many there are, who they are, and why they are here. I can see by the looks on your faces that you are all thinking the same thing I am; this is by no means going to be easy. I believe we are right; however, it has to be done, and I'm confident that if anyone can do it, we can."

Everyone smiled in agreement, but I could still sense their trepidation. I had my own as well. I glanced at my watch; it was 5:01 p.m. We had entered the Conjuring house at approximately 12:30 p.m. We had to be done and ready to leave on or about 12:30 p.m. tomorrow afternoon, which left us about nineteen and a half hours to finish this investigation, give or take.

"All right, people, get your equipment ready. Bill, grab some target objects, and we will meet in the dining room in about twenty minutes."

Everyone nodded and began to bustle around getting their equipment ready to go. I decided to use my main ghost box again; it seemed to get good reception here and was a reliable old friend. I took my ghost box, digital voice recorder, and equipment pouch. I also grabbed a six-foot extension cord so I could plug the ghost box power cord into the wall outlet and still have enough length for it to reach the dining room table. I headed to the dining room, which was only two rooms away. I entered the dining room and walked to a seat at the far end of the table. I attached the extension cord to the ghost box power cord and plugged it into a nearby electrical outlet. I placed the box on the table and sat down. I placed my voice recorder next to the ghost box and retrieved my temperature gun and EMF meter from my equipment pouch.

No one else had arrived yet, so I decided to take some temp and EMF readings while I waited. I turned on the temp gun and fired the red laser at the far wall facing me. The temperature reading was 70 degrees, not warm but not cold either. Next, I turned on my EMF meter and took a reading. The indicator read 0.10. The low reading was not surprising since there were no electrical devices in operation in the dining room or any of the adjacent rooms, which would have produced a higher reading. I made a mental note of the temp and EMF readings and sat back in my chair.

I noticed, looking out the dining room windows, that it was almost dark. I took out my walkie-talkie and called Tom. "Tom, come in."

The walkie-talkie crackled. "Tom here; go ahead."

I answered, "Tom, it's getting dark, bring a couple of low-light lanterns with you, and tell Bill and Sue to make sure their digital cameras have night-vision mode."

Tom answered, "Will do; see you in a minute."

I put the walkie-talkie away and waited for the team. After a few moments, Bill and Sue entered the dining room, placed their equipment on the table, and took their seats.

"Wow, it really got dark fast," said Bill.

"Yeah, I just called Tom and asked him to bring two lanterns with him."

"Good idea," replied Sue.

Just then Tom walked into the dining room, carrying two low-light lanterns. He placed them at either end of the room and turned them on. Tom said, "Be right back. I couldn't carry the lanterns and my equipment." Tom quickly went to retrieve his equipment and returned in less than a minute. He took his seat. The infamous Conjuring house dining room was bathed in dim yellow light from the lanterns; low-light lanterns always lent an air of extra spookiness to a room.

"Ok, now that we are all here and settled, let's begin. I am not going to conduct a structured session; we will take it as it comes. Usual protocol applies. Let's all stay alert and focused. We don't know yet what the dark entity Bathsheba is capable of."

Everyone nodded. I looked at my watch; it was 5:35 p.m.

I reached for my digital recorder and turned it on, hit the record button, and stated the session information, date, time, location, and individuals present. Sue and Bill started their own voice recorders, and Tom had a handheld digital video camera ready in night-vision mode. I flicked the ghost box power switch on; the box began to run smoothly, rendering a loud and relatively clear sweep sound. I was a bit relieved that the reception of the broadcast radio signal in the dining room was good.

As I have in every live ghost box session I have ever done, I asked for my spirit technicians Mike and Lisa. "Mike, Lisa, are you there? Can you assist in this session?" A few seconds went by, and the response of, "Yes, Bruce, here," was heard through the ghost box, delivered in a familiar male voice. "Hi, Mike, how are you?" I asked. The reply, "Good," came through. "Great, is Lisa with you?" I asked. "Yes, here," Lisa responded in a sweet female voice. I replied, "Very good, thank you both. Please give us your protection and help any spirits who want to communicate to do so."

My next question was also generic. "Are there any spirit entities here or on the other side who would like to communicate today?" I always started a live ghost box session with this initial question to get the ball rolling. A few seconds went by, and a faint but audible male voice came through. "I am here," was the reply. I didn't know if everyone was able to catch it, but I did. "The entity who just said I am here, can you tell me your name?" Quite a few seconds went by, and the answer, "Adam," came through the ghost box, this time a little stronger than the previous response. We all heard the communication. "Hi, Adam, are you the spirit I spoke to earlier?" The response, "Yes, me," came through the ghost box. I continued, "Adam, are you here in this room with us now?" We received the answer, "Yes." I followed with, "Adam, did you live in this house?" Again the answer, "Yes," came through the box's speaker. My next question, if Adam answered, would tell me if he was a member of the family who resided in this house in the time of Bathsheba Sherman. "Adam, can you tell me what year you died?" About fifteen seconds passed with no response. I repeated the question. The response, "Don't know," came through. I had to rephrase the question. "Adam, can you tell me what year you were born?" A few seconds passed and the reply of, "1839," came through. I heard the response, but it was always easier to mistake numbers and dates when heard live through the ghost box. I asked Adam, "Adam, can you please repeat that? What year were you born?" The answer came in two quick parts, "18," and a second later, "39."

The splitting up of live spirit communication was very common with ghost box communication. It was an occupational hazard. Sometimes there will be a piece of sound fragment or a pop or hiss that divides the intended communication into two or even three parts. Being able to recognize this occurrence and decipher the communication takes experience. Most times one of the components of the communication is missed, leading to the intended communication going unrecognized or disregarded. This usually happens when a ghost box operator lacks sufficient experience.

I heard Adam's answer and asked him to confirm it. "Adam, did you say 1839?" A few seconds went by, and the answer, "Yes," came through. My next question would have been to inquire as to why Adam was still here in the Conjuring house and had not crossed over to the spirit world. As I was about to ask the question, the large, heavy, wooden dining room table began to vibrate; it would not have been immediately noticeable except for my voice recorder, which was standing on end on the table, falling over. I first thought maybe one of us jarred the table a bit, causing the recorder to fall, but when I reached over to pick it up, my arm rested on the table, and I could feel the vibration. I said, "Hey, guys, the table is vibrating." Everyone immediately placed a hand on the table.

"Oh, yeah, it is vibrating," exclaimed Sue.

"Yeah," said Bill, and Tom nodded.

As I was about to speak, the dining room table went from an almost undetectable vibration to a very perceptible shaking. I immediately grabbed my ghost box and placed it on the floor away from the now shaking table; the others removed their equipment from the table and moved back away from it. Just as we all moved back from the table, it began to shake violently, almost jumping up and down. I yelled to Tom, "Are you getting this on video?" I had not noticed before I spoke that Tom already had the video camera up and pointing toward the shaking table. This went on for about twenty or thirty seconds, and then as quickly as it had started, the table slammed down with a loud thud and stopped shaking. Everything became dead silent except for the sound of the ghost box, which was still running on the floor next to me. I turned and bent down to pick up the ghost box. As I did, a very loud and creepy-sounding laugh came through the box's speaker; it was delivered in a depraved-sounding female tone of voice. It was starkly apparent that the dark entity Bathsheba had joined us.

We all took our seats and tried to shake off what we just experienced. I put the ghost box back on the table and glanced over at Sue, who was seated to my left. She had a look of sullen, fearful anticipation on her face. I asked her, "Sue, are you feeling ok?"

Sue forced a smile and nodded.

I decided to attempt contact with the entity Bathsheba immediately, after making that heavy wooden table shake. I wanted to see if I could gauge where Bathsheba was energy-wise. Did the evil entity deplete energy in the performance of such physical activity, and if so, would the energy drain be apparent in her responses through the ghost box? My goal was to determine whether or not it was possible to goad her into depleting her energy reserve, and to ascertain if she would need to retreat and recharge her energy. I called out to the dark entity Bathsheba, "Bathsheba, was that you who just shook the table?" Almost immediately the response of, "Yes, donkey," came through the ghost box, followed by, "Only the beginning." Bathsheba's responses were strong and loud; they showed no sign of weakness in their tone or delivery.

I decided to make an antagonistic comment in hopes of soliciting another physical reaction. I wanted to see if it was possible to make the evil entity expend more of her energy, making her weaker; however, I also realized that if the shaking of that big table did not cause her to display signs of weakening, my chances were not very good. I made my next comment. "Bathsheba, I don't know who you believe you are, but in this house, you are nothing but a pest. You are like an annoying fly that cannot seem to be swatted." We all sat tensely in our chairs, awaiting an inevitable response from Bathsheba.

In the corner of the dining room sat a heavy antique wooden credenza that had dishes and other various glassware displayed on it. As we sat there waiting for either a physical or verbal response to my scathing comment, the glassware on the credenza began to shudder and shake, making a loud noise as the glassware clanked together. No sooner did the shaking of the glassware start than dishes, glasses, and cups started flying from their resting places, heading in our direction. Everyone jumped from their seats and scurried under the table for cover from the onslaught of flying glass objects. The glassware shattered all around us, breaking on the table and the floor; the sound of the breaking glass was so loud that it drowned out the sound of the still running ghost box. The assault by the evil spirit Bathsheba only lasted about twenty seconds. Crouching under that table, it seemed like an eternity.

After the onslaught was over, we all stayed put under the table for a moment just to be sure the attack was over before emerging.

In the moment or two of our precautionary hunkering down, a loud and clear voice came through the unscathed ghost box. "Will all die," was the comment from Bathsheba, delivered in just as strong and vindictive a tone and volume as before.

I said to my team while we were all huddled there under the table, "I think it's over. Let's get back in our seats." We emerged from under the table like rabbits cautiously exiting their burrow; we all got up and looked around. The tabletop and floor were covered in pieces of broken glass and china. Amazingly my ghost box, which I'd left on the table in my haste to take cover, was unharmed, not a scratch. I wondered if my ghost box being spared any damage was sheer luck, or was it intentionally spared harm because the dark entity Bathsheba knew it was the only way for her to get her comments and threats to our ears? In any case, I was thankful my ghost box had weathered the attack.

Before we could retake our seats, the broken glass had to be removed. Bill walked over to a corner of the room where a broom was propped against the wall, making a loud crunching sound as he walked over the broken glass. Bill proceeded to sweep the shards of glass from the tabletop and then the seats of the chairs. He quickly swept what broken glass he could into a pile and pushed it to a corner of the room.

We all took our seats, the ghost box was still running, but no messages except the ones that had been sent by Bathsheba were heard. We all took a breath, and I told the team I would try to continue the session. I wanted to get Bathsheba to communicate as quickly as I could to determine if I could detect any difference in her responses that would indicate she had weakened in any way after her poltergeist attack. I called out to her, "Bathsheba, that was impressive but useless. We are still not leaving this house." We all listened to the ghost box, awaiting her reply. The now distinctive voice we had come to associate with the evil spirit Bathsheba broke the sweep of the ghost box. "LEAVE MY HOUSE," followed by, "OR DIE." The communication was heard loudly and clearly by all of us. Bathsheba had not seemed to have lost any forcefulness or appeared weakened at all. I could not understand this. In my experience when an entity perpetrated a physical act, or even used the ghost box to communicate for a length of time, they expended energy in the process and would become weak and eventually be unable to continue their immediate interaction. I could not understand how the dark entity Bathsheba was able to execute these strong physical incidents and still appear to have an unlimited supply of energy.

I decided to try to communicate with my spirit technicians Mike and Lisa. "Mike, Lisa, are you there? Are you able to communicate?" Buried in the noise of the ghost box sweep as if far away, I heard a faint female voice say, "Too hard, Bruce," followed by a male voice, "Be careful," and then, "Not right." I was able to hear Mike's and Lisa's messages as they faded until only the sound of the ghost box sweep gibberish was left.

Sue asked me, "Did Mike or Lisa answer? I heard something but could not make it out."

I answered Sue by saying, "Yes, I heard their answer. It's time to end this session." Everyone nodded. I instinctively said goodbye to Mike and Lisa and switched off the ghost box and voice recorder.

As everyone gathered up their equipment, I said, "Ok, guys, let's get over to the operations room." We all made our way across the adjoining living room into the operations area. Bill lagged behind for a moment to gather up the target objects.

I looked at my watch; it was 6:51 p.m. We were seated around the operations table. Sue had offered to get everyone a cup of coffee and was in the process of doing so. When Sue returned, she handed out the cups of coffee and took a seat.

"Ok, let's have some thoughts on what we just experienced."

Tom spoke up first. "This Bathsheba is a bad ghost; she does not want us or anybody else in this house. If you go by all the reports over the years, she has been plaguing this house since the day she died. I knew what you were up to, Bruce, when you made those couple of antagonizing comments to her. It didn't seem to me that she was any weaker after her attack."

Bill broke in. "Yeah, she seems like she has an unending supply of energy. I don't think I have ever come across an entity in all the years we have been doing this that doesn't deplete their energy after such strong activity."

When Bill finished, I said, "I agree; this dark entity Bathsheba is not your run-of-the-mill grounded spirit. We are going to have to figure out how she does not deplete any of her energy after such strong poltergeist attacks."

Sue spoke out. "What about the other spirits either trapped or grounded in this house, the spirit Adam we spoke to at the beginning of the session, and who knows how many others there are here?"

"You're absolutely right, Sue. I have an idea for that very thing. Tom, you have a ghost box, don't you?" I asked.

"Yeah, but since you do the ghost box work, I hardly ever use it."

"Ok, good. In the next phase of the investigation, I want you and Sue to go to the far end living room where Sue did her initial investigation. Bill and I will go back to the dining room. I will initiate another ghost box session in the dining room. When I make contact with Bathsheba and have her attention, I will have Bill signal you on the walkie-talkie. I want you and Sue to do a ghost box session in the far living room. I will ask our spirit technicians Mike and Lisa to oversee your session. I want you to, with Mike and Lisa's help, try to contact and communicate with any other spirit entities who may be present in the house."

Tom and Sue both replied that they understood.

I asked Bill, "Are you good with that? We won't have any spirit technician help unless there is another tech who can attend."

Bill answered, "Absolutely."

"Good. Now let's take a forty-five-minute break, use the bathroom, get a snack, whatever you need to do. We'll gather back at the table in forty-five minutes." Everyone got up and started to move about.

Tom said, "Bruce, I'm going to go get my ghost box out of mothballs and make sure it's in top working condition."

"Good idea," I replied. I glanced at my watch; it was 7:30 p.m. Everyone would gather back at the operations table at around 8:15 p.m.

I got up to stretch my legs, took my cup of coffee, and made my way to the front door. I opened it and walked outside. I took a few steps into the crisp night air. Now that it was dark, the temperature had dropped; it had to be close to freezing. The sky had a few billowy clouds moving lazily across the sky. The front yard and adjoining woods were bathed in a pale white light coming from a full moon that beamed overhead. It was so peaceful, so serene, it was hard to believe that a few feet away lurked such a foul and evil presence. I stood there and soaked in this pristine moment. As I gazed into the distance, letting my mind wander to thoughts of how this scene must have played out a billion nights before, I looked up at the vast sky, black and filled with pinpricks of sparkling light. I couldn't help but think, was there another world out there somewhere experiencing the same type of perfect moment? Were there beings there who were self-aware? Did they contemplate what lay beyond their physical existence?

I was snapped out of this existential daydream, or rather, nightdream, by the crackle of my walkie-talkie. "Bruce, come in." Tom's voice pierced the silence.

I answered, "Yeah, Tom. Over."

Tom asked, "Where are you? Are you ok?"

"Yes, just stepped outside for some air. Over," I replied.

"Ok, just checking on you, buddy."

I told Tom I was on my way back in. I turned and started back toward the front door of the house. I reached for the door handle, fully expecting the door to open. I pushed forward, but the door did not open, it had to be locked from the inside, but who would have locked it? I knew someone would have to be in the operations area, which was just on the other side of the door, so I knocked. I waited a few seconds and could hear someone attempting to open the door from the inside. I heard a muffled voice. "Bruce, is that you?"

"Yes," I replied. It was Bill trying to get the heavy wooden door to open. "Let me in," I said.

"The door won't open," yelled Bill from inside. Bill was pulling, and I was pushing, but the door would not budge.

I yelled to Bill, "Go to the entrance in the far living room and unlock the door there." I turned and started to walk to the alternate entrance when I saw a black silhouette move quickly across my path. I abruptly stopped in my tracks. I felt a rush of cold wind hit me in the face. The wind was accompanied by a foul stench; it smelled like rotting compost. I continued quickly to the other house door. As I got to it, Bill swung it open from the inside.

I walked in, and Bill said, "What the hell? The other door was not locked; it just would not budge."

"No matter," I said, "Let's get back to the operations area." As we walked back to the operations room, I welcomed the warmth of the inside of the house. I must have been outside longer than I thought. I could feel my fingers tingling as the heat inside alleviated the numbness that the cold night air had caused.

When we reached the operations area, I walked over to the front door, which had refused to open. I checked the lock; it was not engaged. I reached for the door handle and pulled the door; it opened freely. I turned and looked at Bill, who just shrugged his shoulders. We both knew the door being unable to be opened was an attempt by the dark spirit Bathsheba to bar my return to what she believed to be her house. I walked over to the big box of coffee we had picked up on our way here. I squeezed the little spigot and filled a Styrofoam cup with steaming black coffee. It would hit the spot since I still carried a slight chill from my time outside.

Bill and I sat at the operations table. I pulled up my sleeve and glanced at my watch; it was 8:10 p.m. Just as I looked up, Sue and Tom walked into the room.

"Did everybody have a good break?" asked Sue.

I quickly recounted my journey outside, the experience with the door, and the dark figure I saw.

Tom said, "Boy oh boy, this witch never takes a break, huh?"

"Guess not," I answered. "Ok, gang, let's discuss the plan for the next phase. Tom, is your ghost box good to go?"

"Yup, fit as a fiddle," Tom replied.

"Great." I quickly reiterated the plan I had outlined before, and asked if everyone understood, and everyone nodded. Our main goal was for Bill and me to distract the evil Bathsheba long enough for Tom and Sue to make contact with any spirit entities here in the house and to try to find out who they are and why they are here.

I told the team, "I will try to keep Bathsheba occupied for as long as I can, but she is pretty aware of everything that happens in this house, so I don't know how long I can keep her distracted from what Tom and Sue are doing, especially since Tom will be operating a live ghost box that will be emitting an energy signal that Bathsheba will almost certainly detect. I don't know if this plan will work at all, but if Bill and I can keep her attention focused on us for even a little while, Tom and Sue may be able to obtain some important information. Tom, Sue, one more important thing, no matter what you might hear coming from our location, stay put, and continue your ghost box session. If either our situation or Sue and Tom's becomes too dangerous or intolerable, use your walkie-talkie and declare a mayday. If either of our teams hears a mayday, we are all to shut down the ghost box sessions and return immediately to the operations area. Does everyone understand?"

Everyone said they understood. I looked at my watch; it was 8:45 p.m. I told everyone the time and that we would give this phase of the investigation a two-hour time limit. Barring any unforeseen catastrophes, we would meet back here at 10:45 p.m.

"Ok, let's do it, everyone please exercise extreme caution, and good luck."

Sue smiled, and Tom and Bill both gave a thumbs-up. We all stood up, grabbed our equipment, and headed out to our respective areas.

CHAPTER THIRTEEN

THE DECEPTION SESSIONS

Bill and I entered the dining room. I plugged my ghost box into the wall outlet and set it on the table with my voice recorder. As I sat down, a thought crossed my mind. Bathsheba was a spirit capable of being in the same room with us without us being aware of her presence; suppose Bathsheba had been in the operations room as I had explained the plan for this ghost box session to my team, and overheard all the details of what we were planning to do. If she had been present and heard our discussion, did she understand it? And if so, what did she have planned for us? Since there was no way of me knowing the answer to those questions, I simply had to go through with the plan and hope the dark entity Bathsheba was not aware of our intentions.

I turned to Bill and asked, "Ready?"

Bill gave a thumbs-up.

"Ok, I'm going to initiate the ghost box session. Once we have contact from Bathsheba and are sure she is here, you tap the morse code button on the walkie-talkie to let Tom and Sue know it is time to start their ghost box session."

"Gotcha," Bill replied.

I looked at my watch; it was 8:59 p.m. I reached for the voice recorder and started it and stated the usual session information out loud. I turned on the ghost box, and it crackled to life with a thankfully strong and relatively clear sweep sound.

Prior to leaving the operations room to come to the dining room, I'd quietly spoken aloud to my spirit technicians Mike and Lisa and informed them of our plan for the two live ghost box sessions, and asked them to please attend the session being performed by Tom and Sue. I also asked them to render all the assistance and protection they could to Sue and Tom. I was confident my longtime friends and spirit technicians heard my requests. Many times in the past I had done experiments where I would ask a specific question before starting a ghost box session, while the ghost box was turned off, and I would receive a relevant and valid answer when I started the ghost box. Those experiments were designed to verify that my spirit technicians, or any entity for that matter, were capable of hearing and seeing me without the ghost box being in operation.

My first comment of the session was, "If there are any technicians present who can help with this session, please let me know you are there, and tell me your name." A few seconds passed, and the clear response of, "Here," and then, "Peter," was heard. "Hello, Peter," I replied. I was familiar with Peter; he was a spirit technician who has attended many of my live ghost box sessions along with my permanent technicians Mike and Lisa. I followed my greeting with, "Peter, how are you? I have not heard from you in a while." The answer, "Good," came over the ghost box speaker. "Glad to hear from you, Peter," I answered.

I went on to ask, "Peter, are there any entities who would like to communicate today?" After a few seconds, the response, "Yes," came through. "Yes, ok," I replied, followed by, "The entity who wants to communicate, can you tell me your name?" After quite a few seconds, the response, "Hi," came through in a childlike voice. "Hi, can you tell me your name?" The answer, "Paul," came through clearly. "Hi, Paul," I answered. My next question was, "Paul, can you tell me where you are?" The spirit entity who identified himself as Paul in a childlike voice answered, "Near window." Both Bill and I heard the response clearly. I asked, "Paul, what do you mean near the window?" The answer, "Middle window," came through, but this time in the same voice that was used by the spirit tech Peter; he had answered for the entity Paul. My next question was, "Paul, are you near a window in this room with us?" The answer, "Yes," again in the child's voice, came through the box. I went on to ask, "Paul, did you live in this house?" A few seconds passed, and a timid response of, "Yes," came through.

Just as I was about to ask my next question, Bill told me the morse code signal was sounding on his walkie-talkie. That was odd since we were supposed to send a morse code signal to Tom and Sue when we were sure the dark entity Bathsheba was here in the dining room and engaged by us. Since there was no sign of Bathsheba here in the dining room with us, I told Bill to go to the far living room where Tom and Sue were and to see what the situation was there. Bill nodded, got up, and started for the far living room.

I spoke to the little entity Paul. "Paul, if you lived in this house, who are you?" A few seconds later the response, "Sherman," came through. I heard this response clearly. I could not be sure how many children Bathsheba Sherman had. I knew she had children, but the accounts of her life that I had either heard or read were inconclusive. I quickly asked, "Paul, are you the son of Bathsheba Sherman?" A quick response came through the box, "Yes," followed by a panicked request, "Help me!"

As I prepared to ask my next question, Bill came hustling back into the dining room. "Bathsheba is communicating with Tom and Sue," he blurted out excitedly.

This was unexpected; the plan I had formulated for this tandem ghost box session now needed to be reversed. "Is there anything else going on there, any physical activity?" I asked.

"Yes, but I'm not sure what happened yet," Bill replied.

"Ok, Tom and Sue are aware of what the goal of the plan is. Go back there and tell them quietly to take the lead, they will keep the witch busy, and we will try to determine how many souls are here, and who they are." Bill nodded, and I added, "Bill, tell them both to be very careful. Bathsheba can be physically dangerous."

Bill gave another nod and headed out to Tom and Sue's location. I put the spirit, Paul, on hold for a minute and called out to my attending spirit tech Peter. "Peter, are you still there?" A yes came from the ghost box. "Ok, good," I replied. "Are Mike and Lisa still overseeing the other ghost box session Tom and Sue are performing?" Again, the answer, "Yes," was received. "Ok, Peter, can you please stay aware of the situation with Mike and Lisa and render any assistance you can if needed? I'm ok here; don't worry about me." I received the response, "Yes, Bruce." I took a breath and said a small silent prayer for Tom and Sue.

I posed my next question. "Peter, are there any other entities besides Paul in this house who are here with me now?" The answer, "Yes," came through, followed by the number, "One." I heard this and asked, "Peter, can the other spirit speak with me? If so, can you have them communicate and tell me his or her name?" A few seconds elapsed, and a male voice came through the ghost box. "Adam," followed immediately by, "Here." I had communicated with Adam in my previous ghost box session. "Hello, Adam, good to hear from you again." The response, "Hello," came through. "Adam, can you tell me now who you are?" About twenty seconds passed, and the answer, "Field hand," came across the ghost box speaker. "Adam, did you work on the farm here when the Shermans owned the land?" The answer, "Yes," was delivered. My next question to Adam was, "Adam, did you die here?" Again, "Yes," was received. "Adam, can you tell me how you died?" I waited a few seconds and received the answer, "Just died," followed by the communication, "In barn."

Amazingly, all the live spirit communication being delivered was relatively clear and understandable. Of course, it had taken almost twenty years of listening to ghost box communication to develop an ear for hearing a good quantity of the live spirit communication as it came through the ghost box, but God knows there was still a lot that I discovered when reviewing a session recording.

My next question was, "Adam, why are you still here in this house? Why have you not moved on to the world of spirits?" After a few seconds the answer, "Seeking my wife," came through the box. "Adam, it has been over 125 years since you were alive on this property; your wife has long since passed away." I followed it with, "Surely she is on the other side, waiting for you." The ghost box was devoid of any communication for the next thirty seconds or so; then the response, "NO, not leave me," was delivered.

I was about to address Adam's last comment when I felt a sharp, slightly painful sensation in my right calf. I reached down to rub the spot and felt my fingers were wet. I lifted my hand and looked at it; my fingers were covered in blood. I pushed my chair back and looked at the floor where my right leg had been. There was a broken shard of glass lying there with the edge covered in blood, a piece of glass left over from Bathsheba's previous onslaught in the dining room. I stood up and quickly placed my right foot on the seat of the chair and lifted my pants leg. I looked down at my leg to find a deep and bleeding slash wound about three inches long. I didn't think, I just acted. I left everything as it was, ghost box and recorder running, and made my way quickly back to the operations area. When I reached the operations room, I fumbled around, looking for the first aid kit, which was still in one of the equipment cases. I found the first aid kit and went over to the table. I propped my leg up on one of the chairs and used a piece of gauze to wipe away the blood. As I did, I could see the cut I'd received was not that deep but would probably still need a few stitches. I held the gauze on the wound and applied pressure and took a deep breath.

I grabbed my walkie-talkie and called for Sue; she was our resident team medic. Sue had worked for three years as a paramedic right after college. "Sue, come in," I called over the walkie.

After a couple of seconds, Sue responded, "Sue here. Everything ok, Bruce?"

I answered, "Not really. Can you come to the operations room ASAP? Tell Bill and Tom to continue."

The response, "On my way," came through the walkie-talkie.

As I waited for Sue to arrive, I took a bottle of hydrogen peroxide from the first aid kit and soaked a fresh piece of gauze. I quickly removed the bloody gauze and replaced it with the soaked one; the peroxide mixed with the blood and ran down my leg, foaming as it went. It ran right into my sock and shoe. I held the soaked gauze on the wound with my left hand and tried to wipe the bloody runs with my right hand; after all, I really liked these socks.

Sue came hurriedly into the operations room and saw me propped up on the chair with bloody gauze in both hands. "Oh my God, what happened?" Sue asked excitedly.

"I'll explain later. Can you take care of this?"

Sue put on a pair of rubber gloves from the first aid kit and grabbed a few pieces of clean gauze. She said, "Ok, move your hand." As I did, the wound began to bleed profusely. Sue began to wipe away the blood as it escaped the wound in order to gauge the severity of the slice. "Oh, not good," Sue exclaimed, "but not really bad." She went on to say, "It's deep, but not that deep. It's going to need about ten stitches, I would say." Sue suggested that she call Tom and he take me to the nearest emergency room to have this taken care of.

I told Sue that by the time we went to an emergency room, depending on how crowded it was, and depending on how busy the doctors were, and depending on how long the treatment took, it could be half the night before I returned here.

Sue just looked at me and said, "This leg needs to be stitched."

I answered, "I know it does, but that can wait. What can you do to take care of it until tomorrow when we leave here?"

Sue shook her head, but I knew she was not surprised at my response. "Well, I can clean it up, place some butterfly stitches, and wrap it; that should stop the bleeding." She went on to warn me, "I can't promise an infection won't set in, and it's going to be painful, especially considering how tight I will have to wrap it to stop the bleeding."

"Do it," I said.

Sue followed with, "If you have any numbness in your calf or foot, we will need to loosen the bandage, let the blood circulate to your leg, and then reapply it. You need to let me know if you experience any numbness."

"I will, I promise," I told Sue.

It took Sue about fifteen minutes to apply the butterfly stitches and bandage the wound. When she finished, I removed my foot from the chair, and when I placed my foot on the floor and put pressure on it, a throbbing pain started to take hold of my calf. I must have winced because Sue smirked and said, "Told you it would hurt."

With my leg patched up, I was able to think a bit clearer again. I asked Sue, "Did you and Tom experience a sudden end to the communication from Bathsheba about ten or fifteen minutes before I called you to come here?"

Sue answered, "Yes, how did you know?"

I explained to Sue that around that time was when the attack on my leg took place, and that I believed that was when the evil entity Bathsheba had used a piece of broken glass to inflict my wound.

Sue replied, "So she left us and went after you. I guess we didn't do such a great job of keeping her occupied."

I told Sue it was not their fault, Bathsheba was an old entity, and this was not her first rodeo. Maybe we should have known better than to try to trick her for too long. At that moment I remembered I had left my ghost box in the dining room running. I told Sue to head back to the others and to continue with the session till they heard from me.

I took a quick step toward the dining room, and a bolt of pain shot through my calf. As I took the next couple of steps, I realized

I was limping. *Great, just what I need!* I hobbled my way back into the dining room, my ghost box was still in its original position, but I did not hear any sound coming from it.

As I got to my seat, I could smell the telltale odor of burnt plastic. I sank into the chair, knowing full well what the cause of that smell was. I systematically flicked the ghost box power switch on and off repeatedly a few times, and turned the volume knob from low to high and back again. I heard only silence; my favorite ghost box of ten years was dead. I had smelled that distinct odor of burnt plastic a couple of times before, emanating from a silent ghost box that only seconds before had been operating perfectly; the electronic components that ran the ghost box had been fried.

This had happened to me many years ago in the middle of a live ghost box session in which I was receiving communication from a negative entity. At the time I was using an old Joe's box, which was a small handheld ghost box that looked like a walkie-talkie. The Joe's box was the second model of custom ghost box in existence at that time. It was created by Joe Cioppi a couple of years after Frank Sumption had created the first-ever ghost box. In the midst of this tense live ghost box session, I had been communicating back and forth with a very angry dark spirit entity when smoke began to come from the Joe's box I was holding in my hand. The box had crackled and hissed and then gone completely dead. The same smell of burnt plastic had filled the room then as it did now. Upon examining the guts of the destroyed Joe's box, I'd discovered that the electronic circuit board had been melted. I knew that when I opened my now deceased ghost box, I would find it had suffered a similar fate. Hopefully, this ghost box, which had served me undyingly for over ten years, and had facilitated countless tens of thousands of live spirit communications, was not beyond repair.

I felt a sick feeling in the pit of my stomach; losing this ghost box would be like losing an old and dear friend. I knew it had been the evil entity Bathsheba who was responsible for the damage to my number one ghost box. With that, I also thought I should never have left my ghost box in the dining room, especially when I was aware of the capabilities of this wicked spirit. The only consoling thought that took some of the edge off my feelings of guilt was that what had happened to my ghost box could have just as easily happened while I was in the middle of the session; my leaving the ghost box alone was not the mitigating factor in its demise.

I did not feel any awareness of a presence there in the room with me at the moment, the temperature seemed even, and there was no indication of any paranormal activity. With my main investigating tool out of commission, this part of the investigation, for me, was over. I picked up the corpse of my ghost box and reached for my voice recorder, which I noticed was still running. I picked it up and switched it off, and I made my way back to the operations room. When I arrived at operations, I walked over to my equipment case and opened it to place my deceased ghost box in it. I could not help feeling like I was opening the lid of a coffin. When I placed the box inside, I thought to myself, *Hopefully, this isn't a coffin for my ghost box, it's simply a temporary hospital bed.* I closed the lid of my equipment case, went over to the table, and sat down.

I looked at my watch; it was 10:37 p.m. The team was supposed to end their respective investigation session and return to the operations area at 10:45 p.m. They had eight minutes to go, give or take. I decided to just sit quietly and wait for them to arrive. As I sat there, I thought to myself, *They must have had quite an eventful session.* I knew the entity Bathsheba had made contact with them, and I had sent Bill back there almost an hour ago, and he had not returned. I hoped they were all safe, and no one had suffered any injury at the hands of Bathsheba.

A couple of minutes passed, and Bill walked into the operations room and took a seat at the table. "Hey," Bill said.

"Hey," I replied. "You look beat," I told Bill.

"Yeah, I feel like all the energy has been drained out of me," he replied.

"Where are Tom and Sue?" I asked.

"They're gathering up the equipment; they should be here in a minute," Bill answered.

With that, I saw Tom and Sue crossing the room leading to the operations room. They walked in, put down their equipment, and took a seat.

"How's the leg?" Tom asked.

"Yeah," said Bill. "How's the leg?"

"Hurts like hell, but bearable," I replied.

Sue followed with, "He is too stubborn to go to the emergency room to get proper treatment."

Tom replied, "I wouldn't either; can't miss the rest of the investigation."

Sue sighed. "Uh, men," she groaned.

"You all look tired," I said.

"Yeah, was like going fifteen rounds with Marciano," commented Tom.

"Let's all take a few minutes to take a breath and gather our thoughts, then you can fill me in on your investigation, and we can decide what we need to do next." About five minutes passed, and I asked, "Is everyone ready to begin the debriefing?" Everyone nodded.

Tom said, "I'll start."

Before Tom could speak, Sue said, "I need a water; anyone else want one?"

We all declined. Sue got up and excused herself, and Tom began. "Me and Sue went to the far living room. I set up my ghost box on the couch next to me, and Sue took a seat opposite me and to my left on the couch. While we waited for the signal from you and Bill, we decided to do an EVP session. Both of us turned on our voice recorders, and I asked, 'Are there any spirits here who would like to talk to us?' We let a little time pass, and then Sue said out loud that any spirits who wanted to could speak directly into the recorders, and we would be able to hear them.

"We were about fifteen minutes into the EVP session, Sue put down her recorder but left it running, and she started to take some random pictures. As Sue snapped the pics, I happened to look to my left. When I did, I saw, for a split second, a black figure come into the room through the doorway. I immediately told Sue what I had just seen, and she turned the camera in that direction and started snapping pics. In the area where I saw the black figure, there is a sort of counter with a TV on it, and some other junk up against the wall. As Sue continued taking pictures, a candle in a glass jar that was on the counter flew off and came straight at my head. Good thing I was quick enough to duck. The candle jar smashed against the wall behind me. We both knew Bathsheba was there in the room with us.

"I told Sue to start hitting the morse code button on her walkie-talkie to get your and Bill's attention. It worked, Bill came in only a couple of minutes later, we told him what was happening, and he left to report back to you. Bill came back a few minutes later and explained that the plan was reversed, and we were to try to keep Bathsheba busy. Evidently, it didn't work too well, judging by the cut on your leg. After Bill returned, I started my ghost box session, and we managed to get some great communication from that evil spirit. The session was going along, with Bathsheba delivering nasty, threatening responses to every one of our questions or comments. Then all of a sudden she was gone; all communication and any further activity just abruptly stopped.

"A few minutes later Sue got your call on the walkie-talkie to come to the operations room. After Sue returned, we continued the ghost box session. We received a few communications from our spirit techs, Mike and Lisa, basic stuff except for a couple of stern warnings about Bathsheba and the danger she was capable of. We kept the ghost box and recorders running until it was time to come back here to the operations room." Tom ended the recounting of his and Sue's experience and ghost box investigation.

I thanked Tom, Sue, and Bill for their professionalism and bravery in a dangerous situation. Bill had been with me part of the time and with Tom and Sue the rest of the time. "Sue, you were present with Tom for the entire investigation other than the time you spent patching me up. Do either you or Bill have anything to add to what Tom said?"

Bill and Sue both answered, "No."

I started my account of the experiences in the dining room. "Bill and I started the investigation in the dining room fully intending to stick to the agreed-upon plan; however, the dark entity Bathsheba had her own plan. When we started the live ghost box session, I established that there was a spirit technician overseeing our session named Peter. At the beginning of the session, we communicated with the spirit entity of a boy named Paul, who claimed to be here in this house. The child Paul gave his last name as Sherman, he also claimed to be the son of Bathsheba Sherman, and he also asked for help.

"During the back-and-forth communication with the spirit Paul, we got the signal from Tom and Sue. I had to pause the interaction with Paul in order to give my attention to the situation at hand. As you know, I sent Bill to check on you guys. He reported back and apprised me of your situation; that's when I sent him back over to your location.

"After Bill left, I confirmed with the attending spirit tech Peter that Mike and Lisa were still with you all and rendering their assistance and protection. I then asked the spirit tech Peter if there were any other entities besides Paul here in the house, and he informed me that there was one more. I asked for that other spirit to come forward and tell me his name. I received communication with the name Adam. We'd had some brief communication from an entity, Adam, in the previous two sessions; he also had claimed to be in this house. I was able to discover through Adam's communication that he had been a field hand on the Sherman farm when Bathsheba was the mistress here. Adam went on to tell me in our back-and-forth exchange of communication that he had died on the property, in a barn. I was also able to learn from Adam that he was still here looking for his wife. I informed him that his wife would be long since deceased and that she was most likely waiting for him in the spirit world. Adam did not accept my assertion, he believes his wife is here somewhere, and he was very adamant about finding her.

"As I pursued further communication with Adam, I felt the attack on my leg. The evil spirit Bathsheba had used a shard of glass from her previous attack in the dining room during our first group ghost box session, when she had destroyed the glass and china, to slash my calf. You are all aware of Sue attending to my injury, so I won't rehash that. What I'm going to tell you now hurt me more than the physical injury to my leg ever could."

Everyone's eyes widened, and they all listened intently with a look of concern on their faces.

"After Sue returned to your location, I limped my way back to the dining room. I intended to attempt further communication with the spirits of Paul and Adam; however, when I entered the dining room, I immediately detected the strong odor of burnt plastic. It did not really register until I approached my previous position and discovered that my ghost box, which I had left running on the dining room table, was now silent."

"OH NO, don't tell me," Tom exclaimed.

I looked at Tom and asked, "Do you remember me telling you what happened to my Joe's box back in the day?"

Tom answered, "Yeah," in a deflated tone of voice. Bill and Sue had never heard the story of the fried Joe's box. I quickly recounted it for them.

Sue asked, "So your favorite, number one, go-to ghost box is fried?"

I answered, "I'm not absolutely sure. I have not opened it up yet, but it's completely dead and smells like burnt plastic."

Bill asked, "Can it be repaired?"

I replied, "I don't know. If it's just wiring, there's a good chance it can be fixed. If the circuit board is fried, it will have to be replaced. That would change the whole ghost box; it would virtually be a new ghost box." I went on to explain, "A new circuit board would cause the box to run completely differently, and the reception and delivery of the sweep would be different, not to mention it has taken me many years of continually using this box and having the exchange of my energy and spirit energy flow through the ghost box to establish a strong personal imprint of my energy on it. A major overhaul and replacement of all the original electronics would pretty much leave me with only the ghost box case being original; that would negate any and all imprinting that made that particular ghost box the best one I have ever used for live spirit communication. With all that being said, we need to stay focused on this investigation. I'll worry about my ghost box after we are through here.

"Ok, back to the task at hand, this evil entity Bathsheba is one of the strongest, if not the strongest entity we have ever encountered. Over our last three investigation sessions and the experiences both verbal and physical we have had with her, it seems she has a never-ending supply of energy. She has not once shown any sign of weakening, and that is what makes her and this investigation so dangerous. From the limited contact and communication we have had with the other two spirit entities here in this house, the child Paul Sherman and the farmhand Adam, it does not seem like she is tormenting them. They seem to be subdued and somewhat distressed, but I believe that is due to their confusion and anxiety, given their circumstances. Don't get me wrong, I believe she rules the ethereal roost here with an iron hand, she is the boss, but I don't think she is a constant threat to the other spirits here."

CHAPTER FOURTEEN

THE AWAY GHOST BOX SESSION

"My plan for the next phase of the investigation is a little unorthodox. I have never done this before, so bear with me while I explain, and please don't offer any comments or opinions till after I'm finished. For the next phase of the investigation, I alone want to leave the Conjuring house property."

Sue opened her mouth to speak. I put up my hand and stopped her before she could utter a word. "Please let me finish. I have a very good reason for wanting to leave the property. The dark entity Bathsheba Sherman is an all-encompassing presence here, not only in the house, but I believe on all of its property also. Believing this, there is no way any of us could obtain any information about her without her being aware of it. I feel the only way we can receive answers as to why Bathsheba is endowed with unlimited energy is to be able to communicate freely with our spirit technicians Mike and Lisa without being subject to the prying eyes and ears of the evil Bathsheba. That cannot be accomplished here in this house or on the property it sits on. I will have to leave the property completely and get far enough away so that I can conduct a live ghost box session, contact Mike and Lisa, and try to get some answers about Bathsheba Sherman and her invincibility. I would only be gone for a short time, only as long as it takes for me to get some answers.

"While I am on this away investigation, I would like you three to conduct the next investigation here. Tom, I would like you to do a group ghost box session with your box; you pick the location and apply the normal protocols, well, as normal as they can be. Recorders, cameras, electronic readings, target objects, the works. I need you guys to try to establish communications with the entities Paul and Adam and try to get as much information from them as you can before the entity Bathsheba interferes, which she definitely will at some point. Try not to antagonize Bathsheba, and maybe she will keep the interaction to verbal as opposed to physical. I should not be gone longer than half an hour to forty-five minutes; hopefully, in that time, I will be able to receive the information we need to deal with this problem entity."

Although showing signs of not liking my leaving the property, everyone agreed that my plan was a good one, and if I were able to obtain any valuable information that would help us combat the evil Bathsheba, it was worth the effort.

"Let's all take a break and then get our equipment ready for the next phase of the investigation." I looked at my watch; it was 11:35 p.m. We had just about reached the halfway mark of our investigation, with twelve and a half hours to go. I called out to everyone, "It's 11:35 p.m. I am going to get my other ghost box and get ready to leave. Let's all meet back here in fifteen minutes to confirm everyone and everything is ready." Everyone agreed.

The fifteen minutes passed quickly, and the team gathered at the operations table. "All right, everybody ready to start?" I asked, and everyone nodded.

"Bruce, be careful and hurry back," said Sue.

"Yeah, it's not the same without you," Bill added.

Tom just winked and gave me a thumbs-up. I knew Tom was more than capable of taking the lead in my absence. Hell, he'd been at this as long as I had. I told Tom as I opened the front door, "Anything, just call me on the cell phone."

Tom replied, "Don't worry, get going."

With my equipment pack around my waist and my backup ghost box in my hand, I walked out of the Conjuring house. As I walked to the vehicle, I had a very uneasy feeling, sort of like someone was following me. I even stopped and looked behind me, but of course, no one was there. I got into the vehicle and glanced at my watch; it was 12:01 a.m. I placed my ghost box on the passenger seat next to me. I even went as far as fastening the seat belt around it; better safe than sorry. I was not about to lose another ghost box. I started the engine and turned on the head-lights. I looked into the rearview mirror. As I was about to adjust it, what I saw in the mirror's reflection made me do a double take. There was a large tree behind me in the distance; it was adjacent to the water that was on the property just behind the house. When I looked into the rearview mirror, it was dark, but everything was bathed in pale moonlight. I could swear I saw a hangman's noose swinging from the old tree's lowest branch. I rubbed my eyes and took another look, but there was no noose to be seen. Was it a trick of the eye, or a trick of the evil entity Bathsheba?

I pulled up the long dirt driveway and turned onto Route 96. I knew we had passed a combination gas station and luncheonette on the way here; it was about ten miles down the road. I headed for that. As I drove down the road, I spoke out loud to my spirit technicians Mike and Lisa. I knew they were probably already aware of my plan, but I verbalized it to them anyway. I would need all the help my spirit technicians could give me with this upcoming remote ghost box session. Actually, my spirit techs Mike and Lisa would be the main source of information about the evil entity Bathsheba Sherman and her ability to retain her energy without depletion after perpetrating any level of paranormal activity.

As I drove toward my destination, I noticed the silhouettes of other large farm-type houses scattered about the landscape on both sides of the road. I couldn't help but wonder if any of those houses contained spirit entities, and what their situation might be.

As I navigated a bend in the road, I could see the small gas station and luncheonette looming in the distance. As I drove up to it, I could read the old neon sign standing on the edge of the road "John's Food and Gas, Open 24 Hours." I could not help but chuckle at the sign. My first thought when reading it was that John's food gave you gas. I wondered if that was the intent of the owner or just an absence of thought.

I pulled in. Just to the left of the luncheonette was a small parking lot that accommodated about ten vehicles. I drove to the end and parked in the farthest spot. I could have had my pick of parking spaces since there was only one other vehicle parked in the lot. I wanted the most privacy I could get, so I chose the farthest parking space from the building. Thankfully it was very dark, and the spot was on the side and close to the back of the building. With no vehicles around me, the chances of any nosey people coming up to my vehicle were slim.

I switched on the vehicle's interior light and pulled an adapter from the glove box that plugged into the cigarette lighter of the vehicle; the adapter would allow me to plug my ghost box power cord into it and therefore be able to run the ghost box from the vehicle's power supply. I pulled my voice recorder from my equipment pouch and released my ghost box from its seat belt restraint. I plugged the box's power cord into the adapter and placed the ghost box on the passenger seat next to me. I turned off the interior light and the vehicle's engine.

I sat there quietly for a moment before beginning the session. My first thought was of my team; surely they had begun their part of the next phase of the investigation. I said a small silent prayer for their safety. I looked at my watch; it was 12:45 a.m. Once more I called out to my spirit technicians Mike and Lisa. "Mike, Lisa, I am going to start the ghost box session in a minute. I know I'm repeating myself, but can you please do your best to get the communication through?" I followed it with, "I know I don't have to tell you how important this is." With that, I turned on my voice recorder and stated the session information, location, time, date, and special session topic. I placed the running voice recorder into the vehicle cup holder that was located in the center console.

I picked up my ghost box and turned it on. The box came to life. My first impression of the box's reception and the sweep was good; the ghost box was rendering a surprisingly clear and sound-fragment-filled sweep. I tweaked the sweep speed a bit. I felt it was a bit slow. Since it was late at night, the radio broadcast signal the ghost box was receiving had more music content than it would have had if I were performing the session in the daytime hours. Radio stations tended to broadcast more music content at night as opposed to more informational talk content that was distributed during daytime hours. This did not pose any serious problem, although some of the communication might be delivered in a harmonic tone, which was indicative of live spirit communication built by an entity that had to utilize fragments of music sound in the construction of their communication along with the fragments of broken-down human speech.

I asked for my spirit technicians Mike and Lisa. "Mike, Lisa, are you guys there to help with this session?" Almost immediately the answer, "Yes, Bruce, here," came through the ghost box. The initial communication from Mike was loud and clear. I was relieved, and I knew Mike and Lisa were rendering their best effort to make sure their communication was received and heard live by me. I replied, "Great, thank you, guys, for being with me and helping with this session."

Before I could deliver my next question, a message came through the box. "Bruce, sorry about box." I heard the communication, but since I was focused on my intended goal for this session, I did not realize at that moment what the message meant. "What do you mean, sorry about box?" I asked. The response of, "Broke box, sorry," came through. It immediately dawned on me that Mike and Lisa were sending their condolences for my now defunct number one ghost box. I thanked them for their sympathy and assured them I would do what I could to revive number one.

I uttered my next question. "Mike, Lisa, I know you are aware of why I am out here doing this particular ghost box session; are you able to help me with the information I need?" I waited a few seconds, and the answer, "Yes, Bruce," came through the ghost box speaker. I noticed the communication was extraordinarily clear and understandable. I attributed this to my being out here far from the negative influence of the dark entity Bathsheba. Mike and Lisa had unrestricted access to the ghost box, and with a long-time energy connection between my spirit technicians and me, they were able to render high-quality communication. Both I and my spirit technicians were ready to begin the questioning about Bathsheba Sherman.

"Mike, Lisa, are you both aware of the ongoing situation with Bathsheba Sherman at the Conjuring house?" I asked. The answer, "Yes," came through. I told Mike and Lisa, "My main concern is her ability to perform paranormal acts without depleting any of her spirit energy." Again the response, "Yes," came through. I asked, "Mike, Lisa, can you tell me how she performs these strong poltergeist incidents and does not exhaust any of her energy?" I waited a few seconds, and the answer, "Has help," came through the ghost box. Has help, what did that mean? Was there another entity there or possibly a nonspirit presence that was resupplying Bathsheba with energy as she expended it? "Can you tell me what you mean by 'has help'?" I asked. After a few seconds, the answer, "Portal," came through. I replied, "A portal, what do you mean? Is Bathsheba using the open portal the ghost box creates?" I knew every running ghost box creates an open portal between our world and the spirit world; the open portal is necessary to facilitate the mutual exchange of energy between the ghost box operator and the communicating spirit entities, which is necessary for live spirit communication. The answer to my question came through from Lisa. "No, not box portal," was the response. I paused for a minute to think. If it was not the open ghost box portal being used by Bathsheba, then what was it? Was there another open portal in the Conjuring house? If so, where did this portal lead to, and who or what was on the other side of it?

"Mike, Lisa, is there another portal that is open and active in the Conjuring house?" I asked. "Yes," was the answer received. I then asked, "Can you confirm your answer; is there another open portal in the house being used by Bathsheba?" Again the answer, "Yes," came through. Ok, that was my first significant piece of information: the Conjuring house contained an active open portal being used by Bathsheba.

I now needed to obtain details about the open portal; who or what was on the other side of it? How was Bathsheba utilizing this portal to retain her energy at full strength? Was Bathsheba traveling back and forth through this open portal, or was there an exchange of energy coming through the portal that was keeping Bathsheba supplied with energy? Were there any other entities traveling through the portal into the Conjuring house? If so, what type of entities, and what type of threat did they pose? All these questions and a few more needed to be answered if we were to be capable of dealing with the evil spirit of Bathsheba Sherman. I realized this ghost box session would be longer than I had planned.

I asked my next question of Mike and Lisa. "Mike, Lisa, can you tell me what type of portal it is, and where it leads?" A short time passed, and the answer, "Evil portal," came through in Mike's familiar tone. I replied, "Mike, I think I heard you say the portal was evil. Is that what you said?" A reply of, "Yes, evil," came through. "Ok, Mike, thank you. Can you tell me, if the portal is evil, where does it lead to?" Mike answered, "Dark place," followed by, "Demons there." I heard my spirit technician's communication clearly; what he had to tell me gave me a nauseous feeling. My next question was, "Can you tell me, are the dark entities from that realm supplying Bathsheba with constant negative energy?" A resounding, "YES," came through the ghost box, first in a male voice and then repeated in a female voice. I replied, "Ok, guys, thank you," followed by, "Mike, Lisa, can you tell me, are there any demonic or evil entities traveling through the open portal into the Conjuring house?" I received the answer,

"No." This response took away some of the sour gut feelings I was experiencing. At least we would not have to deal with multiple dark entities, only Bathsheba, which in my experience up to now, was enough.

"Mike, Lisa, is there any way for us to close that open portal?" Quite a few seconds passed without a response. I repeated the question. A few seconds later the response of, "Portal there one hundred years," came through the ghost box. It was followed by, "Too strong." I thought for a moment before my next interaction with Mike and Lisa. If that open portal to the dark realms had been in existence in the Conjuring house for over a hundred years, there was no way we as physical beings could close it. I contemplated the situation a bit longer; then an idea struck me. I didn't know if it was even possible, but I would ask my spirit techs anyway. I called out, "Mike, Lisa, I know there is virtually no way for us as physical beings to close that evil portal." I followed it with, "Can you or Lisa or both of you do anything to eliminate that open portal?" After a few seconds the answer, "No," followed by, "Too strong," came through. My next question was, "Is it possible to enlist the help of a higher and stronger entity to close this foul portal?" My spirit technicians told me to, "Wait." I replied, "Ok, I'll wait."

A little over a minute had passed as I waited for my techs' answer. "Mike, Lisa, you guys still there?" I asked. "Yes, wait, please," came back through the ghost box.

As I sat there, I caught a flash of red and blue lights out of the corner of my eye. I turned my head to see a police patrol car pull up behind me. As the police officer walked over to my driver's side window, I lowered it. "Good evening, Officer," I said.

The officer did not speak; he had his right hand on his gun and shined a bright flashlight into my vehicle with his left. After a few seconds of looking around the vehicle, he asked me, "What are you doing here, and what is that contraption?" He was referring to my running ghost box.

I answered, "Officer, I am a paranormal investigator. My team and I are conducting a paranormal investigation of the Conjuring house up the road. I'm sure you are familiar with it."

The officer took his hand off his gun and removed the bright flashlight beam from my eyes. "Oh, you're one of those," he said with a smirk on his face. He went on to ask, "If you are investigating that creepy old house, why are you sitting here in your vehicle miles away?"

I informed the officer that I was conducting a remote ghost box session and that I needed to be away from the property to get an accurate reading.

He nodded although I knew he had no idea what I was talking about. He said, "Ok, let me see your ID, and I'll confirm your story. Just sit tight; I'll be back." The officer took my driver's license and returned to his patrol car.

The interaction with the police officer had taken around five minutes or more, during which time I was able to hear attempts at communication coming from the still running ghost box; however, I didn't catch the communication that had been sent, as I was focused on my explanation to the officer. I was sure my spirit techs Mike and Lisa were aware of my situation and would redeliver whatever communication I had missed. I looked in my side-view mirror, and I could see the officer sitting in his car. His silhouette was illuminated by the lights from his dashboard and in-car computer.

After another few minutes, the officer walked casually back to my driver's window, handed me my license, and said, "Ok, Mr. Halliday, have a good rest of your night, and be careful with all this ghostie stuff. I hear that Conjuring place is a real ass-kicker." The officer tipped his hat and went back to his patrol car.

As I watched the police car drive away, I called out to Mike and Lisa, "Mike, Lisa, I'm sorry about that. Are you still with me?" The response, "Yes, Bruce," came through. I replied, "Great, thank you for your patience." My next question was, "Do you have an answer to my question about having a higher entity help us?" The response, "Yes, Bruce," came back through, followed by,

"It is possible." When I heard the answer from my spirit techs, a slight surge of excitement ran through me. "Ok, great," I replied.

I had learned through all my years of live spirit communication that there were different levels in the spirit world. There were higher levels than the ones occupied by the spirit entities who communicated with me through the ghost box. I also knew these upper spiritual levels were where the higher, more advanced spirit entities dwelled. I had come to understand that the more an entity matured and learned, the higher the spirit would ascend to more sanctified spirit levels. I also knew the higher level a spirit attained, the more spirit energy and spiritual enlightenment it attained. This led to a higher entity having more power and knowledge. This was the type of entity we needed to help us with this evil portal and the dark spirit Bathsheba. I also knew that a spirit who had risen to a higher level could return to a lower level on occasion, but a spirit from a lower level could not rise higher until they were deemed ready, not even for a visit. I had never asked, but I was sure Mike and Lisa were spirit entities from a higher level who chose to remain on a lower level in order to work with and help physical human beings with live spirit ghost box communication and the pursuit of knowledge.

My next question was, "Mike, Lisa, what do I need to do?" I waited a few seconds, and the response, "Return house," came through. I replied, "Ok, what do I do when I get to the house?" Mike replied, "Use box and wait," followed by, "Help will come." I agreed and thanked my spirit technicians for all their help and guidance. I switched off the ghost box and then the voice recorder.

It had taken me many, many years to learn and perfect the understanding of live spirit communication messages. Due to their inherent structure, they were not fluid like normal human speech; most of the time they were broken up and cryptic. It took a large learning curve for a ghost box operator to be able to hear the live communication and piece together its intended meaning. I knew what my spirit technicians Mike and Lisa wanted me to do. I needed to return to the Conjuring house and perform another group ghost box session. I would need to keep the session going and wait for the higher spirit entity to make contact. With the knowledge I had attained about the portal and Bathsheba, I headed back to the Conjuring house, secure in the knowledge that help was on the way.

I pulled up to the Conjuring house, turned off the vehicle, and grabbed my ghost box. I opened the front door and walked in to find my team members seated around the operations table.

"Hey, you're back," said Tom.

"Thank God," said Sue. "We did not have a very good time while you were gone."

I immediately asked, "Is everyone ok?"

Tom replied, "Yes, physically anyway."

I followed by asking, "What happened?"

Tom said, "We'll get to that; first, how did your outside session go?"

As long as no one had sustained any physical injury, there was time for me to take a seat and explain my experience and listen to the account of my team's investigation in my absence. I removed my coat and draped it on the back of the chair, placed my ghost box on the operations table, and took my seat. I looked at my watch; it was 2:51 a.m. on Saturday. We had approximately nine hours and fifty minutes left to finish this unprecedented investigation.

"Ok, I guess I will start with how my away investigation went. Let me start by saying you are not going to believe what I discovered, and what I plan to do about it. If you remember, we passed a small gas station and luncheonette on the way here, about ten miles up the road. I decided to do my remote ghost box session there. I made it there and parked in the back of a small parking lot they had. I settled in and started my ghost box session, the signal was excellent and no interference from pesky evil spirits, so the communication was strong and clear.

"Of course, I enlisted the help of our spirit technicians Mike and Lisa, whom, by the way, I had informed verbally of my inten-

tions for the session on my way there. Mike and Lisa were there
and ready to go as soon as I turned the ghost box on. After the
usual pleasantries between the techs and me, I began to ask questions about Bathsheba. I won't go into explaining every single
question I asked, and the answers Mike and Lisa delivered; I'll
just tell you what I found out from them. I was informed that the
reason the dark entity Bathsheba is able to retain a never-ending
supply of energy is because there is an open portal in this house,
separate from the portal that is created when we use a ghost box.
Mike and Lisa told me that this open portal is over a century old
and connects the Conjuring house to a dark and negative spirit
realm."

Sue blurted out, "Oh God."

I replied, "Exactly." I went on to explain, "Bathsheba is being
fed an unlimited supply of negative energy through this open
portal. Whatever dark entities are on the other side of it are
feeding her a constant supply of energy, which is why she never
weakens, even after a strong paranormal attack."

Tom asked, "I have never heard of that before, have you?"

I answered, "No, not this exact situation." I went on to say, "I
have heard of there being open portals in locations that were
found to exude negative energy, but nothing like this particular
situation."

I continued, "This is a very bad and dangerous situation;
however, Mike and Lisa did inform me that no evil or demonic
entities were entering the Conjuring house through the open
portal, only sending energy through for Bathsheba to utilize."

"I guess that's a plus," said Bill.

Before I could continue, Sue asked, "So what are we going to
do about it?"

I replied, "I was just coming to that. Are all of you aware of the
different levels of the spirit realm?"

Everyone nodded.

"Ok, I asked Mike and Lisa if it were possible to have a higher-
level entity from one of the upper levels come to help with the evil

open portal and Bathsheba. By the way, before I could get their answer, the session was interrupted. I'll explain that after I'm through. When I was finally able to receive Mike and Lisa's answer about the higher entity, they told me it was possible and that a higher, more powerful spirit entity would come to help."

"That's great," said Tom. "Can we be sure that it will happen?"

I told Tom, "In all my years doing live spirit ghost box communication, Mike and Lisa have always been with me in pretty much every ghost box session I have ever done, even in the first days when I was restricted to doing manual sweep sessions because there were no operating ghost boxes available at that time." I went on to assure everyone that Mike and Lisa had never abandoned me, lied to me, or not done everything in their power to help me.

Tom replied, "I know that, Bruce. Sorry for the stupid question."

I winked at Tom to let him know I did not give it a second thought. "Mike and Lisa told me to return here and to do another group ghost box session. They also said to wait, and help would come. I ended the ghost box session and made my way back here."

Sue asked, "So we are supposed to do a group session, and the higher spirit entity will come during the session and hopefully be able to deal with the evil portal?"

I answered, "Yes, that's right."

Bill added, "Wow, that's a lot to take in, so that's why that witch Bathsheba never gets tired."

"That's about it," I said.

Then Tom asked, "What was it that happened to delay your session? Can you tell us now?"

I laughed and said, "This is kind of funny. I mean, it wasn't really funny at the time, but I can understand why it happened."

"What?" Sue asked. "Don't keep us in suspense; we can use a laugh too, you know."

"Ok, ok." I started my explanation, "In the middle of the

session, just as I was asking Mike and Lisa about the help of a higher entity, I catch sight of red and blue flashing lights coming right at me."

"Oh no," Bill exclaimed.

"Oh yes," I replied. "Two seconds later a Harrisville deputy sheriff was standing at my driver's side window with his hand on his gun."

Now Sue cried out, "OH NO."

"Oh yeah," I replied. "The officer visually inspected the interior of the vehicle with a very bright flashlight, all the time keeping his hand on his gun. When he finished, he asked me what I was doing there. Remember now, the ghost box on the seat next to me was still running, spitting out pretty loud nonsense sounds. I must have looked like some kind of nut," I said, laughing again.

With this, everyone else began to smile and chuckle.

Sue said, "Go on. What happened then?"

I went on to say, "Well, I told him I was a paranormal investigator, doing a remote ghost box session, and that I and my team were investigating the Conjuring house. Once I told him that, he eased up, took his hand off his gun, and lowered his flashlight, and smirked at me. I'm assuming he and other residents here are aware of the Conjuring house and familiar with paranormal investigating teams visiting their town."

"So he let you off the hook?" Bill asked.

"Well, first he took my driver's license, went back to his patrol car for a few minutes, came back, handed me my license, and told me to be careful. Then he got in his car and drove away. I went back to the ghost box session and finished it up."

Tom said, "Well, can't say your trip was uneventful. The main thing is you were able to accomplish what you wanted to and more."

"Yes, I did," I replied. "Ok, now that you heard my story, who wants to tell me about the events that took place here during your investigation and ghost box session?"

Bill and Sue both elected Tom to recount the events of their investigation.

Tom began, "Ok, after you left, we grabbed our stuff and went to the dining room. I set up the ghost box and voice recorder while Sue and Bill put a few target objects on the table along with a running K2 meter. We all took a seat, Bill took out an EMF meter and took some readings, and Sue took out her temperature gun and did the same. I turned to Sue and Bill and asked if there were any unusual readings. Sue said the temperature was a bit low but nothing out of the ordinary."

Just then Sue broke in and said, "Boy, did that change."

Bill spoke up and said at the time he took the EMF reading, there was no significant EMF detected.

Tom continued his account of the investigation. "Everything was pretty quiet. I asked if everyone was ready, and then told them to start their voice recorders. I turned on my recorder and then my ghost box. The sweep was pretty good, with not too much static noise and a good amount of sweep sound. I knew our spirit technicians Mike and Lisa would be attending your ghost box session, so I called for any technician who would be attending ours. After a second or two we got the response, 'Yes, here.' The spirit technician gave his name as Peter. I remembered from Bruce's explanation of the last phase of the investigation that a spirit technician named Peter had been assisting him in the dining room. I greeted Peter and asked him to help us with the session.

"The session started pretty ordinary. I asked some basic questions and received the basic answers. About ten minutes into the session, we started getting communication from an entity who said his name was Adam, the same one you communicated with, Bruce. I tried to get Adam to give us more information on his situation; we communicated with him for about five minutes or so. Adam told us he lived nearby with his wife. He also told us his wife worked here as well. I can't be sure until I listen back to the session recording, but I think he said his wife helped out with the household chores. I was about to ask for the child's spirit Paul when all of a sudden the room got extremely cold, I mean like a bitter cold."

Sue offered, "So cold you could see your breath and feel the cold nipping at your skin."

Bill added, "Yeah, and it happened in about five seconds."

Sue continued, "When I took the initial temperature reading, it was 69 degrees. After the temp drop, I pulled out the temp gun, and the temperature had dropped to 28 degrees in, like Bill said, about five seconds."

I replied, "Oh, that's what you meant a few minutes ago when you said, 'Boy, did that change.'"

Sue replied, "Yup," and then Tom continued his account of the investigation. "With the severe temperature drop, we knew something was up. Bill took out the EMF meter, and the reading was off the charts. I looked at the K2 meter, and it was lit up like a Christmas tree. I was about to ask the spirit tech Peter if there were any spirits here with us who made the temperature drop and caused those readings when two of the target objects Bill put on the table started to float about six inches in the air. None of us had remembered to bring a handheld video camera with us, so Bill jumped up and headed for the operations room to get one. As Bill came rushing back into the dining room, he already had the video camera recording. The two target objects, a small stuffed bear and a Rubik's Cube, were still bobbing in the air above the table. Bill confirmed he'd captured it. Just then I realized the stationary video camera that was in the dining room had captured it anyway. It was all good though, because now we have video evidence from two separate cameras. After a few seconds, the two target objects fell and hit the table.

"With the ghost box still running, I asked the tech Peter who was in the room with us besides the entities Paul and Adam. There was no response from Peter, but the answer, 'Me, here,' came through the box in a loud nasty voice. We all heard it loud and clear. I already knew who sent the communication, but I asked anyway, 'Who just said "me here"? What's your name?' A few seconds later a growling female voice came through and said, 'Leave now, or die.' I responded with, 'Bathsheba, is that you?' We all waited for the reply, but instead, one of the dining room chairs that was at the table flew backward and slammed into the wall. We all jumped in our seats.

"While we were still in shock from the chair being thrown against the wall, loud, angry screams started to come through the ghost box. The screams were bone chilling. The strange thing was that the screams did not sound like they were made up of the usual ghost box fragments of sound; they were above and separate from the sound of the box but still coming from the ghost box speaker. I knew at that point there was no dealing with that evil witch Bathsheba, and as long as she was there and in a fury, there was no more communication from any other entities to be had, including from Peter the technician. I decided to end the session, so I did, and we all came back to the operations room and waited for you." With that, Tom finished his accounting of their investigation.

I loved it when Tom gave the briefing of an investigation. Tom was an old-school Brooklyn Italian, and he had this heavy Brooklyn accent, which was like comfort food to me. You see, I was also an old-school Brooklyn Italian, with just as heavy a Brooklyn accent as Tom, and I felt very much at home when listening to Tom speak.

"Ok, boys and girl, I would say that both our sessions were very productive and for the most part went off without a hitch. Now we need to discuss and come up with a plan for the next phase of the investigation, which will be a group ghost box session in the dining room." I told everyone, "Let's not mention anything about the upper level or anyone pertaining to it, Bathsheba has sharp ears, and I'm sure she is listening to everything we say. I already informed everyone in my last briefing about what we can expect. My explanation of the following part of the investigation will be short and sweet."

CHAPTER FIFTEEN

THE EVIL PORTAL AND THE HIGHER SPIRIT ENTITY

I began to explain briefly what the plan was for the upcoming group ghost box investigation, paying close attention to not revealing out loud any information about the expected visit by the spirit entity from the higher spiritual level. "Ok, guys, we are bringing the battle to you-know-who. This is what I would like to do for the next phase of the investigation. I want to do another group ghost box session in the dining room. I would like to attempt to communicate with the entities who are here in this house, the child spirit Paul, the farmhand Adam, and of course, the mistress of the house, Bathsheba Sherman." I winked at Tom as I said that.

Tom smiled and winked back.

"Tom, I would like you to run a voice recorder and K2 meter. Sue, a voice recorder and also take temperature and EMF readings. Bill, I would like you to also run a voice recorder and take still photographs. Since it will be dark, Bill, please set up two low-light lanterns at either end of the dining room." I then asked slowly and succinctly, "Does everyone understand what we are about to do?"

Everybody verbally confirmed they understood.

"Ok, let's all take a fifteen-minute break and then meet back here to gather our equipment and get started." I sat down at the operations table and looked at my watch; the time was 3:41 a.m.

I began to contemplate the events to come when a thought crossed my mind. What if the evil entity Bathsheba was capable of reading our thoughts? This was not an unheard-of concept; the theory of spirit entities being able to read our thoughts has been bandied about by paranormal researchers and parapsychologists for many, many years. The theory of telepathic reception on the part of a spirit entity was one that I personally subscribed to. Through my many years of paranormal research and investigation with a ghost box, I had had countless instances where I had received valid and relevant answers and comments to specific questions in the form of live spirit ghost box communication while the question was still a thought in my mind and had not been verbalized yet. I tried my best to clear my mind of any thoughts pertaining to our upcoming investigation and ghost box session, especially all thoughts about what I hoped would happen.

My ghost box sat on the table next to me. I reached over and faced it toward me and said, "Ok, champ, number one is on the disabled list. I'm putting you into the big game in his place. I'm confident you will sweep the radio bands well and facilitate the best communication you can. I know you'll make me proud, so let's get out there and win one for old number one." As I was giving my ghost box a pep talk, Tom walked back into the operations room.

"You feelin' ok, buddy?" Tom asked.

"Yeah, what's the matter? You never saw a man talk to a ghost box before?" I replied.

Tom followed with, "Not unless there was something on the other side talking back." We both laughed out loud, and Tom sat down.

"Where are Bill and Sue?" I asked.

Tom said, "They are checking the stationary cameras and

placing some target objects," followed by, "They should be here in a minute."

A few minutes later Bill and Sue arrived in the operations room.

"Everything set to go?" I asked.

Bill answered, "Ready as it will ever be."

I looked at my watch again; it was 4:00 a.m. Saturday morning. I told everyone we had eight and a half hours left to finish this investigation, and I was confident that we would all do our best to bring it to a successful end. I followed with, "Let's all grab our equipment and head to the dining room."

We all entered the dining room together. I could feel the anticipation and also the tension in the air. Everyone found a seat around the big wooden dining room table. Bill had placed a couple of target objects in the middle of the table. The dining room was bathed in a faint light from the two low-light lanterns placed at either end of the room. I went over to the electrical outlet on the wall near my chair and plugged the ghost box power cord into it, returned to my chair, and sat down. I held off plugging the other end of the power cord into the ghost box until we were ready to begin the session; better safe than sorry. I didn't want any live current running to the ghost box before it was needed. One fried ghost box was bad enough; two fried boxes would have been catastrophic.

"Sue, can you take some temp and EMF readings; let us know if there are any readings that are out of the ordinary. Bill, please snap some pics of the room in both normal and infrared modes. Tom, get that K2 meter running, keep an eye on it, and alert us if it shows signs of activity." I allowed a few minutes for the team to take electronic readings and get some still photographs. I then asked everyone to start their respective digital voice recorders. I turned on my voice recorder and stated aloud the basic session information. I looked at my team and said, "Everybody ready? Here we go."

I plugged the power cord into the ghost box and switched it on, two or three seconds passed, and we heard nothing but a static hiss coming from the box. My heart skipped a beat. I got a hot flash that ran through my brain. Before I could process this immediate panic, the ghost box began sweeping, and the welcome sound of clear fragments of gibberish came through loudly. I had forgotten for a second that this particular ghost box incorporated a sweep circuit that took a few seconds to warm up before the box began to sweep. My fear of losing the only working ghost box I had left on this investigation that had any of my energy imprint on it just got the best of me. I took a breath and enjoyed the momentary rush of relief before beginning what most likely would prove to be an extraordinary live spirit ghost box communication session.

With the ghost box sweeping comfortably, I asked for my spirit technicians Mike and Lisa. "Mike, Lisa, are you there? Can you assist with this session?" Immediately the answer, "Yes, Bruce, here," came through the ghost box. I replied, "Good, great to have you with us." The response, "Thanks," was received.

I then asked for any entities who were present in the house with us to come forward and communicate. The first voice we heard was that of a small child: "Hi." That communication was followed by, "Adam here," in a male voice. I replied, "Hello, Adam, was that you who said hi? It sounded like a child's voice?" I, of course, knew an entity could send a communication in any tonal form: a male could deliver communication in a female voice, a female in a male voice, an adult in a child's voice, and vice versa. A spirit entity uses whatever fragments of sound are available at the time of constructing the words needed to deliver the communication, which can result in an entity, male, female, or child, communicating in any vocal scenario. The response, "Both here, Paul, Adam," came through. In this instance, the response of hi had come from the child spirit Paul, which meant that both entities, Adam and Paul, were present and communicating through the ghost box simultaneously. I greeted both entities and asked, "Adam, Paul, which one of you would like to communicate first?"

As we waited for a response, a familiar-sounding male voice came through. "Ready, Bruce," was the message that was sent. I knew this to be my spirit tech Mike, and I also knew what his message meant. The higher entity who was to help with the evil portal and Bathsheba was present and ready; at least I hoped that was what Mike meant.

Immediately following the communication from Mike, the response to my question came through. "Me first," was delivered through the box in a child's voice. I replied, "Ok, Paul, you first. Is there something you want to say?" As I waited for a response, the majority of my thoughts were on Bathsheba and the evil portal. If, as I hoped, the higher entity was standing by, waiting for the right time to act, it would most likely be when the evil spirit Bathsheba made her appearance here at this session. I was listening for little Paul's response, but I was also listening for any indication coming through the ghost box that Bathsheba was here or on her way. The message, "Mommy," came through the ghost box speaker. I responded, "Mommy? What about mommy, Paul?" The answer, "Coming," immediately came through, followed by, "Scared," delivered in the quivering voice of a scared child. "Paul, is Bathsheba coming?" I asked. The answer, "Yes," came through. We all looked at each other; it would not be long now. I told the little spirit Paul to go and hide, away from here and his evil mother Bathsheba.

I waited a few seconds and then called out to the entity Adam. "Adam, are you still here with us?" The answer, "Yes, here," came through quickly, followed by, "Will help." We were all surprised by this response. I did not expect the spirit entity Adam to stay here with us, with Bathsheba close by, let alone offer to help. I thought for a second and then told the brave spirit, "Adam, we appreciate your offer, but you can help us more by taking little Paul to a safe area and watching over him." A few seconds went by, and the response, "Yes, I will," came through the ghost box.

Now with the entities Adam and Paul away from this room and out of danger as much as they could be, we waited for the evil Bathsheba to make her presence known.

I took the moment to speak to my spirit techs Mike and Lisa. "Mike, Lisa, can you tell me, is Bathsheba here?" We waited for an answer from my technicians, but instead, a low, distinct, gravelly female voice came through in a serious and menacing tone of voice. "I am here, fools," Bathsheba replied. She did not send the communication in a loud threatening tone, but in one of more staunch resolve and determination. I needed to get more communication from her in order to get an idea of whether or not she was aware of our real plan. "Oh, hello, Bathsheba," I said. The response, "Hello, ass," came through. "Now, now, Bathsheba, no need for name-calling," I replied. Bathsheba's next communication was a bit chilling. "Ready to die now?" followed by, "Pigs." I did not respond to her heinous question.

I paused for a moment to think. I did not believe she was aware of what we were planning. She seemed too confident, too stoic in her approach; she must not know. I was a bit nervous. I did not know when or how the higher entity who was enlisted to help us would act. Bathsheba was here with us, apparently strong and confident. Should I continue to engage her, and if so, for how long? Was the higher entity already in the process of dealing with the evil portal? It was evident by Bathsheba's demeanor and aggressive confidence that she was not aware of any immediate threat to herself or the evil portal. Whatever the immediate situation on the spirit side was, I had no choice but to continue my interaction with Bathsheba and pray that the higher entity would intervene before the evil witch had a chance to inflict a serious physical attack on one or all of us.

I waited a few seconds, focused my thoughts, and then spoke. "Bathsheba, we intend to leave your house in a few hours. We are only here to communicate with you and the other spirits in this house." I followed it with, "There are people who have lived here who have told the world only bad things about you. I would like to hear your side of the story." I was curious to find out what kind of response my comment would elicit.

As the ghost box continued its unending delivery of broken-down sound fragments, we waited, fully expecting a verbal response from Bathsheba through the ghost box. Instead, the K2 meter that was running on the table next to Tom, which had the indicator lights fully illuminated from green to red, suddenly flew straight up in the air and came crashing down on the table, breaking into pieces. We all jumped in our seats. Tom yelled, "Whoa." This physical act by Bathsheba I don't believe was intended to do harm; it was simply to remind us that she was in charge here and capable of doing anything she wished without any of us having the slightest clue when or how it would occur, or having the ability to stop it. I guessed Bathsheba was not in the mood to chat.

I wasn't sure how long we could keep this up without having Bathsheba tire of the interaction and deliver a more devastating and, possibly, physically damaging attack. We were stuck between a rock and a hard place. I had asked for help from a higher spirit entity and was granted it, I'd initiated this group ghost box session, and I was committed to seeing it through. I prayed that if Bathsheba was to inflict any harm on one of us, it would be me. I didn't want any of my team members to suffer any injury at the cost of continuing a plan that I had orchestrated and put into effect.

Before going on, I spoke to my team. "Before we continue, I want to say that if any of you want to leave this session, I completely understand. I would not think any less of you as individuals or paranormal investigators."

Tom just chuckled, Bill spouted, "No way," and Sue said, "All for one, and one for all, to the end."

I felt a genuine wave of emotion flow through me. I was proud of my team, my friends! "Ok, that being said, let's continue. Bathsheba, why did you do that? I told you we will be gone in a few hours. If you want us to leave sooner, why don't you cooperate and help us with the information we're looking for?" About thirty seconds passed before a response came through the ghost box. The response was delivered in an angry, aggressive, and forceful tone. "Fools," followed immediately by, "Can't trick me." Before I could offer my next reply to Bathsheba's comment, a loud screaming was heard through the box. It started out loud and progressively became fainter and fainter as if Bathsheba were moving away from our immediate location.

As the screaming became almost undiscernible, a familiar female voice came through the ghost box. "Bruce, Samuel here," was delivered by my spirit tech Lisa. We heard her communication loud and clear. "Lisa, who is Samuel?" I asked. Lisa immediately responded with, "Ascended spirit." I understood this to mean Samuel was the higher-level entity we had been waiting for. I followed Lisa's answer with, "Lisa, can you tell us what is happening?"

I knew it was not possible to receive a detailed explanation by way of a ghost box communication; the way a ghost box worked to allow live spirit communication to be delivered and heard was not conducive to a spirit entity being capable of delivering a lengthy and detailed communication. The communication was predominantly sent in a patchwork of coinciding words, which led to the meaning of what the communicating entity wanted to convey.

Lisa responded to my question, "Bad struggle." I took this to mean that the higher spirit Samuel was in a struggle with either Bathsheba, attempting to close the evil portal, or both simultaneously. I asked my next question, "Is Samuel winning?" This time it was my technician Mike who answered. "No," was the response. "NO, what do you mean no?" I replied. After a few seconds the answer, "Too strong, too evil," came through the ghost box speaker. We continued to listen to the faint sounds of distant voices emanating from the ghost box, enveloped in the ever-present gibberish of the ghost box sweep. "Mike, Lisa, what's happening? Is Samuel ok?" Approximately another thirty seconds or so passed. We expected to hear an answer from our spirit technicians; instead, the evil familiar voice of the dark entity Bathsheba emanated from the ghost box. "Stupid fools," followed by, "Can not beat me."

I sank in my chair, as did the others. Samuel was not successful. I could only conclude that the evil portal was still here and open. I knew by the last communication that Bathsheba was still here and as strong as ever, and that Samuel must have retreated to the spirit realm. I looked at my team; they all had looks of staunch disappointment on their faces. I was sure I had the same look myself.

I thought for a second and decided to attempt another question to my spirit techs. "Mike, Lisa, is Samuel still here with us?" After a few seconds, a faint and deflated response came through the box. "No, gone," rang in all our ears. I knew Bathsheba would not let this attempt at her destruction and that of her energy source go unpunished. I decided the best course of action for us would be to end the session and retreat to the outside of the house for a while, which would give us the best chance of avoiding a severe physical attack by Bathsheba, which could possibly injure one of us, and possibly give Bathsheba some time to cool down, which was unlikely but possible. I told everyone I was ending the session and for them to gather up the equipment.

As I reached for the ghost box's power switch to turn it off, a female voice came through. "Not over," was the communication. I knew it was my spirit tech Lisa, and I knew she was telling me that we were down but not out; the fight would continue. I looked at my team, who were busy getting the equipment we had used in this session. "Did you hear that?" I asked.

"No, what?" responded Sue. Tom and Bill shook their heads.

"Lisa just said, 'Not over,' which I'm sure means we still have a chance. Everyone, let's drop the equipment in the operations room and head outside for a while; let things calm down in here."

"Good idea," said Tom. Sue and Bill nodded in agreement. I

turned off the ghost box, unplugged it from the wall, and headed for the operations area. Tom, Sue, and Bill followed close behind.

I looked at my watch; it was 5:37 a.m. We dropped our equipment in the operations room, I secured my only remaining ghost box in its protective case, and we headed for the front door. I opened the door and went to step out when I heard a loud crashing sound behind me. I spun around to see Tom and Sue huddled together right next to me. Bill was lying on the floor about five feet away. Just in front of him was a broken and shattered glass and brass light fixture that had been hanging from the ceiling about three or four feet from the front door. I rushed over to Bill. He was shaken and holding his right ankle. I kneeled beside him. Tom and Sue knelt down on his opposite side.

"Bill, are you hurt?" I asked excitedly.

"Yeah, my ankle," Bill replied.

"Where did it hit you?" was my next question.

"It didn't hit me," Bill said.

"If it didn't hit you, how did your ankle get hurt?" Sue asked.

"I heard the light coming away from the ceiling, and I jumped back. I must have twisted my ankle," answered Bill. "It really hurts," he added.

"Ok, Tom, get his other side. Let's get him up and outside before anything else happens." Tom and I lifted Bill to his one good foot. We wrapped Bill's arms around our shoulders and moved toward the front door, with Bill hopping on his one good leg. The three or four feet to the front door seemed like a mile. We were all tensed in anticipation of another attack by the evil and now vengeful entity Bathsheba.

We made it outside without further incident. I immediately felt the nip of the cold night air. Tom and I helped Bill over to the vehicle, with Sue following close behind with a flashlight illuminating the way. Tom opened the vehicle door, and we helped Bill into the back seat. His face was wincing in pain.

"Ok, Bill, try to take it easy. Would you like to go to the emergency room?" I asked him.

"No, no way, and miss all the rest of the fun," he answered.

Sue said, "I'll go back in and get the first aid kit. There are some painkillers and Ace bandages in it."

Tom, being the quintessential old-school gentleman, said, "No way. I'll go get it."

Sue was about to rebut Tom's offer when I said, "Neither one of you will go. I'm going to get the first aid kit. I'll be right back."

No one responded.

I turned and made my way back into the house. I walked over to the case containing the emergency medical kit, stepping on the remains of the fallen light fixture as I walked. I opened the case and retrieved the kit. As I turned to leave the house again, the heavy wooden front door abruptly slammed shut; it startled me. I started to walk to the door anyway. I had that strange tingling feeling, like when you're around someone using a hammer, and you uncontrollably anticipate the hit of the hammer blow, or like waiting for a balloon that is being overinflated to pop. I reached the front door and grabbed the handle. I fully expected the door to be unable to open; human nature made me tug on it anyway. I was shocked when the door swung open easily. I made my way back over to the vehicle. I handed the med kit to Sue. She proceeded to remove the items she would need to treat Bill.

"Why did you slam the door shut behind you?" Tom asked.

"I didn't," I replied.

Tom finished with, "Oh, ok, well, you made it, thank God."

I nodded.

Tom and I both shined our flashlights where Sue would be working. Sue handed Bill four aspirin and a bottle of water she had in her coat pocket. Bill could not swallow the aspirin fast enough. Sue told Bill, "Drink all that water; you need to stay hydrated."

Bill continued to drink.

Sue went on to tell Bill, "Ok, I'm not going to lie, this is going to hurt, but you're tough, you can take it. I'll try to be as quick and gentle as possible."

Bill tried to muster up a manly grin, as if to express that he was, in fact, a tough guy and could take it. Bill swung around on the car seat and stuck his bad ankle out the door for Sue to attend to. Sue rolled up Bill's pants leg. The ankle had already swelled and begun to turn black and blue. As Sue touched the ankle to position it for bandaging, Bill winced, but did not let out a peep. As Sue began to wrap the Ace bandage tightly around Bill's foot and ankle, Bill said in a shaky voice, "I heard that a sprain is worse than a break, is that true?"

Tom, in full Brooklyn style, trying to alleviate some of the tension, answered, "Well, if you want, I could always break the ankle for you if you think that would make it feel better."

Everyone chuckled, including Bill.

Sue finished rendering first aid, rolled down Bill's pants leg, and said, "Ok, all done; now just sit there quietly and relax. I'll check it in half an hour." She explained that the Ace bandage was wrapped tightly around the ankle and that the ankle would most likely swell further. She went on to say, "If I don't check it and rewrap it to accommodate for the extra swelling, it will cut off circulation to your foot, and we don't want that." Sue closed up the med kit and placed it in the back of the vehicle.

We all gathered around the open vehicle door where Bill was seated. Tom had started the vehicle's engine and turned on the heater full blast; the warm air felt good against the cold of the outside. I noticed there was a glint of light breaking the horizon. I glanced at my watch; it was 6:15 a.m. We only had six hours and fifteen minutes to bring this investigation of the Conjuring house to its conclusion.

"Ok, everyone," I said, "let's take a short break out here and give things inside a chance to calm down. We don't need any other injuries. We have about another six hours left in this investigation, give or take. I don't want to waste too much time, so I'll go over the next phase while we are standing here. We will need to perform another group ghost box session in the same spot. If I interpreted Mike and Lisa's final communication in the last session correctly, the higher entity Samuel was not finished; he simply stepped back to reevaluate the situation. I myself do not believe his initial intention was to bring about a final solution. I believe his plan was to step in, get a feel for the level of evil energy, size up the portal and Bathsheba, and then move back to formulate his final plan of action. I can't say for sure, but that's the impression I got."

As I explained, I thought to myself, *I really have no idea why the higher entity acted the way he did, or if he has given up for good*. I could only go by what the last message from Mike and Lisa was: "Not over." Those two words from my trusted spirit technicians and friends were the only thing keeping a spark of hope alive in me. Of course, I could not let my team know that; they needed to face this next phase with as much confidence and as little fear and apprehension as possible.

I continued my explanation of the next phase of the investigation. "We will go in this time with as little equipment as possible, mean and lean. We will each have only a single voice recorder, and I will, of course, have my ghost box. There is really no need for data-monitoring equipment; we will surely know when Bathsheba arrives. We will do a group ghost box session and take everything as it comes."

Everyone agreed.

I addressed Bill, "Bill, I want you to sit this one out. We don't know what is going to happen or how fast we will have to react to any possible physical attack. Obviously with your injury, you will not be able to move quickly or dodge an attack if necessary."

Bill immediately balked at my request. "Come on, man, you're not going to make me sit here in the vehicle while my three teammates go rushing into harm's way?"

I replied, "Sorry, my friend, not only could you suffer another possibly more serious injury at the hands of Bathsheba, but your inability to react and move quickly enough could endanger one of us as well." I followed it with, "I am truly sorry, you will be sorely missed, but you have to sit this one out."

Bill opened his mouth to respond.

I stopped him and said, "That's final." Bill didn't like it, but I knew he understood. I went on to tell Bill, "Just because you're sidelined doesn't mean you have to miss everything. Keep your walkie-talkie on, and I'll place a walkie on the table during the whole investigation with the transmit lock on. It will be like an intercom system; you will be able to hear everything that happens." I could see that made Bill feel a bit better about being absent from the investigation.

"Ok, guys, ten more minutes and we will head back in."

Tom and Sue nodded, and Bill checked the batteries in both walkie-talkies to make sure they were fresh. He didn't want to miss a minute of the action. Sue, Tom, and I made our way back to the Conjuring house. As we approached the front door, I could not help but feel a small deep-down twinge of envy; a small part of me wished I was staying in the vehicle.

We entered the house into the operations room. I said, "Let's gather our equipment and head over to the dining room."

Tom and Sue each grabbed a voice recorder. I grabbed my ghost box and voice recorder. "Ready?" I asked, and both answered yes. "Ok, let's go." I reminded Tom to grab a walkie-talkie to set up the intercom link with Bill.

As we walked toward the dining room, I could literally feel the air start to get heavy. It felt like gravity had gotten stronger all of a sudden, like I weighed more than I actually did. We entered the dining room cautiously. I paused for a second and looked around. All was calm, for the moment. I did not know if it was because of our previous experiences in this room, I was sure that had a part to play, but I had a foreboding feeling of impending danger, a feeling I could not rationalize away. I reached down and plugged the ghost box power cord into the wall outlet, and we all took a seat.

I looked at Tom and Sue. "Do you guys have this strange feeling of dread?" I asked.

Sue responded, "Kind of, I can't exactly say what the feeling is, but it's there."

Tom just grinned and winked at me. Tom was a longtime paranormal veteran; it took a lot to shake him. Honestly, I thought he liked the danger. I told Tom to set up the walkie-talkie for Bill. He set it up and placed it in the middle of the table. I asked, "Everyone ready?"

Both Tom and Sue nodded.

"Ok, here we go again. Start your recorders," I exclaimed. Tom and Sue powered up their voice recorders.

I checked my watch; it was 6:51 a.m. on Saturday morning. The morning sun shone brightly through the dining room windows. It was a white winter sun, not like that warm inviting golden summer sun. This sunlight made everything seem a bit monochrome. I turned on my voice recorder and reached for the power switch on the ghost box. I flicked it to the on position, and the ghost box began to warm up. A few seconds later the box began to emit its usual sweep sounds.

I took a breath and asked for my spirit technicians Mike and Lisa. "Mike, Lisa, are you there? Can you assist us in this session?" A few seconds passed, and the answer, "Yes, Bruce, here," came through. I followed it with, "Mike, Lisa, is everything ok on that side?" The response, "Yes, Bruce, good," was delivered. I replied, "Great, we're ready here." Of course, I knew the evil Bathsheba was listening to every word that was said between myself and my spirit techs, and she was well aware that she would be meeting the higher entity Samuel a second time. Bathsheba was an arrogant and evil entity, but I didn't think the impending reunion with Samuel frightened her at all.

While we cautiously awaited the appearance of Bathsheba, I decided to ask for the other two entities we believed to be in this house. "Adam or Paul, are you here? Can you speak with us?" My request for communication from the two entities went unanswered. I then asked for each spirit individually, first the child spirit Paul.

"Paul, are you here? Would you like to speak with us?" A few seconds went by; we all expected Paul to reply in the child's voice we had come to associate with his communication from previous sessions. Instead, a gruff male voice that was unfamiliar came through. No words were spoken; just a sinister-sounding laugh was heard from the ghost box. I did not immediately suspect anything nefarious. I knew live spirit communication through the ghost box could come in any form, and because of that, it was not indicative of the gender, age, or specific identification of the delivering entity. "Paul or Adam, was that you laughing?" The answer was delivered in the same unnerving male voice. "I am Anwir." I did not understand the name given by the communicating entity, so I asked Tom and Sue, "Did either of you understand that name?"

Sue shook her head, and Tom just shrugged his shoulders.

"The male entity who is speaking, we did not understand your name. Can you repeat it slowly?" A few seconds went by, and a response that sounded like, "And we're," came through in the male voice. I asked, "Did you say 'and we're'?" The reply, "Anwir," followed by, "Demon of lies," was delivered through the ghost box. I paused for a second and looked at Sue and gestured for her to use her cell phone to search the name Anwir and demon of lies.

A moment or two went by. Sue slid her cell phone to me across the dining table. I picked up the phone and read the description Sue had settled upon. It explained that Anwir was the name of an imp, or lesser demon, associated with deception and lies. I slid the cell phone back to Sue, who, now along with Tom and myself, had a look of serious concern on her face. If the communication with this entity was to be taken seriously, we now had a bigger problem. Was this alleged demon of lies Anwir really who he claimed to be, or was this a clever deception by the evil Bathsheba? There was not much we could do, only time would tell if this communicating entity was actually Anwir, the demon of lies, or not.

I called out to my spirit technicians Mike and Lisa in what I knew would probably be a futile effort to learn the truth about this supposed demon. "Mike, Lisa, the entity who is communicating now, is he really a demon?" I knew that if it were at all possible, Mike or Lisa would truthfully answer my question. A moment passed, and we could hear verbal activity amidst the chatter of the ghost box sweep; finally a faint female voice came through that sounded like the tone Lisa used to communicate. "Yes, real," followed by, "Demon," was delivered through the box. My mind raced. Did this demon come through the evil open portal? If so, how long had he been here? Did his presence here, combined with that of Bathsheba, present insurmountable odds against the success of the higher entity Samuel in his next attempt at combating the evil in this house? These were all questions that could only be answered by the continuation of this investigation and the ghost box session.

I spoke again to my spirit techs. "Mike, Lisa, are you ok?" Again, a faint seemingly distant voice came through; this time it was Mike. "Yes, Bruce, ok," followed by, "Can not interfere." I was glad to hear that my beloved spirit technicians were safe, but it was a bit unsettling to know that they had been sidelined. Truth be told, the three of us were basically spectators in this unfolding drama. Of course, I had a small active role in that I communicated with the entities through the ghost box, but that was inconsequential compared to the task the higher entity Samuel had ahead of him. I knew I had to keep this live ghost box session going.

I instinctively asked a question of the self-proclaimed demon Anwir in an attempt to garner some kind of information, or at the very least keep him occupied. "Tell me, Anwir, did you come here to this house through the open portal?" After a few seconds the answer, "Of course, fool," came through. I didn't know what I was thinking, but I replied to his answer with a sarcastic joke. "Anwir, just because you're a demon, there is no need to be rude." After the comment left my lips, I regretted it. I should know better than to antagonize this evil demon, especially not knowing what he was actually capable of. Instead of replying to my comment with anger and disdain, we heard the sound of a loud chuckle come across the ghost box speaker. Before I could say anything else, "Unaware of," followed by, "Who you deal with," came through the ghost box.

Sue gestured to me that she wanted to speak. I nodded in approval. "Is Bathsheba here with you, Anwir?" Sue asked. "She is present," was the answer that was delivered.

While Sue had control of the session, I looked at my watch; the time was 7:30 a.m. The ghost box session had been in progress for about thirty minutes. We had been interacting and exchanging communication with the demon Anwir since the opening moments of the session. There was still no indication that the higher entity Samuel was present or even close by.

Sue asked a second question. "Anwir, if Bathsheba is here, why has she not spoken or made her presence known?" The answer, "Bathsheba, my control," came back.

I nodded to Sue, letting her know I would resume control of the ghost box session. She nodded back in understanding. I didn't know if the demon Anwir realized it, but he was forfeiting information about his and Bathsheba's situation that could prove useful to us and to the higher entity Samuel. The boastful answer to Sue's last question, delivered by the demon, informed us that the evil Bathsheba was not actually in control here; she was being controlled by the deceitful demon Anwir. If this demon were in complete control of the spirit of Bathsheba, it could indeed prove very valuable in the effort to eradicate the evil influences reining over this house.

I heard verbal chatter amidst the sweep of the ghost box. I was unable to tell if it was being produced by the demon and his lackey Bathsheba, or from my spirit techs and hopefully the higher entity Samuel. I asked a question in an attempt to find out who was initiating the chatter we heard. "Who is speaking in the background?" A few seconds went by, and the answer, "Me, Mike," came through. I followed with, "Mike, is Samuel there?" I immediately heard the answer, "Yes, here." Before I could deliver my next question, the message, "End session now," came through the ghost box. The message from Mike was loud and clear, but before I just abruptly ended the live ghost box session, I asked Mike for confirmation. "Mike, did you say end session now?" The immediate answer, "Yes, now," came back across the ghost box speaker. I did not pursue any further explanation. I trusted Mike and Lisa; if they said to end the session, I listened.

I asked Tom and Sue, "Did you guys hear that?"

Both Sue and Tom answered, "Yes."

I did not say goodbye to my spirit technicians. I reached for the ghost box power switch and turned it off. I said, "Ok, let's go back to the operations area." I looked at my watch; it was 7:55 a.m. The whole session had only taken about fifty-five minutes. I stood up, unplugged my ghost box from the wall, grabbed it, and turned to leave the dining room. Tom and Sue were already walking out since they had only the two small voice recorders and a walkie-talkie to carry.

As I walked from the dining room across to the operations room, it struck me. Bill, he must have heard the whole investigation; he was not able to send any messages or interact at all since the walkie-talkie we had running on the dining room table had the transmit button in constant operation to allow Bill to hear everything that was taking place. I reached the operations room seconds after Tom and Sue.

"I'm going to go out and check on Bill," I told them.

"Ok, give him a kiss for me," said Tom jokingly. "If you are planning on bringing him back inside, let me know. I'll help you."

I smiled and went to the door. I stepped outside. The early morning sun was starting to warm the remnants of the night air. When I reached the vehicle, Bill swung the back door open. I asked how his ankle felt, and he said it was ok. I thought he was just setting the stage for me to have him come back inside.

Looking at his watch, Bill said, "Wow, 8:15, that was a really quick session."

I replied, "Yeah, the spirit techs told us to shut down. Were you able to catch all of it over the walkie-talkie?"

Bill said yes, but added that he had a hard time hearing any of the spirit communication that came through the ghost box. That was understandable considering the poor sound quality of the walkie-talkie. Bill went on to say that he was able to get the gist of the session and understood what had taken place.

"Ok, cowboy, you ready to get out of this car and come back inside?"

"I thought you would never ask," Bill replied.

"Ok, hand me that walkie-talkie." I turned on the walkie and called for Tom. "Tom, come in. Over."

The walkie-talkie crackled back, "This is Tom. Over."

I told Tom to come out to the vehicle and give me a hand bringing Bill inside.

He replied, "Will do. Over and out."

While Bill and I waited for Tom to come out to the vehicle, Bill asked, "Was there any physical activity during the investigation?"

"No," I replied. "Not a bit. As you heard, the whole session was basically about the demon Anwir making himself known." I told Bill that I thought that was either brave, arrogant, careless, or very stupid on the part of the demon Anwir, knowing that the higher entity Samuel was planning an assault on him, Bathsheba, and the evil portal that existed in the house.

Before Bill had a chance to reply to my comment, Tom came walking up pushing a hand dolly that we used to move the heavy equipment cases. "Ok, Bruce, load him on," Tom exclaimed, and we all broke into laughter.

"Very funny," Bill said, "but it might not be that ridiculous."

"No, no," I replied, "not the way Tom drives. You will wind up with more than a sprained ankle." We had another laugh and then proceeded to help Bill out of the vehicle. Again Tom and I took Bill's arms and put them around our shoulders. We slowly made our way back to the house and inside. We sat Bill in a chair at the operations table.

Sue asked, "How do you feel, Bill?" followed by, "Any numbness or tingling in your leg or foot?"

Bill replied, "No, not yet. It does feel kind of hot though."

"That's normal. Your body increased the flow of blood and liquid to your ankle; that is what is giving you the sensation of heat." Sue added, "Don't forget, let me know if there is any numbness."

"Ok, I will," Bill replied.

Tom turned to me and said, "So what's our next move?"

I told Tom and the others that I thought a quick bathroom and snack break was in order. "Let's take fifteen minutes and then gather back at the table, and I'll explain my plan for the next phase."

Bill asked if Tom and I could help him get to the bathroom.

"Of course," I said. Tom came over, and we proceeded to help Bill to the bathroom. Luckily, it was only a few feet from the operations room.

Sue said, "I'll use the upstairs bathroom," and headed for the staircase leading up to the bedrooms.

As Tom and I waited outside the bathroom door for Bill to finish, I looked at my watch; the time was 8:50 a.m. It seemed like the time was passing more quickly for some reason. I guessed it felt that way because we only had about three hours and forty minutes to conclude this investigation, no matter what the final outcome was.

Bill opened the bathroom door. Tom and I helped him back to his seat at the operations table. Sue came down the stairs and joined us. We were all seated at the operations table. I asked, "How is everybody holding up?"

Tom answered, "Tired, but holding up."

Sue echoed what Tom said, and Bill said, "Except for the ankle, Ok."

I took a deep breath and exhaled. "All right, to be perfectly honest with you, I'm not quite sure how to go about this next phase." I paused for a second and said, "I would like your input; feel free to make any and all suggestions." The room was silent for a moment or two while my team members contemplated offering any suggestions. "Come on, guys, we are all equal here; no idea is silly or irrelevant; just shoot them out there so we can discuss them."

Sue broke the silence. "I know I am the junior member of the team, and I don't have near the experience you all have." She continued with, "What if, and please don't laugh, but what if we did nothing?" Sue went on, "What if we just initiated the live ghost box session and then allowed our spirit technicians and the higher entity to take control of the session and do whatever they needed to do?" Sue finished her comment with, "We could monitor whatever came through the box, sort of like observers."

When Sue finished, I thanked her. I wanted to give everyone the opportunity to make suggestions for the upcoming phase of the investigation. Sometimes what someone thinks is silly or ridiculous turns out to be a gem. "Tom, Bill, do you have any suggestions or anything to add to Sue's suggestion?"

Bill said, "I'm stumped."

Tom said, "I want to comment on Sue's idea."

"Ok, Tom, go ahead," I replied.

"Sue's idea is not bad, but I don't think we can be totally inactive during the ghost box session." Tom went on, "For us to know exactly what is happening, we will have to ask questions and interact with our technicians and most likely the evil ones too." Tom continued, "If we were to be completely silent and not actively participating in the session, we would most likely miss some of the important parts of what was happening. Our techs Mike and Lisa would have to act like sports commentators, giving a blow-by-blow account of what was happening. I don't think they will be able to do that." Tom finished with, "That's about all I got to say."

"Thanks, Tom," I said. "Sue, your idea is good, and what Tom said is true. I think we should be active in the live ghost box session, but keep our interaction to a minimum. We need to interfere as little as possible in order to allow Mike, Lisa, and especially Samuel the ability to focus on the task at hand. I believe they are going to have their hands full without having to deal with continuous questions and comments from us. We will do a basic group ghost box session in the dining room and try to keep our involvement to only what is necessary. The reality is, I'm afraid that is going to be easier said than done, but we'll give it our best shot.

"Before we get started—"

In the middle of my sentence, Bill broke in and said, "You don't have to say it. What about crippled old Bill, right?"

I replied, "Well, I would not have put it quite that way, but yes."

Bill went on to say, "While you guys were talking, I was thinking about that very question. I know how you feel about me, in my condition, being in attendance at the actual investigation. I know you're all concerned about my safety and that of everyone if a quick reaction is necessary." He finished with, "How about this? If a situation arises that warrants a quick reaction for protection's sake, I will simply drop to the floor out of my seat and take cover under the table. That way I will be in the best position to avoid harm, and I won't put anyone else in jeopardy. I think that is an acceptable risk for me, and I'm more than willing to take it." Bill finished his plea.

I thought for a second and said, "Ok, you guys heard Bill. I won't make the decision for everyone; we'll put it to a vote." I then asked Bill, "Is that good; will you abide by whatever the vote is?"

Bill acknowledged that he would quietly agree to whatever the vote turned out to be.

I put the decision to a vote. "Ok, everyone in favor of Bill attending the next investigation, raise your hand."

Sue put her hand up immediately, and mine went up as well. We all looked at Tom, who just sat there quietly. "Tom, are you going to vote?" I asked.

Tom replied, "Will I have to drag his ass out from under the table and pick him up?"

I smiled and said, "Probably."

Tom replied, "Oh well, ok, won't be the first time I had to take care of him, and probably won't be the last." With that, Tom laughed and raised his hand.

"Ok, Bill, looks like it's unanimous."

Sue yelled, "All for one, one for all, to the end." We all felt a twinge of emotion, I could not be sure, but I thought Bill wiped a tear from his eye.

"All right, everyone, same protocol as the last time, voice recorders and my ghost box only. We are going to have to be extra cautious; it may get nasty in there."

Everyone agreed.

I asked Tom to get Bill a voice recorder and, when he was ready, to help me get Bill to the dining room. Tom nodded. I grabbed my ghost box and asked Sue if she would not mind carrying it into the dining room for me. She smiled, took the ghost box, and headed for the dining room. Tom gestured to me that he was ready to help Bill. I walked over, and all three of us made our way to the dining room.

CHAPTER SIXTEEN

BEYOND THE FRAY OF THE HIGHER ENTITY
SAMUEL'S RETURN

W e entered the dining room and helped Bill into his seat. I went over and plugged my ghost box power cord into the wall outlet, took my seat, and put the other end of the power cord into my ghost box, which Sue had placed on the table in front of my chair. Sue, Tom, and Bill were seated around the table with their respective voice recorders placed in front of them. The mood was serious, but surprisingly calm, considering what could possibly occur in the upcoming investigation and ghost box session.

I gave everyone a moment to settle, and then asked, "Ok, everyone ready?"

Everybody nodded in acknowledgment.

"I would just like to add before we get started, I'm very proud to be working with all of you."

Everyone responded with similar remarks. Bill tried to lighten the mood a bit by saying, "Listen, if you can't find me after this is over, somebody please check under the table."

Everyone chuckled, which served to alleviate even more of any anxiety we were feeling.

"Everybody start your recorders and focus," I said. "Here we go."

I checked my watch; it was 9:10 a.m. I reached for the power switch and turned on the ghost box. After a few seconds the box began to emit a smooth sweep. I took a breath and asked for my spirit technicians. "Mike, Lisa, you guys around? Can you assist with this session?" The immediate reply, "Yes, Bruce, here," followed by, "Not alone," came through the ghost box. "Not alone, do you mean we are not alone?" After a second or two the response, "No, we not alone," came back. That was one communication I was happy to hear. It indicated to us that the higher entity Samuel was in attendance.

As soon as Mike had delivered his last communication, the sound of faint growling could be heard coming through the box's speaker just above the sound of the ghost box sweep. This was a sure indication that either the demon Anwir or the dark entity Bathsheba, or both, was not far away. Since the evil in this house was already aware of my spirit technicians and the higher entity's intent, there was no need for me or my ethereal assistants to camouflage our communications.

"Mike, Lisa, is everything ready?" I asked. The answer, "Yes, ready," came through. I replied, "Ok, great, what do you need us to do?" A few seconds passed, and I noticed the evil sounds were starting to get louder. Lisa answered, "Be safe." I understood Lisa's communication to mean don't take any unnecessary chances; let us do the work. I acknowledged Lisa's message and took the opportunity to pause our participation in the live ghost box session.

We all listened intently to the chatter of the ghost box. Muffled voices were mixed with the sound of growling, and all were embedded in the continual sound of broken-down fragments of human speech, music, and singing produced by the ghost box sweep.

I wanted to inform my spirit techs Mike and Lisa that we would be taking a minimal active part in this session, and I also wanted to ask them to keep us informed of the events taking place that were beyond our physical comprehension. I spoke to my spirit technicians. "Mike, Lisa, we will be here on the sidelines listening to the ghost box; we will interact as little as possible." I went on to ask, "Will you please keep us informed from time to time of what is happening that we are not aware of?" A few seconds passed, and the response, "Yes, Bruce, we will," came across the ghost box speaker. I thanked my spirit technicians, and we went back to our silent vigil.

As we continued to listen to what was being delivered through the ghost box, Bill asked, "Should we just sit here and do nothing but listen? It's weird, but I feel uncomfortable not taking an active role in what's happening."

Tom concurred with Bill, "Yeah, me too. I feel like a coward."

Sue just sat quietly, since it was her idea originally to take a passive role in this session.

I replied to Bill and Tom, "I know how you feel, I'm not used to sitting idle either, but we have to remember that it's not out of fear or incompetence. We are doing what's best for the situation and for our friends facing this powerful evil beyond the veil." I ended my response with, "Don't worry, if we need to act, we definitely will. We are not going to be completely disengaged."

Both Tom and Bill nodded understandingly and refocused on the emissions of the ghost box. A few moments passed. There was a distinct sound of what I could only describe as a melee coming from the ghost box; the sounds were reminiscent of being the spectator to a verbal altercation between two opposing groups, kind of like listening to a bar fight. I looked at my team. "Are you guys hearing this?" I asked.

Sue replied, "Yeah, sounds like people having a bad argument."

Tom could not resist and added, "Sounds like my family at any Sunday dinner." We all managed a smile at Tom's remark.

The air of levity created by Tom's joke quickly dissipated, and the sounds of an altercation that were coming from the ghost box became louder and more aggressive sounding. We all listened intently, wishing we could be privy to what was happening first-hand. It was hard and confusing to just have access to the sound of the activity. Listening to the apparent altercation between good and evil that was unfolding, enveloped by the incessant gibberish that came from the ghost box sweep, was like being a blind person in a crowded room, trying to piece together the events taking place with limited senses. It was very difficult being beyond the fray.

As we listened, the sounds of the obvious altercation started to dissipate. After a few minutes, they had silenced completely. The disturbing sounds of the conflict had only lasted about twenty minutes; now the only sounds coming from the ghost box were that of the broken-down fragments of radio broadcast, an average, normal sweep. We listened to the benign ghost box sound for a moment or two, expecting the action to resume.

When no extraordinary sounds were heard, I asked, "Mike, Lisa, Samuel, are you still there? Is everything ok?" Shortly after my question, the answer, "Yes, Bruce," followed by, "Demons moved away," came across the box speaker. My next questions were, "Did we win? Are the demon Anwir and Bathsheba gone? Is the evil portal closed?" We waited for a response with concerned but excited anticipation. "No," followed by, "Still there," and then, "Just away," came through. I believed this to mean the demon Anwir and Bathsheba had retreated to a safe distance. If they did retreat, it meant the higher entity, along with Mike and Lisa, had managed to inflict enough damage to drive them back.

"Mike, Lisa, did the demon Anwir and Bathsheba go through the evil portal?" I knew this was extremely wishful thinking on my part. "No," was the answer delivered by Mike. The communication, "Still with you," came through, followed by, "Portal open." The demon and the evil witch were still in the Conjuring house, and the evil portal was still open. This was unfortunate. It meant the higher entity and my spirit techs were not able to eradicate the evil presence or close the evil portal. It also meant the demon and Bathsheba were most likely replenishing their evil energy by way of the portal right now and would be back stronger than ever. I knew I did not have to explain this to my team; they all had enough experience to come to a similar conclusion on their own.

"Ok, everyone, apparently the problem is not resolved."

Everybody nodded.

I went on to say, "I'll try to find out from our techs what they would like us to do moving forward." I called out to my spirit technicians. "Mike, Lisa, should we continue this live ghost box session?" A moment passed without a response. I repeated my question. A few seconds later the answer, "Won't help," came through the ghost box. Won't help, that could have different meanings. I asked for clarification from my techs. "Mike, Lisa, what do you mean won't help?" The response, "Must rest," came through followed by, "Over for now." I replied, "Ok, I am going to end the session now." The reply, "Ok, goodbye," was heard through the box from Mike. It was apparent that our spirit technicians, as well as, I'm sure, the higher entity Samuel, had exhausted their own supply of energy and needed to recuperate.

As I reached for the power switch to turn off the ghost box, I realized the threat of any physical reprisal on us from the demon Anwir and Bathsheba was not likely in the immediate future, since they were off licking their wounds. I verbalized that thought to my team members, and they all nodded in relief. I said to my team, "Let's all go back to the operations room and take a break."

I got up from my seat and unplugged the ghost box power cord from the wall outlet. I turned and told Bill to hold on; Tom and I would give him a hand getting to the operations room. Bill nodded. Sue grabbed Tom's and Bill's voice recorders and headed to the operations area. Tom and I helped Bill to his feet.

Tom said jokingly, "At least you didn't wind up under the table." We all chuckled and helped Bill to the operations room.

We entered the operations area and helped Bill into his chair. Sue had considerately placed a hot cup of coffee on the table in front of all three of our seats. "Thank you, Sue," I said.

"Yeah, thanks," exclaimed Tom, Bill offered his thanks, and we all took a seat.

I looked at my watch, it was 10:05 a.m. on Saturday morning, and we had approximately two and a half hours left to the scheduled end of the time allotted to us for the investigation.

Tom stood up. "I don't know about you guys, but I'm starving. We didn't take a meal break, and I haven't had anything to eat since breakfast yesterday. I'm gonna grab some peanut butter crackers from the supply box. Does anybody want any?"

"I'll take some," said Sue.

"Me too," said Bill.

I told Tom to bring whatever snacks he could carry to the table, we were all pretty hungry, and we could snack while we talked. Tom returned with a plethora of snacks, peanut butter and cheese crackers, potato chips, packages of mini doughnuts, and assorted candy bars. Tom dropped everything in the middle of the table; everyone reached for their favorite.

"Tom, when was the last time you checked the monitors and video cameras?" I asked.

"Must have been in the middle of the night sometime," Tom answered.

"Ok, after we finish our coffee and snacks, please do a quick equipment check and make sure everything is still working."

"Will do," Tom replied.

As we sat there noshing on our respective snacks, I said, "We don't have a lot of time left till the end of the investigation. I don't want to waste too much time on this break, so I'll talk while we snack."

Everyone nodded with a full mouth.

"We will be returning to the dining room for another group ghost box session; there's not much else we can do." I continued, "Very simple, same protocol, same plan, we will initiate the live ghost box session and then follow the lead of our spirit counterparts." All agreed. "I am hoping the higher entity along with Mike and Lisa can manage to successfully deal with the demon Anwir and Bathsheba and hopefully be able to send them fleeing through the open evil portal to whatever dark realm is on the other side of it, and then hopefully be able to close the evil portal in this house for good."

Bill spoke up. "What happens if our spirit friends cannot accomplish all of that by the time we have to end the investigation? Is it possible to extend the investigation?"

I replied, "I'm not sure, but I believe the gentleman John who greeted us when we arrived mentioned there was another paranormal investigation scheduled to take place immediately after we finish ours."

Tom spoke out and said, "You're kidding. Suppose the spirit techs and higher entity can't resolve the evil presence here; those poor investigators will be walking into a buzzing hornet's nest of evil we stirred up."

I replied, "I know, I thought of that earlier. All we can do in the event that our spirit friends are not successful is brief the next team on what we discovered and dealt with, and tell them to use extreme caution and protective measures on their investigation."

Sue offered her input. "Why would they schedule another investigation immediately after ours? Why didn't they give the place time to settle down, or at the very least hear our report before giving unsuspecting and possibly inexperienced paranormal investigators access to a location with a volatile situation?"

I did not have a satisfactory answer for my team members. "The owners of the Conjuring house are free to allow access to the house to whomever they wish, whenever they wish. I don't believe the owners, or anyone else, are aware of the seriousness of the evil presence plaguing this house. I also believe the activity and evil entities we have encountered here during this investigation are unprecedented. I have never heard of any reports made by residents of this house, or individuals who have conducted paranormal investigations here in the past, having dealt with anything we have encountered. Ultimately, our hands are tied; all we can do is report what we have found and experienced to the owners of the house, and advise the team following us of the situation and conditions they are sure to encounter."

Everyone acknowledged that they understood.

Time was of the essence. Hopefully, in the next and final phase of our investigation, the spirits of good could prevail over the forces of evil, and all would be right for the Conjuring house. I could not help but think, if that was the case and the Conjuring house was cleaned of all negative and evil presence, the next paranormal investigating team would have a pretty boring investigation.

Before we set out on this next crucial phase of the investigation, Bill brought up a very good point; he said, "Let's assume the higher entity and the techs are able to dispense with the evil demon and Bathsheba and close the evil portal; what happens to the two innocent entities still grounded here, little Paul and the farmhand Adam?"

I could not believe the fate of little Paul and Adam had not occurred to me until Bill just mentioned it; their fate was just as important as dealing with the evil demon Anwir and Bathsheba. The two grounded spirits here, Adam and Paul, were innocent; they were simply victims of their own confusion, emotions, and suppression of the evil Bathsheba. We had to do something to help them. I had to think about it; what could be done? The clock was ticking; the time we had left grew shorter with every minute. Not only did I have to focus on the task of eliminating the evil in this house, but now I had to come up with a way to not leave two innocent souls stranded here. I looked down at my watch; it was 10:35 a.m. Two hours left to do a group ghost box session to try to aid in the eradication of the demon Anwir, Bathsheba, and the evil portal, and to help the two spirit entities, Adam and Paul, leave this house and move on to the spirit realm. No pressure, yeah, right, not much! I would have to think on the fly. I didn't have the luxury of sitting here while I formulated a plan.

I told everyone to grab a voice recorder and head over to the dining room. I asked Tom to help take Bill over there; he nodded. I made a specific mental note: the first thing we would do after this investigation was to buy a pair of crutches and have them available in the vehicle if we ever needed them again. Sue grabbed three voice recorders and headed out of the operations room, Tom and I helped Bill, and the three of us headed for the dining room. We entered the dining room. Sue had once again placed the voice recorders in front of our seats.

Tom blurted out as we helped Bill into his chair, "Hey, Bill, maybe this time you can actually make it under the table." We chuckled, and Bill took his seat.

I proceeded to plug my ghost box into the wall outlet and take my seat. The dining room had an eerie calm about it; the sun shone strongly through the windows and gave the room a warmer feeling. I looked at everyone; they were all calm and serious. I told everyone we would begin in a couple of minutes. My mind raced, trying to hatch an idea as to what to do about the entities Adam and Paul. The harder I thought, the more difficult it became to form an idea. We were pressed for time, so I decided to start the live ghost box session and deal with the issue of Paul and Adam as the session was in progress.

CHAPTER SEVENTEEN
THE FINAL CONFLICT

I told everyone to start their voice recorders. I turned my recorder on and reached for the ghost box power switch. I turned on the ghost box, and in a few seconds, the box began its usual sweep of the radio broadcast stations. I called on my spirit technicians. "Mike, Lisa, are you there?" The response, "Yes," came through. "Hi, guys, are you all ready for this session?" A few seconds passed, and Lisa answered, "Yes, Bruce, all here." I wanted to confirm, so I asked, "Is Samuel there with you?" The answer, "Yes, here," came through the ghost box, followed by, "More also." I did not understand, so I asked, "Lisa, what do you mean more also?" A few seconds passed, and Lisa answered, "Two high spirit." "Lisa, did I hear you correctly? Did you say two high spirits?" Lisa responded, "Yes, Bruce, two." I replied, "Ok, Lisa, thank you." Two high-level spirits, if this was true, they, combined with Mike and Lisa, would surely have a good chance of beating the demon Anwir and the evil entity Bathsheba. None of us were able to discern any indication through the ghost box that the evil entities were present.

I took the opportunity to ask my spirit techs about the stranded spirits Adam and Paul. "Mike, Lisa, I know you are extremely busy with the task at hand, but I have to ask you if it is possible for you to assist the two spirit entities grounded in this house?" A moment passed, and Mike responded, "Yes, Bruce," followed by, "Must be now."

I called out loudly to the spirits of little Paul Sherman and Adam the farmhand. "Adam, Paul, if you can hear me, please come here where I am." A few seconds passed, and the response, "Here," came through in a monotone male voice. "Adam, I am glad you're here. Is little Paul with you?" The answer, "Yes," was received. I told Adam that my two spirit friends would help him and Paul to cross over to the spirit world, and that they would be safe there and have a whole new happy existence. I went on to tell Adam that his wife was most likely in the spirit world waiting for him, which was why he had not been able to find her here. I then asked, "Adam, are you willing to cross to the spirit world and take the child Paul with you?" A simple one-word answer was delivered by Adam, "Yes." A feeling of relief washed over me. Now we would not have to worry about the two innocent spirits; we could concentrate on the eradication of the evil in this house.

"Mike, Lisa, the entities Adam and Paul are here. Can you lead them to the other side?" "Yes, Bruce," was delivered through the ghost box. I took a deep cleansing breath and let it out. "Whew, I'm glad we got that taken care of," I exclaimed.

Everyone acknowledged it with a short positive comment. "Yes," "Great," "Thank God," everyone replied.

As we savored the moment, and what we believed to be no small victory, I could not help but wonder why the evil Bathsheba and her keeper the demon Anwir allowed this to happen. Where were they, and why did they not try to intervene? I was about to ask my spirit technicians for a confirmation of the two entities crossing over, when a loud, angry, and growling voice came across the speaker of the ghost box. "Not likely," was all the demon Anwir said. I felt a cold chill run down my spine. I became immediately deflated. I called to Mike and Lisa, "Mike, Lisa, were you able to cross over Adam and Paul?" I expected a response from my techs; instead the only sound we heard was the distant cries of a small child and the panicked scream of a frightened man. The two evil entities had just been quietly waiting to sabotage the attempt to cross over the two innocent spirits. The only hope Adam and Paul now had for crossing over to the spirit realm was the eradication of the evil presence that imprisoned them here in this house. The failed crossing-over attempt was a stark reminder to all of us, including our spirit counterparts, that no task was going to be easy when it came to dealing with the demon Anwir and Bathsheba. What we'd savored as a victory a moment ago was now a stinging defeat.

I asked my spirit techs, "Mike, Lisa, what happened? Why were you not able to get the two entities across?" Mike responded with the answer, "Boy too weak," followed by, "Demon strong." I could not help but feel that the failed crossing attempt, and whatever the two innocent entities were now having to endure at the hands of the evil forces in this house, was my fault. I had acted too prematurely. I had allowed myself to be lulled into a false sense of security by the calmness and serenity of the moment. All my years of knowledge and experience should have told me to never let my guard down and never trust that an evil entity is incapable of acting, not even for a second. My momentary lapse in judgment had cost Adam and Paul possibly their only chance to escape from this house. I would never make that mistake again!

The atmosphere in the dining room was now heavy and oppressive; the sour air of evil was almost palpable. I looked at my team members. Sue looked tense and was wringing her hands, Bill sat expressionless in his chair, and Tom projected a look of disappointment and anger.

I called to my spirit technicians and the high spirits. "Mike, Lisa, and Samuel, can you tell me the name of the new high spirit entity who has joined you?" A few seconds passed, and the answer, "Yawar," came through. I recognized that Lisa had delivered the name of the additional high spirit, but none of us understood her communication clearly. I asked Lisa to repeat the name slowly so that we could understand it. My spirit tech Lisa delivered the name again, this time in two separate parts. "Ya" immediately followed by "War." She then repeated it again as one word, "Yawar." This was a common way for an entity to deliver a communication through the ghost box that was difficult for the ghost box operator to understand. I repeated the name and asked, "Yawar, Yawar, is that correct?" Lisa delivered the answer, "Yes." I thanked her.

During this brief interaction between Lisa and myself, the sound of angry grumbling could be heard amidst the ghost box fodder. I realized that although we were all aware that the demon Anwir and Bathsheba were here with us and their presence was obvious, besides blocking the crossing over of Adam and Paul, they had not delivered, physically or verbally, any aggressive activity. I could only attribute this to the presence of the new higher entity and the combined strength of my two spirit technicians, Mike and Lisa, and the two high entities, Samuel and Yawar.

I took advantage of the two evil entities' benign position and asked, "Mike, Lisa, is the higher entity Yawar from the same spiritual level as Samuel?" I was curious to know whether the entity Yawar was stronger, weaker, or on the same level as the entity Samuel. His added strength must be formidable, because his mere presence seemed to be capable of keeping the demon Anwir and the evil spirit Bathsheba at bay. The answer, "Samuel spirit," followed by, "Yawar angel," was delivered through the ghost box. I followed my tech's answer with a request for confirmation. I was praying I'd heard the communication correctly. "Did you say Yawar is an angel?" A few seconds passed, and Mike answered, "Yes, angel."

At hearing this confirmation that the new addition to our spiritual group was an angel, Tom, Sue, and Bill all perked up in their seats; an air of optimism came over all of us. "Thank you, Mike, and welcome, Yawar." The response, "All will be good," came through the ghost box speaker; the voice was one I had not heard before during this whole investigation. I asked, "Yawar, was that you who just spoke?" The answer, "Yes, Bruce," came back. I had been practicing live spirit ghost box communication for many, many years, but having a heavenly angel address me by name was a first, and admittedly a thrilling experience. I replied, "Thank you for being here and for helping us, Yawar." The response, "No need for thanks," was returned. I was amazed at how easily and strongly the angel Yawar was able to communicate through the ghost box. I attributed this to the angel having superior spiritual energy.

At this point, any further attempts at communication with my spirit technicians or Yawar and Samuel would just be generic. I decided we would be silent for a while and see how things unfolded. I told my team, "Let's sit quietly for a bit and see what happens."

They all nodded in agreement. The nagging thought of our time restraint was constant. I looked at my watch; it was 11:16 a.m. One hour and fifteen minutes left. I took advantage of the moment of solace and said a short prayer for the success of the spiritual team, the safety of my team and that of the innocent spirits of Paul and Adam, who were still stranded in this house. I truly believed God was aware of the pestilence plaguing the Conjuring house and had sent his angel Yawar to help eradicate this rotting infestation. I hoped it could be done while we were still here and engaged in this live ghost box session. I decided then and there that we would continue to keep the ghost box session alive until there was either a conclusion to this final conflict, or we were forced by time constraints to leave the Conjuring house.

My focus was snapped back to the live ghost box session. The extraordinarily loud sound of conflict came through the ghost box speaker, so loud that it almost drowned out the sound of the box sweep. Voices could be heard. Although we could not understand exactly what was being said, it was evident that the angel Yawar and his spiritual aides had begun their assault on the demon Anwir and the evil spirit Bathsheba. How the spiritual group was carrying out this assault was a mystery to us. The angel Yawar and his spirit assistants, as far as we knew, were in the spirit realm, while the demon Anwir and Bathsheba were here in this house in the physical world. Did the spiritual team led by the angel come through the open portal created by the ghost box, or were they capable of extending their power directly from the spirit world into our physical world? This was a question I must remember to ask Mike and Lisa in a future ghost box session.

We were all aware that the angel and his team were not employing any type of conventional weapons in their assault on the evil spirits. The weapon used to combat the demon and his minion had to be energy. I secretly wished we could not only hear the melee but see it. I was sure from what we were hearing through the ghost box, it must be an amazing spectacle. If you were to take the time to consider this conflict, it was very basic and easy to understand. It simply came down to good versus evil, and we all knew that good always prevailed, hopefully!

The sounds of the conflict started to become lower, as if moving away from the immediate proximity of the ghost box. As we intently listened, the voices that a moment ago were loud and aggressive became fainter and fainter. My immediate impression was that the demon Anwir and Bathsheba were being pushed back away from our location; at least that was how it sounded. I could not help but allow myself to believe the angel Yawar, the higher entity Samuel, and my spirit technicians Mike and Lisa were winning. They were pushing the evil entities back, hopefully to the mouth of the open evil portal that was supplying them with their evil energy, and pushing them through it, back into the dark realm where they belonged. If the spiritual team were able to force the demon and Bathsheba through the evil portal and then manage to close it, the Conjuring house would be clean.

The conflict was not over yet; sounds of the struggle, although faint, could still be heard by us through the ghost box. The two spirits Adam and Paul crossed my mind. If the spiritual team were successful in cleaning this house, it would be an easy task for our spirit techs Mike and Lisa to help them cross over to the spirit world.

As I let my mind wander to thoughts of victory, my name was called through the ghost box. "Bruce." I immediately acknowledged the communication and said, "Yes, I'm here. Go ahead." What we all heard next was music to our ears. "Bathsheba and the demon gone." I paused for a second to let that single message sink in. Could it be? Did we all actually cleanse the Conjuring house? I responded to my techs, "Mike, Lisa, are you telling me that this house is clean of any evil presence?" As we waited for the confirmation from our technicians, I looked at the members of my team. Everyone had a big smile and a look of easiness on their faces. A few seconds later the answer, "No, Bruce," followed by, "Not clean," rang through the ghost box speaker. I knew I heard the message that Mike delivered through the box. I just could not believe my ears. I asked, "Mike, did you say no, not clean?" The immediate response was, "Yes," followed by, "Not clean," came back. "What do you mean, not clean? If the demon and Bathsheba are gone, how can the house still not be clean?"

A moment went by with no response. I knew my question warranted a more detailed response from my spirit techs, and that they were probably struggling a bit on how to word the communication so that we could understand it. A few more seconds passed and the answer, "Evil portal," came through. In my attempt to get answers, my next question actually stepped on the communication that was immediately following the one delivered. "Sorry, Mike and Lisa, I interrupted your message. Please go ahead." The continuation of the answer was, "Still open." I replied, "The evil portal is still open, why?" A few seconds went by. As I waited for the answer from my techs, I realized my question could be construed as rude and even ungrateful. I was about to render an apology for my rude question when the response, "Energy too strong," came through. I knew the close relationship between my spirit technicians and myself was strong enough to weather a rude question or remark now and then, and my techs decided to ignore the rudeness and simply answer my question, but I felt bad, so I rendered my apology. "Mike, Lisa, please forgive the rudeness of my question." The response, "No problem," came through in a forgiving tone.

"Mike, Lisa, what do we do now?" I asked, and the answer, "Wait now," came back. My next question was in concern for the angel Yawar and Samuel, the higher entity. "Mike, Lisa, are the angel Yawar and Samuel still present? Are they ok?" Lisa answered, "Both good," followed by, "Not here." I responded, "I'm glad they are ok. Are they coming back?" After a few seconds the answer, "Not now," came through the ghost box. "Will they try again to close the evil portal here?" The answer, "Yes," was returned. "Good, when will they try again?" I replied. "Not now," was repeated by Mike. I went on to ask, "Should we wait for their return?" The answer, "No," was delivered. "Ok, what should we do?" I asked, and, "End Now," was the answer delivered.

I was a bit confused, but I did not want to press my spirit technicians for any further information that would most likely have been repetitive. "Mike, Lisa, before I close the session, I would like to attempt to cross over the two stranded spirits Adam and Paul." I assumed they were still here in the Conjuring house without asking. A few seconds passed, and Mike answered, "Already here." I replied, "Already there, what do you mean?" Mike responded, "Already crossed," followed by, "Here safe." With Mike's communication I realized my spirit techs must have seized the opportunity to cross over Adam and Paul amidst the confusion of the encounter between the evil entities and the angel Yawar and the higher entity Samuel. We were all overjoyed. "Thank you very much, Lisa and Mike, thank you for everything, and please give our humble thanks and regards to Yawar and Samuel." The reply, "Yes, Bruce," came through. I told Mike and Lisa I was about to close the session and said goodbye. My spirit technician's final communication was, "Goodbye all."

I told my team to turn off their voice recorders. I did the

same and then turned off the ghost box. We all sat back in our chairs for a moment and took a deep breath to absorb the events that just took place. The heaviness of the atmosphere in this room, and I'm sure the whole house, was gone. "Ok, gang, let's go back to the operations area. I'm sure it's almost time to leave."

Tom checked his watch and told us the time; it was 12:10 p.m. on Saturday afternoon. Tom and I helped Bill up and started for the operations area; Sue led the way. We entered the operations room and helped Bill into his seat. We had taken a seat around the operations table when my cell phone rang. I hit the answer button and said, "Hello."

A voice boomed over the phone, "Hello, Bruce, this is John. I'm on my way over there. Are you ready to leave yet?"

I answered, "Yes, John, uh, no, not quite. We ran into some unforeseen complications. I'll explain when you get here."

John replied, "Ok, but I believe I told you yesterday before I left there that another group is coming."

I answered, "Yes, John, you did."

He replied, "Ok, I should be there in the next five minutes. Goodbye."

"Goodbye, John," I said and ended the call.

I told Tom and Sue to start breaking down the cameras and equipment; we needed to get ready to leave as soon as possible. Tom and Sue got up and left the operations area to retrieve the video cameras that were placed around the house.

Bill said, "Bruce, sorry I can't help."

I told him, "Don't worry, you were injured in the line of duty."

We both smiled. I started to disconnect the video monitors that were on the operations table, winding the power cords and placing them into their respective cases. Tom and Sue came back, each carrying a video camera in each hand; they proceeded to place the cameras in their cases.

Tom said, "Only two cameras left in the basement. I'll get them and collect all the cables."

Sue replied, "Ok, good. I'll start collecting the miscellaneous stuff."

As Tom and Sue continued to pack up, I glanced at my watch; it was 12:37 p.m. Our contact John should be here any minute. I picked up my ghost box and placed it in its foam bed inside my equipment case. I removed my equipment pouch and laid it next to my ghost box. As I closed the case cover, the front door opened, and in walked John. John had a sort of forced smile on his face as he made his way over to me. I assumed he was concerned about the arrival of the next paranormal team. I extended my hand, and John grabbed it and shook it.

"How are you, John?" I asked.

John replied, "As good as an old man like me can be." This time his smile was genuine. I smiled back. John said, "I just got a call from the next group; they are running late, traffic or something." John looked at Bill and smiled. He noticed the Ace bandage wrapped around Bill's ankle and asked, "What happened to your ankle?"

Bill replied, "Just twisted it, nothing serious."

"Oh, that's too bad; nasty things those twisted ankles."

Bill smiled and nodded.

I asked John, "When do you think the next group will get here?"

"Can't say. They said they were running about an hour to an hour and a half late," John answered.

"That's too bad," I replied. I asked John if he would like a cup of coffee, it was a day old, but the coffee usually held up pretty well in those thermal containers. John accepted my offer. I walked over to where the coffee was and poured him a Styrofoam cup full. "How do you take it?" I asked him.

"Black, no sugar," he replied, which was good since Sue had already stowed away the creamer and sugar. I handed John his coffee, and he took a seat at the table. "So how did it go?" John inquired.

I told him it was tough, but in the end, everything turned out ok.

"What do you mean by tough? You didn't run into that old witch who is supposed to be haunting this place, did you?"

Since we had some more time now, I took a seat at the table and said, "Oh yes, we ran into her and a lot more," I told John.

John replied, "Well, since we have to wait, why don't you tell me what happened?" He added, "Make it simple. I ain't too up on all this ghost stuff."

I chuckled and said, "Ok, I'll keep it short and simple."

Just then, Tom and Sue came back carrying the remainder of the equipment. "Oh, hello," Sue said.

"Hi," said Tom.

"Hello, you two, got you doing all the work, huh?" John exclaimed.

Sue answered, "Yeah," with a smile.

John then said, "Ok, Bruce, go ahead with your story."

I said, "Ok, let me start from the beginning." As I started to recount the initial events of the investigation, Tom stepped behind the old man John, raised his eyebrows, and pointed to his watch, as if to ask, what's going on? I thought we had to leave? At the risk of John noticing, I slightly shrugged my shoulders at Tom, and he reciprocated by shrugging his own shoulders as he moved to take a seat. We were all seated around the now empty folding table, and I started my abridged Reader's Digest version of our investigation.

"First, let me tell you that there was much more paranormal presence here in this house than just the evil spirit of a woman."

John interjected by saying, "Oh really? That seems to be all you people ever ask about."

I replied, "Yes, well, I guess we can thank the books and movies for that." I continued, "Without going into details, I will tell you that there were multiple spirits stranded here in this house. We made contact with the spirit of a little boy who claimed to be the son of the woman Bathsheba Sherman, who originally lived here in the mid-1800s. We also made contact and communicated with the spirit of a man who was a farmhand here at the time Bathsheba Sherman was mistress in this house."

John jumped in again. "Bathsheba, Bathsheba, yeah, that's the name of the ghost everybody claims is haunting this place."

"Yes, that's right," I told him. "We can tell you, with evidence to back it up, that an evil entity named Bathsheba Sherman was in fact here in this house."

"What do you mean was?" John asked.

"Hold on, I'll get to that," I answered. John nodded, and I continued, "Like I said, there was much more here than a couple of spirits. We discovered there was actually a portal, or doorway, that was open and active here in the house. This open portal connected this world here in the house with an evil and dark place in the spiritual realm."

"You mean like Hell?" John asked me.

"Well, I can't say if it was Hell, but it was a very dark and negative place for sure. There was also an entity here that was not the spirit of a deceased human being; he was a lower-level demon who probably used that open doorway to travel back and forth between this world and the evil realm."

"A demon, holy cow, you have proof of all this?" John asked.

"Yes, we have video proof of physical attacks on myself and my team, and of objects being thrown and smashed. We also have audio recordings of actual verbal communication from all the entities that were here, the demon included."

John exclaimed, "OH my God, you really have things on film, and voices of ghosts on recordings?"

I answered, "Yes, in a manner of speaking." John was an older gentleman, and I didn't believe he was at all tech savvy; no one has said "on film" in two decades.

I contemplated whether or not to explain the conflict between the angel Yawar, the high spirit Samuel, and my spirit technicians to John for fear that the complexity of it would only serve to overwhelm and confuse him. I decided to forego the

details of that aspect of the investigation. I continued my explanation from the point of the spiritual team's victory. "I can tell
you that the evil spirit Bathsheba and the demon were chased
out of this house by good and righteous spirits who came and
forced them back through that open doorway into the dark
spirit realm. I can also tell you that those good spirits helped the
two spirits of the little boy and the farmhand who were stuck
here to cross over to the heavenly spirit world." I did not
usually use vernacular like "heavenly" to describe the spirit
realm; in this case, I opted to for the sake of John's understanding.

John asked, "So you're telling me the bad ghosts that were
here in this house are gone; all the ghosts that were here are
gone?"

I replied, "Yes, as far as we can tell, the house is clean of all
spirits."

John put a hand to his forehead and exclaimed, "Oh boy, that's
not gonna be good for the owners."

"Excuse me?" I replied.

John said, "Yeah, the owners of this house charge a nice fee for
people like you to come here and look for ghosts. If there are no
ghosts, there's no business."

I had no response to that comment. I ended my explanation
with, "John, I have to tell you that we are relatively certain that
the open evil portal, or doorway that I told you about, is still here
and still open."

Tom interjected, "Yeah, maybe with a little luck, something
else will find its way here, and business will pick up again."

I looked at Tom. He knew what I was thinking; there was no
need to add a sarcastic remark; there was no malice in what the
old man John had said. I guess you can take the man out of Brooklyn, but you can't take Brooklyn out of the man.

John asked, "You can produce all this evidence, the films, the
recordings, everything?"

"Yes, of course," I answered. "We will submit a detailed report of the entire investigation and make all evidence available for review by the owners of the house."

John replied, "That's great. When can I expect it?"

I told John we would be submitting the evidence and the report directly to the house owners; if they chose to share it with anyone, that was at their discretion.

John nodded and said, "I understand. When can I expect it?"

I looked at John and told him I was sorry, but I believed he was a bit confused.

He replied, "I'm not confused. I'm the owner of the house."

I sat back in my chair, stunned for a second with surprise at John's revelation. "Oh, I see, why didn't you inform us that you were the property owner from the beginning?"

John answered, "Well, I don't make it a habit of telling the people who come here that I own the place; leaves the door open for negotiation of the price and what have you. I leave it unsaid unless it's necessary; fewer problems that way."

"I understand," I told John.

"Did you mention some kind of damage, damage to what?" John inquired.

I told John that during the investigation, there had been some attacks perpetrated by the evil spirit Bathsheba, dishes and glassware and a couple of ceiling light fixtures.

John asked, "Did you manage to get the damage happening on film?"

"The video footage has not been reviewed yet, but we had cameras running in the areas at the time the incidents took place, so I am relatively sure that it was caught on video."

"Good, I can't wait to see it," John replied.

"Do you mind if I ask a personal question?" I asked John.

"No, not at all, go ahead," he answered.

"Do you live in this house? I mean when it's not being investigated, that is."

John answered, "I used to live here up until a couple of years ago; then I moved into an apartment in town."

"Too many investigations?" I asked.

"Well, that, and…" John hesitated. "I have seen and heard some things in this house myself."

John piqued my paranormal curiosity. "Really, what type of things?" I asked him.

"Well, one night I woke up in the middle of the night to go to the boys' room, and when I got out of bed, there was a black figure standing in the bedroom doorway, just standing there looking at me." John continued, "Then there was this time I was walking down to the lake in back of the house and something just swept my legs out from under me. I hit the ground hard, still have a twinge of pain in my back because of that."

"Anything else?" I asked.

"Yeah, just weird noises, bangs, and knocks, and so forth, and also from time to time there would be this foul stench, like rotten meat, and it would get cold all of a sudden, I mean really cold, even in the summertime."

"I understand," I told John. "We experienced some of the same things while we were here."

John nodded.

Sue spoke up and asked John, "How about another cup of coffee?"

John replied, "Sure, don't mind if I do."

Sue grabbed John's cup and went over to where the remainder of the coffee was. She poured what was probably just enough left to fill the cup, and started to bring it to John.

As Sue walked over with the cup of coffee, John was checking his watch. "Won't be long; those other folks should be here within the next half hour or so," John exclaimed. Sue handed John the coffee and returned to her seat.

Bill asked, "Does anyone feel that cold breeze?" Just then I realized the temperature in the room had changed dramatically.

John asked, "It sure is cold in here; did one of you folks leave a door open?"

"I don't think so," I answered. "Tom, please go check the doors and make sure they are all closed and secured."

Tom got up and proceeded to go and check all the house doors leading to the outside. John's demeanor with the onset of the unusual temperature drop did not change; he sat there sipping his hot coffee. However, I and my team knew what a sudden temperature drop could mean, but it couldn't be. The evil presence had been chased from this house; it must be atmospheric in nature.

I was facing John, who had just taken another sip of coffee. I was about to speak when the old man John and the chair he was seated in rose about four feet off the ground. In an instant, John and the chair were sent flying across the room, and both John and the chair were violently slammed into the far wall. Sue and I jumped to our feet. Bill instinctively tried to jump up, but the pain in his ankle sent him down to one knee, knocking over the folding table in the process.

Just then Tom came rushing back in. "What's going on?" he shouted.

The old man John was lying unconscious on the floor next to the front door. Sue and I rushed over to him while Tom went over to check on Bill. Everyone was in a crouching position in anticipation of a further attack.

Sue put her ear next to John's mouth while feeling his wrist for a pulse. She looked up at me and said, "He's alive. I think he was just knocked out." Sue ordered, "Nobody try to move him; he may have back or neck injuries."

Just as Sue finished her statement, a groan came from the old man John. His eyes opened, and he asked with a weak voice, "What the blazes happened?"

"You were thrown against the wall," I told him.

"Help me up," he commanded.

"Hang on, don't move; you may be seriously hurt," said Sue.

"I'm fine, just got the wind knocked outta me," John said.

I told John, "Stay put; we are going to call an ambulance."

John replied forcefully, "Ambulance, no ambulance. I'm ok I said. Now help me up."

Tom asked, "Bruce, what should I do? Call the ambulance or not?"

I told Tom we could not force the old man John to accept an ambulance if he did not want one.

Tom put away his phone and came over to where we were crouching near John. "Ok, you take one side, I'll take the other, and we'll lift him on three."

I nodded.

"Ok, one, two, three." Tom and I lifted the old man to his feet; he was surprisingly light for a stout gentleman. We helped him over to a chair and sat him down. Tom in his usual manner said, "You know, I'm gonna put in for extra pay if I have to keep carrying guys around." Even with the suppressing circumstances, we all managed a chuckle, including the old man John.

The temperature in the room was slowly returning to normal, and there were no other indications of any impending activity. Tom started to speak, but I stopped him short. "I know what you're going to say; Bathsheba is back."

Tom spoke. "Yeah, that damned open portal, those demons must have sent her back through."

Sue handed John a bottle of water and two aspirin from the med kit. We all sat silently for a moment, each of our minds racing, *What do we do now?*

I turned to John and asked, "John, are you feeling ok?"

John replied, "Yeah, I'm ok, for somebody who just got tossed across the room." He added, "I believed there was something here in this house, but I never thought it could do what it just did to me."

I told John that we believed the evil spirit Bathsheba had returned through the open portal, and that if she was back in this house, which we believed she was, it was not good.

"So what can be done?" the old man John asked.

I told John I had no information on the paranormal group that was due to arrive shortly, but if they were not seriously experienced in dealing with such a powerful negative entity, the odds were that they would have to leave this house, and most likely with some physical injuries.

John said, "Ok, so I ask again, what can be done? I don't want to have anyone else get hurt."

I told John that if he could delay the onset of the next group's investigation by an hour or so, we would attempt to deal with the evil entity Bathsheba.

John replied, "I guess I have no choice. I'll give them a call and explain." He went on to say, "You all do what you have to do."

I answered, "Ok, we will do our best, but no guarantees."

John smiled and nodded. He slowly rose to his feet. A small grimace crossed his face; I was sure he was feeling the effects of his encounter with Bathsheba. The old man John opened the front door and walked out into the front yard, closing the door behind him.

I turned to my team. "Ok, I guess we are not finished quite yet. Any objections?"

Two answers of "no" and one "none" were delivered by my three team members. I guessed we all felt a sense of responsibility as paranormal investigators and researchers to deal with the problem of Bathsheba Sherman, and an obligation to our fellow paranormal colleagues to not allow them to walk into a volatile situation. I told Tom to grab the voice recorders and one handheld video camera from the equipment case. I retrieved my ghost box and my recorder.

"Ok, this is the plan. We will initiate another live ghost box session, and I will attempt to have Mike and Lisa try to bring the angel Yawar and Samuel back. I don't know if only Bathsheba came back through the evil portal or if she was accompanied by the demon Anwir. I'm sure we will find out. Let's head over to the dining room. Bill, I would like you to stay put; there is no need for you to risk any further injury. I have a feeling this session will not be pleasant."

Bill started to protest. I stopped him and told him that was my decision, and he acquiesced. Bill didn't like being left behind, but he understood.

Tom, Sue, and I headed toward the dining room. As we walked, I called out loud to our spirit technicians Mike and Lisa. "Mike, Lisa, here we go again. I'm sure you are aware of the situation. If possible, can you call upon Yawar and Samuel to return and help us deal with this evil once and for all?" I knew my spirit techs were very aware of what had occurred, and were already in the process of making arrangements; however, force of habit dictated that I make my statement to them regardless.

CHAPTER EIGHTEEN

THE EVIL BATHSHEBA AND THE INVESTIGATION COME TO AN END

We entered the dining room to find it as we had left it a short time ago, calm and quiet. Tom and Sue took their previous positions at the table. I plugged my ghost box into the wall outlet and took my seat. "Ok, guys, I know we thought this was finished, but I guess the evil forces had other ideas. Stay cautious, and let's end this once and for all."

Tom and Sue both nodded, a look of staunch determination on their faces. I turned on my voice recorder. Sue and Tom did the same. I stated the session information and then turned on my ghost box. As I waited for the ghost box sweep to commence, I could not help but think, *Is Bathsheba alone? Is the demon Anwir with her again? Are they stronger, having gone over to the dark realm for a time? Will the evil portal be able to be closed this time?* These were all questions I was sure would be answered in due course.

The ghost box was sweeping nicely, the reception was strong, and the sweep was clear. "Mike, Lisa, are you there?" The answer, "Yes, Bruce, here," was delivered quickly. "Very good, thank you for your assistance," I replied. "Mike, Lisa, were you able to contact the angel Yawar and the higher entity Samuel?" Mike answered, "Yes, Bruce, are coming." We all felt a sense of relief at Mike's answer. I then asked, "Do they know about the current situation?" The answer, "Yes, Bruce," came through. "Good, what should we do until they get here?" I asked. "Wait," was the answer from Lisa.

I looked at Tom and Sue. "Did you get all that?" I asked.

Both answered, "Yes."

We all sat there waiting for the arrival of Yawar and Samuel, all three of us focused on anything that would indicate an assault by Bathsheba was about to take place; all remained quiet. I thought to myself, *If the angel and Samuel are aware of the situation with the dark entities, then surely Bathsheba and whoever else may be here with her are aware of the impending return of the spiritual group.* I could not help but wonder if I was getting just a little too old for this.

As we sat vigil, waiting for the spiritual team to arrive, I started to get that familiar tingling that always preceded some type of paranormal presence and/or activity. I looked at Tom, who was seated opposite me at the dining table. Behind him was the credenza that had housed the dishes and glasses that had been used as projectiles by Bathsheba in her previous attack. I noticed there was one lone item left in place on the second shelf of the credenza, a soup tureen with a lid on it. I began to hear a faint rattling sound. Tom heard it also and turned around to face the credenza, evidently where the sound was emanating from. The sound became louder, and the lid of the soup tureen started to shake violently; then the whole object began to shake. Before I could utter a sound, the soup tureen flew from its perch on the credenza and struck Tom on the forehead, knocking him from his chair. Sue let out a scream as we both jumped from our seats and headed frantically toward Tom. He was lying on the floor; he was barely conscious and bleeding from a cut above his left eyebrow.

"Tom, don't move; you'll be ok," Sue told him.

Tom was trying to wipe away the blood that was running down into his left eye. I reached into my pocket and pulled out a bandana I had, handing it to Tom, who used it to wipe away the blood. Sue took the bandana from Tom and folded it. Placing it on the wound, she told him to hold it there and keep pressure on it. I told Tom to hold on, he would be ok, and that we would get him out of there. "Sue, we need to get him to the operations area."

She agreed. We positioned ourselves on either side of Tom and both grabbed him under the arms. We attempted to drag him, Sue not being strong enough to lift him with me.

Tom cried out, "Stop. Help me up. I can walk."

Sue and I lifted as Tom struggled to his feet. We each put one of Tom's arms around our neck and made our way to the operations room. We helped Tom into a chair.

Still holding the bloody bandana on his forehead, Tom said, "See, I told you I could walk." As Tom made his comment, his words trailed off, his eyes closed, and his head dropped. He began to slump in the chair. Sue and I grabbed his arms and eased him to the floor; he had passed out.

During all of this, Bill had made his way around the table and onto the floor next to Tom. Bill grabbed the bandana and held it over the cut on Tom's brow, applying pressure to keep the bleeding under control.

Sue said, "This is not good. When a person with a head trauma passes out, it could mean a serious concussion. We need to call an ambulance."

I of course agreed. I stood up and dialed 911 on my cell phone. After a few rings, the emergency operator asked, "911, what is your emergency?" I explained Tom's condition and the basic details of the incident and requested an ambulance be sent immediately. The emergency operator told me to keep his feet elevated and to keep him as comfortable as possible; the ambulance was en route. I walked back over to Tom and crouched down beside him. In the interim of my 911 phone call, he had regained consciousness. "Tom, be still; an ambulance is on the way."

Tom began to squirm. "An ambulance," he said. "I don't need an ambulance."

Sue pressed on Tom's shoulders, easing him back into a lying position. "Now, Tom, stay calm and still. You may have a serious concussion. You have to go to the hospital so they can check you out."

Tom calmed down and stayed still. I thought he realized a concussion can be very serious. A few more minutes went by, and we heard the faint sounds of a siren in the distance.

Just then the old man John came in from outside. "Oh my goodness, what happened?" he asked.

I told John that Tom had been injured in an attack by the evil entity Bathsheba, and that an ambulance was about to arrive.

"Oh, that must be the sirens I hear."

The ambulance siren became progressively louder until it was just outside the front door. John walked over and opened the front door just as the EMTs were about to knock. They rolled in a stretcher and came quickly over to where Tom was lying on the floor. Tom was conscious and coherent. Sue and I stepped back to let the medical technicians do their job. As the EMTs worked on Tom, it dawned on me that I had left my ghost box running in the dining room. I asked Sue if she would accompany Tom in the ambulance to the hospital, and of course, she agreed. I told her I would stay here and finish the session alone.

Sue protested adamantly. "Alone, are you crazy? It's too dangerous," she exclaimed strongly.

"I know it is dangerous, but what would you do, what would any of us do? We can't just turn and leave at this point; we are committed to seeing it through to the end." I followed with, "We can't send Tom to the hospital alone, and besides, Bill will be here if I get in serious trouble."

Sue did not like it, but she understood and begrudgingly agreed.

The ambulance techs loaded Tom onto the stretcher and proceeded to wheel him out to the ambulance. As Tom wheeled by me, he grabbed my hand. He knew instinctively that I would not leave until it was finished. He smiled at me and said, "Give it to 'em Brooklyn-style, buddy."

I winked at him, his hand slipped out of mine, and they

wheeled him out the door. Bill hopped back to his seat at the table, and the old man John sat down. "I pushed the other group back two hours," John said.

"Ok, great, that should be enough time," I replied. I then told the old man John it could potentially get very dangerous here. "You just saw my man Tom wheeled out of here on a stretcher, and you yourself experienced a forceful attack by the evil entity Bathsheba. I will be short two investigators, so I am going to have my hands full. I need you to please leave until I call you. I cannot risk having you sustain any further attacks and possibly bodily harm."

John looked at me and said, "Young man, you don't have to ask me twice. If I were a younger man, I would stay and fight with you, but I'm not a younger man, so I'll take my leave. Call me when you want me to come back."

I shook John's hand, and he left.

I looked at Bill and said, "I am going back to the dining room to finish this." Bill was surprisingly silent. I walked over to an equipment case and retrieved two walkie-talkies. I gave one to Bill and told him to turn it on; I would do the same when I got to the dining room. "You can monitor the activity like before. If you hear that I'm in trouble or I do not confirm that I am ok, call 911."

Bill nodded, smiled, and just said, "Ok."

I turned and headed back to the dining room. As I approached, I could hear the still sweeping ghost box. I thanked the powers that be for protecting it, and not having it wind up another casualty of this investigation. I entered the dining room, passing the broken remnants of the ceramic soup tureen used by the evil witch Bathsheba to send my friend to the hospital. I walked over to my chair and took a seat.

I turned on the walkie-talkie and called to Bill, "Bill, come in. Over." I heard nothing but the hiss of static. "Bill, are you there? Come in."

A voice came back, but not through the walkie-talkie. I turned my head and saw Bill hopping on one foot into the dining room.

"Hey, what did I tell you? I don't want anyone else to get hurt," I shouted.

"Listen, I understand your concern, and I know you're the boss and all, but I'm not about to leave a friend alone to face danger, not as long as I'm still breathing. You want me out, fire me." With that, Bill took a seat at the dining room table.

I just shook my head, any one of us would have done the same, so how could I chastise Bill? I looked at him, smiled, and nodded. He smiled and nodded back.

The ghost box sweep was rattling along at a good pace. I called out, "Mike, Lisa, are you still there?" The response, "Yes, Bruce," immediately came through, followed by, "Help here now." I immediately knew what that meant; the angel Yawar and Samuel had returned. I asked my spirit techs what we should do; they replied, "Nothing, Bruce." Bill and I sat back in our seats and listened intently to the sounds emanating from the ghost box.

At first nothing but the normal sound of the sweeping ghost box could be heard, and then a rough and angry female voice was heard: "Bruce." I replied, "Yes, I'm here. Who is that?" as if I did not know. "You are mine," was the next message delivered by who I knew was the evil entity Bathsheba. I responded, "Bathsheba, I know that is you. I thought you were sent to Hell." Bathsheba's next comment chilled me a bit. "You with me," she exclaimed. As I exchanged communications with Bathsheba, I wondered why the angel and High spirit had not acted; were they waiting for Bathsheba to be preoccupied with me?

I then asked, "Bathsheba, where is your master Anwir?" A few seconds passed without a response, and then, "Not master of me," followed by, "Only me," was sent by Bathsheba. Only her, did the demon abandon her? Was he too afraid to face the spiritual group again? Did the demon Anwir decide to hang back in the dark realm and send Bathsheba to face the angel and the higher entity alone? Before I could ask any of those questions of the witch Bathsheba, a swift and sharp blow was delivered to my left cheek. My head jerked sharply to the right, so much so that I felt a buzz-like numbing in my neck. Stunned, I reared back in my seat and instinctively raised my hands to protect my face, anticipating another attack, but none came.

Bill asked excitedly, "Are you ok?"

"Yes," I replied. "She only stunned me." I was telling Bill a half-truth; the numbness in my neck was still there and now carried a twinge of pain. I did my best to shake off Bathsheba's assault. In an attempt to keep her attention, believing it would help the spiritual group, I said to her, "That was not very lady-like." I could hear the sound of laughter coming through the ghost box, a sinister laugh; it reminded me of a laugh that would come from a drunken hag in a sleazy bar who had just done something inappropriate. As I prepared for my next comment to Bathsheba, I realized the laugh I had heard from her a second ago had turned into a scream. I could hear other voices, garbled voices, as the female screams became more distant sounding. As we listened, I knew the angel and the higher entity had made their move; the evil Bathsheba was now alone and embroiled in an altercation with the powerful angel Yawar and Samuel, the higher entity.

A male voice came through the ghost box. I recognized it to be my spirit technician Mike. "Bruce, two angels." I immediately asked Mike, "What do you mean two angels?" The reply, "Yawar and another," was delivered. If I understood Mike correctly, the angel Yawar had brought another avenging angel with him upon his return. If this was the case, Yawar, along with a second angel and Samuel, would be more than a match for the evil Bathsheba, and more than enough power needed to close the evil portal after throwing Bathsheba back through the portal to the dark realm. I thanked my spirit tech Mike for the information and returned to silently listening to the sounds emanating from the ghost box.

As we continued to listen, we could hear chaotic activity and the distressing sound of a female voice I was sure was that of Bathsheba. A small part of me actually felt sorry for her. I knew she was getting what she deserved, but I couldn't help but think about the betrayal she must be feeling after being sent back here alone while the demons that controlled her cowered back on the dark side of the evil portal, knowing what Bathsheba would face when they sent her back to this house. The thought also crossed my mind that this was the absolute nature of evil and demons, fear, cowardice, betrayal, deception, and treachery. Yes, Bathsheba was an evil spirit, but she was an amateur compared to the demons that she followed.

The sounds of the altercation became faint; it was obvious it was coming to its conclusion. Bill and I could no longer hear any sounds that were reminiscent of the evil spirit Bathsheba. All sound from the ghost box returned to the normal sound of the ghost box sweep.

I called out to my spirit technicians. "Mike, Lisa, is it over? What happened?" A short time passed, and Lisa's voice came through the ghost box. "Yes, Bruce, over." I repeated the question, "What happened?" The response, "Bathsheba gone," was delivered by Mike. "Very good," I answered. "Is the evil portal closed?" I asked. We waited about thirty seconds without an answer. I repeated, "Mike, Lisa, is the evil portal closed?" A few seconds later the answer, "No," was delivered through the box. I quickly responded. "NO, how could it still be open?" I asked excitedly. "Very strong energy," was the answer I received. "So what happens now?" I replied. "Will try again," was the answer delivered. I waited a few seconds and asked, "When will they try again?" I could count on one hand the number of times my spirit technicians Mike and Lisa had become annoyed with my pressing them for an answer. "Will be," followed by, "When is," was the answer I received.

I realized at that moment that it was not my place to question the wisdom, intent, or actions of angels and higher spiritual beings. Mike, Lisa, and I enjoyed mutual respect and a caring relationship; however, there were boundaries I should have been experienced enough to respect without having to be told. I apologized to my spirit techs for overstepping; their response was, "Love you, Bruce." That response was indicative of the close bond my technicians and I shared, built over many years of working together. Lisa called my name, "Bruce." "Yes, Lisa, go ahead," I replied. "You finished there," was the message delivered. I answered, "Is there nothing more we can do to help?" The response, "No, finished for now," followed by, "Go home now," and then "All you great sacrifice," and finally, "Well done," came across the ghost box speaker. Mike and Lisa had let me know that my team and I had done all we could do at the Conjuring house, and that they appreciated our efforts; it was time to end our investigation.

Before I shut down the ghost box, I called out to Mike and Lisa one last time. "Mike, Lisa, I am going to shut down now, thank you so much for your help, and please convey our thanks to the angels and the higher entity." The response that followed gave Bill and me a warm and secure feeling. Mike said, "God knows you all. Goodbye, Bruce." I turned off the power to the ghost box, and it fell silent.

I got up and unplugged the power cord from the wall. I walked over and offered Bill my shoulder, which he gladly accepted. I helped Bill back to the operations room and returned to the dining room to retrieve my ghost box. I stood still for a moment and looked around the dining room; you would never know that such a battle between good and evil had taken place here. I walked back into the dining room and placed my ghost box into its protective case. I felt a twang of sadness as I saw my now defunct number one box sitting next to the box I'd just laid in the case. I went over to the table and sat down.

Bill asked, "How long were we in there?"

I looked at my watch; it was 3:05 p.m. "A little over an hour," I told Bill.

"Wow, it seemed longer than that," he replied.

I told Bill I was going to call Sue, took out my cell phone, and dialed Sue's number. The phone rang a few times, and Sue answered, "Hello."

"Hi, Sue, it's me. How is Tom?"

Sue answered, "He's ok, no concussion, but he got four stitches, and he's going to have a hell of a headache for a while."

I replied, "Oh, thank God, no concussion. Tell him to listen to the doctors. Bill and I will finish up here. I'll call you when we are leaving, and I'll pick you guys up at the hospital."

Sue replied, "Ok, how did it go? Did you get things settled?"

"I'll explain when I see you" I answered.

Sue understood and said goodbye.

I then dialed the old man John's number.

He picked up. "Hello."

"Hello, John, it's Bruce Halliday. We are finished here, so you can head back here anytime."

John replied, "Ok, Bruce, on my way."

I hung up the phone and placed it back in my pocket. I asked Bill if he was ok, and he replied, "Fine." I told him I would finish packing up the few things that were left and then take the cases out to the vehicle.

Bill said, "Gee, I'm sorry I can't help. I feel terrible."

"Don't give it a second thought," I replied and set about the task of gathering up the miscellaneous items that were still unpacked.

I stowed away the remainder of the items and closed the cases. I went over and retrieved the hand truck, placed a few of the bigger cases on it, wheeled it to the front door, and set it down. I remembered that all the broken china and glass from one of Bathsheba's previous tantrums was still strewn all over the dining room floor. I told Bill I was going to clean it up, grabbed a broom, dustpan, and cardboard box, and headed to the dining room. It took longer than I expected to locate and clean up all the small pieces of broken glassware. I returned to the operations room carrying the cardboard box full of broken glass. As I entered, I saw John sitting there.

As I placed the box down, John said, "Hello, Bruce."

"Hello, John," I replied.

"How is everything?" John asked.

I knew he was asking about the situation in the house. "Well, John, we were successful in sending Bathsheba back to the dark realm; for all intents and purposes, the house is clean of spirits at this time." I continued, "However, the portal I told you about was not able to be successfully closed. As far as we know, it is still open but not active at the moment."

A look of disappointment came over John's face. "Oh, I was sure you all would be able to finish everything." He went on to say, "I know you did your best, and a couple of you were hurt in the process. I appreciate all you did."

I explained to John that it was beyond our physical capability to do anything about the open portal. I also explained briefly about the angels and the spiritual group and how they would continue to try to close the evil portal even after we were gone. John nodded understandingly. I asked John about the next group and when they would arrive.

John said, "They're at a motel up the road, waiting for my call. I didn't tell them about any of the goings-on here with you and your group. I told them there was a problem with the heater and that's what caused the delay."

I told John I was going to begin loading our equipment into our vehicle, and if he wanted to give the other group a call, I would wait for them to arrive and brief them on our investigation and the current situation. John agreed and made the call. I opened the front door and wheeled the already loaded hand truck to the vehicle. I placed the equipment cases into the back of the vehicle and went back to the house for another load. I pushed the empty hand truck over to where the other equipment cases sat.

John said, "The other group will be here in about fifteen or twenty minutes."

"Ok, great," I replied, and proceeded to load the next set of equipment cases onto the hand truck.

"Can I lend a hand?" John asked.

"No, thank you, one more trip and I will be finished."

John smiled and nodded.

I wheeled the loaded hand truck out the front door and pushed it toward the vehicle. I felt the cold air fill my lungs as I breathed through my mouth under the strain of pushing the heavy equipment cases. I reached the vehicle and loaded the remainder of the equipment cases into the back. There were only a few odd boxes and the folding table left to retrieve from the house, and we would be packed and ready to leave. I made my way back to the house with the now empty and much lighter hand truck.

As I made the short walk back to the house, I could not help but notice that everything around me was completely still. I looked at the trees; not a leaf was stirring. It was dead silent, no birds, no rustling of leaves, and no wind. It gave me an eerie feeling as if time had stopped. I stopped walking and concentrated on the strange atmosphere. I noticed that in the distance I could see the tops of the trees blowing in the wind, but the Conjuring house property seemed to be apart and devoid of any natural forces. I started back to the house, taking with me a very weird feeling I could not explain.

I entered the house. Bill and the old man John were talking. I asked John, "John, when you were outside, did you notice anything odd, like no wind and no sound, like everything was completely still?"

John answered, "Tell you the truth, I hadn't really taken notice." With that, John got up from his seat and walked to the front door. He opened it and took a couple of steps out into the front yard. I could see him looking around. He turned and came back into the house, closing the door behind him. "Everything looks normal to me. Matter of fact, there is a bit of a biting wind out there today," John exclaimed.

I walked back to the front door, opened it, and looked out. The wind was blowing some dead leaves across the yard, I could see the treetops swaying back and forth with the force of the wind, and the sounds of nature filled my ears, birds chirping and a dog barking in the distance. I closed the door and returned to the table. I sat down and thought out loud, "Strange, a minute ago it seemed like this property was frozen in time."

John replied, "Well, it seems ok now."

I nodded and committed the experience to memory.

Bill, John, and I sat there chatting about the history of the Conjuring house and the events of the investigation while we waited for the other paranormal group to arrive. John offered, "I was born and raised about two miles up the road and heard the stories about this place all my life."

I asked John, "Did you know any of the people who lived here in the past?"

John answered, "Oh, sure, knew them all."

I replied, "Did you know the Perron family?"

John answered, "Sure did, nice folks, a little odd, but nice. They lived here quite a few years, as I recall." He went on to say, "I believe that family got the worst of whatever was happening here. We all heard some wild stories."

I commented, "Yes, the Perron family reported experiencing some strong paranormal occurrences here in this house; those reports were actually what made the Conjuring house and its property famous." Just as I finished, there was a knock at the door.

"Come on in," John shouted.

The door opened, and in walked three gentlemen carrying various cases. One of the men, dressed in a long cowboy-style duster coat, walked up to the table and said, "Hi, my name is Jack Dwyer. I am a lead investigator for the Rhode Island Paranormal Investigative Institute."

The other two gentlemen walked over. John, Bill, and I all stood up, introduced ourselves, and shook hands with the new arrivals.

"So how did your investigation go?" asked the man Jack.

"Very interesting and very eventful," I replied.

"Great, we love eventful," Jack answered.

I told Jack and the other two men not to get too excited until they heard what I had to say. They responded with a confused nod. "Let's all take a seat, and I'll explain." Everyone sat around the empty folding table. The men from the RIPII listened intently. I began at the beginning of the investigation. Needless to say, I did not recount every little detail of the whole investigation or the ghost box sessions; I did, however, cover the details of all the physical encounters and went on to explain the angel Yawar, the spiritual group, and their struggle against Bathsheba and the demon Anwir. The three men sat in amazement as I recounted our investigation and our time here in the Conjuring house.

After I finished, there was a moment or two of silence. The old man John was equally stunned by the story since he had not heard about the spiritual group or the demon before.

One of the three men spoke, a man named Joel. "That is the most amazing story of paranormal activity I have ever heard. You have documentation of all of this?"

Bill answered, "Yes, absolutely, video and audio evidence of all of it." Bill's answer carried a bit of a defensive tone in response to the man Joel's question, which carried an air of disbelief.

The man Jack spoke up. "That is unbelievable. I would love to hear and view some of that evidence sometime."

I replied, "You are more than welcome to, just give me a call, and I'll send it to you for review."

"Thank you, and let me say we are honored to be following up you and your team."

Bill and I smiled and thanked them for their compliment.

"Ok, just to confirm, the spiritual team is not through here. From what my spirit technicians told me, they fully intend to make another attempt at closing the evil portal." I went on, "With that evil portal still open and active, there is no telling what may happen, so stay vigilant and aware of what's happening around you at all times. These evil entities injured two of my team members and sent one to the hospital. Be very careful."

The lead man Jack acknowledged my advice and thanked me.

I finished by saying, "Please give me a shout after your investigation. I will be curious to know how it went."

Jack assured me he would call me.

I stood up and said, "Ok, if there is nothing else, I have two team members at the hospital, waiting to be picked up."

Bill made his way around the table, we all shook hands again, and we wished the three men of the RIPII good luck. The three men proceeded to begin unpacking their equipment as John gave me a hand folding up the table.

As we turned the table upside down to fold the legs closed, the man Jack asked, "Hey, Bruce, you wouldn't want to sell me that table, would you? We don't have one, and it sure would come in handy."

I smiled and said, "You know what, Jack, take it, it's yours. Consider it a gift from one para investigator to another."

Jack put on a big smile and said, "Thanks, hope I can return the kindness one day."

I told him, "Just pass it forward; someday you may be able to help out another paranormal team."

Jack nodded in an assuring way. John and I flipped the table right side up and walked over to the door. John said, "I'll walk you out."

I smiled, and we both helped Bill out the front door.

CHAPTER NINETEEN

WE BID THE CONJURING HOUSE GOODBYE AND FIND AN ADDED BONUS

W e all made our way over to the vehicle. Bill said goodbye to John and shook his hand before getting into the passenger seat of the vehicle. John and I walked around the vehicle to the driver's door.

"You know, Bruce, I feel like I have come to know you, like a friend," John said.

"Yes, me too, John," I replied.

"Anytime you want to come back, just give me a call and the place is yours for as long as you want it."

I thanked John and said, "I may just take you up on that." We shook hands heartily.

I got into the vehicle and started the engine. I looked at Bill. "Ready?" I asked.

"More than ready," Bill answered.

As we drove down the dirt driveway, I could see John fading into the distance, waving, silhouetted by the infamous Conjuring house.

I couldn't say that I didn't feel a certain relief as we pulled out of the driveway and onto the road; the Conjuring house was one of the toughest, most dangerous, and most thrilling investigations I had ever done. We would have literally months of evidence review ahead of all of us. The situation we had left behind concerning the still open evil portal also occupied my thoughts as we drove to the hospital to retrieve our other two team members. I could not help but feel a deep concern. The evil spirit Bathsheba had returned to the Conjuring house once after being ejected through the portal to the dark realm; what was stopping her from a second return? I was concerned for the safety of any paranormal investigating team that might venture to take on the Conjuring house if they were not experienced enough or didn't have the wherewithal to deal with Bathsheba and any other evil demonic entities that could have access to the house through that open portal. I had to trust that my spirit technicians along with the higher entity and the assisting angels would be able to combat any evil entities that might reinvade the Conjuring house, drive them back to the dark realm, and close the evil portal once and for all.

As we neared the hospital, I resigned myself to the fact that I would have to endure these nagging thoughts and concerns. We passed the final big white and blue sign with the letter H and an arrow on it, indicating that the hospital was close by. I turned to Bill and asked, "How's the ankle?"

"Still hurts, but not as bad," Bill answered.

"When we get to the hospital, would you like to get it looked at?" I asked.

"I don't know; maybe that might be a good idea," Bill replied.

I spotted the hospital sign that said "Emergency Room" in big red letters. We pulled into the hospital parking lot and were lucky enough to find a parking space close to the emergency entrance. I got out of the vehicle and made my way around to the passenger side. Bill opened his door.

"Do you want to get the ankle checked?" I asked. "At least you can get it rewrapped and get some pain meds; that's what medical insurance is for, right?" I added.

Bill nodded and said, "I know Tom and Sue have been waiting

a long time. I don't want to have them have to wait longer for me."

I answered Bill, "It's fine. I'm sure they won't mind."

"Ok, I'll get it looked at," Bill said.

"Ok, great," I replied. I told Bill to sit tight for a minute. I walked into the emergency room entrance, and as luck would have it, there were two empty wheelchairs just inside the doors. I grabbed one and made my way back to the vehicle. "Your chariot, sir," I said jokingly.

Bill hopped out of the vehicle and sat in the wheelchair. "Boy, we could have used this back at the Conjuring house," said Bill.

"We sure could have," I replied. I wheeled Bill across the parking lot and through the emergency room entrance. As we made our way inside, we came to the waiting area.

I heard Sue's voice. "Hey, Bruce, over here."

I looked to my left to see Sue and Tom sitting there. I made my way over to them, navigating Bill through the rows of chairs.

"You made it in one piece," Sue said.

"Well, not all in one piece," Tom added, looking at Bill in the wheelchair.

"Yes, we made it, barely," I replied and went on to ask, "I know you guys have been waiting a while, but do you mind if Bill gets his ankle looked at?"

"Absolutely, he should definitely have it looked at," Tom exclaimed. Tom had a bandage over his eye, covering the stitched laceration, and a golf-ball-sized lump on his forehead.

"You look beautiful," Bill told him.

"Good enough to kiss," retorted Tom. We all managed a small chuckle.

I left the three talking and went over to the reception desk, where a young girl dressed in a blue scrub uniform sat. "Hi, can I help you?" she asked.

"Yes, I just brought my friend in with a badly sprained ankle that needs attention," I explained.

"All right, can you bring your friend over? He will need to give me his information," she asked.

I thanked the young lady and went to retrieve Bill. I wheeled Bill over and positioned him facing the young ER attendant. "I'm going over to Tom and Sue, wave when you're finished here, and I'll come and get you," I told Bill. He nodded.

I walked back to where Tom and Sue were seated. I took a seat next to Sue.

"So what happened after we left?" she asked.

I started to explain, "We were right, the evil Bathsheba had returned through the evil portal, but only her; the demon Anwir decided to stay behind in the dark realm and send Bathsheba to face the angel Yawar and the spiritual group."

"So did the angel and the spirit group come back to face her again?" asked Tom.

I answered, "Yes," and went on with my recounting. "Not only did the angel Yawar and the spirit group return, but Yawar brought another angel with him; together they were able to force Bathsheba back through the portal, but not before she delivered a stinging slap across my face."

"Oh, are you ok?" Sue asked.

"Fine," I replied.

"Was the spirit team able to close the evil portal?" Sue asked.

"No, which is a problem," I answered. "Until that portal is closed, anything can come through into the Conjuring house, entities that could be even stronger and more vile than the ones we dealt with."

Sue silently shook her head.

I continued, "The para group that followed us is there now. I briefed them on the situation and the potential danger; they elected to stay and conduct their investigation in spite of the possibility of being confronted with forces they could not handle."

"So what can we do?" Sue asked.

"Nothing at the moment. The owner of the house, John,

extended us an open invitation to return whenever we want, for as long as we want," I answered.

"Are we going back?" Tom asked.

"Possibly at some point. I will keep in touch with the old man John. The team that is there now agreed to contact me and brief me on what they encounter."

"Ok, good," Sue replied.

As I finished my explanation to Sue and Tom, I saw Bill waving at me from the other side of the waiting room. I walked over and wheeled Bill back to where we were sitting.

"What did they say?" asked Sue.

Bill answered, "They said to sit tight, and they would call me."

"Guess there's nothing to do but wait," Tom exclaimed.

About twenty minutes or so had passed when a hospital attendant opened a door and called Bill's name. Bill answered, "Here." The attendant came over and asked Bill for his date of birth to confirm he had the correct patient. The attendant told Bill he would be taking him to the treatment area to take vital signs and have him seen by a doctor. Bill smiled and said, "See you later," as the attendant wheeled him away.

"We'll be here," Tom called out.

"It should not be too long," I said.

"I hope not," replied Tom.

Sue asked if we wanted a cup of coffee or a snack.

"No, thanks," I said.

"I'll take a bottle of water," Tom replied.

I reached in my pocket and took out a ten-dollar bill and offered it to Sue.

"No, I got it," Sue said.

"No, I insist," I replied.

Sue reluctantly accepted the money and walked over to the vending machines located at the far end of the waiting room.

Tom asked me, "So what's on your mind? I know you're not just going to leave loose ends at the Conjuring house."

I replied, "I really don't know right now. I have to give it some thought. It's a good thing the old man John extended us an open invitation. Whatever we decide to do, we can return there anytime we want."

Tom nodded in acknowledgment. Sue came back and handed Tom a bottle of water; she had gotten a bag of chips and a soda. She handed me the change from the ten-dollar bill and thanked me.

"Yeah, thanks," said Tom. I smiled and placed the change in my pocket.

The attendant who had taken Bill back to the treatment area returned and told us Bill was resting comfortably in his assigned spot, and if we wished, we could go back and stay with him. We all got up and made our way to where Bill was. He smiled when he saw us come through the curtain that separated his little area from the other examination cubicles.

"Did they say anything?" Sue asked.

"Not yet, they just took my temperature and blood pressure and said a doctor would be in to examine me."

There were two chairs next to the stretcher Bill was now lying on. I told Tom and Sue to sit. I remained standing. There was a small TV in the cubicle. There was no sound coming from it; closed-captions streamed across the bottom of the screen. Bill said, "Hey, look what's on the TV." We all turned and looked at the television. The paranormal investigation show *Ghost Hunters* was playing. We all chuckled.

After about fifteen minutes Sue stood up and took a small digital voice recorder from her pocket. "I'm going to take a walk and do an EVP session," she stated.

"Be careful; try not to draw too much attention to what you're doing," I told her.

She nodded and walked out of the cubicle.

Tom, Bill, and I were talking about the events at the Conjuring house when a doctor came through the closed curtain. "Hello, my name is Dr. Sherman. I'll be examining you today."

Tom and I got up, excused ourselves, and stepped outside the curtain. "Did you hear his last name?" Tom whispered.

"Yes, I wonder if there is any family relation to Bathsheba Sherman?" I replied.

About ten minutes passed, and the doctor walked out into the corridor. "You can go back in now," he said with a smile.

Tom and I nodded and went back into Bill's cubicle. "What did the doctor say?" I asked Bill.

"I have to have an X-ray of the ankle."

"Yeah, I figured that," Tom said.

Bill asked, "Hey, did you catch that doctor's name?"

Tom replied, "Way ahead of you, buddy." We all grinned.

Tom and I had just retaken our seats when a booming voice came over the hospital PA system. "Bruce Halliday, please come to the hospital security office." The page was repeated twice.

"Uh-oh," Tom exclaimed.

"Yeah, they must have Sue," I replied. I told Tom and Bill I would be back, and headed out of the cubicle. I stopped a nurse and asked directions to the security office; she blurted out some quick rights and lefts. I was relatively confident I had heard her correctly and set out for the hospital security office. I paused for a second before entering the hospital security office. I knew Sue was very protective when it came to the tolerance of people for the paranormal and anything associated with it, and I did not know what exactly to expect. I took a deep breath and opened the door.

Sue was seated in a chair in front of whom I assumed to be the security administrator for the hospital. I walked in, and Sue mouthed the word, "Sorry," with a sheepish look on her face.

I said, "I'm Bruce Halliday. I was paged to this office."

"Oh yes. Come right in, Mr. Halliday. Have a seat," the gentleman sitting behind the desk replied. I went over and sat in the chair next to Sue. "My name is Peter Tuttle. I am head of security for the hospital. I'm assuming you know this young lady."

I replied, "Yes, Mr. Tuttle, she is a member of my paranormal investigating team." I continued by asking, "Did she do something wrong?"

The security officer answered, "No, not something wrong per se, more like something weird."

"I'm sorry, something weird?" I responded.

"Well, not weird, but out of the ordinary, I should say," he said.

"Can you tell me what she was doing that was out of the ordinary?"

"Yes, she was wandering the halls of the hospital, talking to herself and holding a running sound recorder. For us here at the hospital, that's a bit out of the ordinary." He went on to say, "She was eventually approached outside the entrance to the morgue, on the basement level."

I responded, "Ok, is that against hospital rules?"

"Not exactly, but the lower level of the hospital is off-limits to non-hospital employees." Mr. Tuttle went on to say, "Before we get too far into a misunderstanding, this young lady is not in any trouble; quite the contrary, we were hoping your team could help us with a little mystery that has plagued this hospital for years."

I asked, "Let me understand, you want the help of my paranormal investigative team here in the hospital?"

Tuttle answered, "Yes, Mr. Halliday, that's correct."

"All right, and please call me Bruce."

He responded, "Ok, call me Pete." We all smiled.

Sue spoke up and said, "I played the recording I made for Pete, and don't you know, there was a very clear EVP on it."

Tuttle exclaimed, "Yes, I would never have believed it if I didn't hear it with my own ears; it said, clear as day, help me!"

Sue was still holding the recorder; she lifted it up and pressed the play button. Sue's voice was the first thing heard from the recording. "Are there any spirits here who would like to speak to me?" A few seconds of static white noise was heard, and then a raspy male voice cried out, "Help me." Sue had captured what I would score as a class A EVP.

"Nice capture, Sue," I said.

"Yeah, I know, thanks," she replied.

Pete just sat there with his mouth open in dumb amazement.

I told Pete, "Ok, evidently there is at least one spirit entity here in the hospital, and he is asking for help. I can bet you that he is not the only one." I then asked Sue, "Did you get that EVP downstairs by the morgue?"

"Yup," she answered.

"Ok, Pete, I have two team members here in the hospital. One has been treated and released, and the other is receiving treatment as we speak. When my current team member has finished being treated and is released, Sue and I will look into any activity you may be having here."

Pete agreed and offered his cell phone number. "Give me a call as soon as you are ready."

I nodded, shook Pete's hand, and Sue and I left the security office. We headed back to the emergency room area where Bill was being treated. "I think there are a lot of entities in this hospital who want to make contact," Sue said. She continued, "That EVP was not the only one I captured in the short time I had to wander around. I heard at least five more just by quickly playing back the recordings."

I agreed and told Sue that in my experience, hospitals usually had a good supply of lingering and confused souls.

We arrived back at the emergency room cubicle where Bill was being treated. "Hey, guys," Sue said.

"Hey," said Bill.

"You got pinched, huh?" said Tom.

"Yes, but not for the reason you think," Sue answered.

"Bill, has the doctor told you anything?" I asked.

"Not yet, just waiting for the results of the X-ray," Bill replied.

Tom turned to Sue and asked, "What did you mean, it's not what I think?"

Sue answered, "Security caught me downstairs near the morgue, doing EVP."

Tom interjected, "So it is what I think."

Sue replied, "No, if you let me finish. I played one of the EVPs I captured for the head security guy, and he wants us to do an investigation here in the hospital."

Tom and Bill both raised an eyebrow. "Is that right, Bruce?" Bill asked.

"Yes, Sue is right, the head of security explained that he receives reports all the time of paranormal activity here in the hospital, and he wants us to check it out."

Tom asked, "You mean now today, or down the road?"

"Hopefully today. I don't want to have to drive all the way back to Rhode Island when we are already right here," I answered.

"Makes sense," Bill added.

I went on to explain that I did not want to do a full-blown investigation. Since most of the EVPs were captured in the basement level of the hospital, we could concentrate on that level and do a basic sweep and ghost box session, no stationary camera setups or video monitors, handheld equipment only.

"So when do we get started?" Tom asked.

I told everyone that we would wait until we knew what the situation was going to be with Bill, and based on that outcome, I would contact the hospital security administrator and coordinate the investigation with him. Everyone nodded in understanding.

A few minutes later the doctor walked into the cubicle, carrying a clipboard. "Ok, we have the results of the X-ray," he told Bill. We all started to make our way out of the cubicle.

"No, wait, you guys stay," Bill said.

The doctor continued, "The good news is that it's not a sprain."

"What's the bad news?" Bill asked.

"Well, you have two fractures, one of the ankle bone, and the other is located on the instep of your foot," the doctor replied and then asked, "What type of accident did you have that caused this injury?"

Bill answered, "Just turned wrong, I guess."

A vague look of disbelief crossed the doctor's face, but he did not pursue a more detailed explanation. "Ok, well, the ankle and foot will have to be put in a cast for about six to eight weeks," the doctor explained.

"Six to eight weeks, that's just great," said Bill. "Hobbling around on crutches for eight weeks, great," he added.

I asked the doctor, "When will the cast be put on?"

The doctor answered, "A nurse should be here shortly to prep Bill for the procedure and then take him to have the cast applied."

Bill was noticeably frustrated and annoyed. "I guess I'll be sidelined for a while, guys," Bill stated.

"Not necessarily," I said.

"You can get around on the crutches, right," added Tom.

"Yeah, and I don't think we have anything major coming up, right, Bruce?" Sue asked.

"Not that I can think of," I answered. "You just concentrate on the here and now," I told Bill.

He reluctantly nodded.

I excused myself and walked out of the cubicle into the hallway. I took out my cell phone and dialed the number Pete, the head of security, had given me. The phone rang a number of times and then was picked up. "Hello, Peter Tuttle."

"Hi, Peter, Bruce Halliday here," I said.

"Oh, hello, Bruce, how is your friend making out?" Pete asked.

"He has to get a cast put on his ankle," I answered.

"Oh, too bad," he replied.

"Pete, I'm calling about the paranormal investigation we spoke about."

"Oh, yes, are you still willing to do it?" Pete asked.

"Yes, of course," I answered.

"Great, when can you do it?"

"We can start in about an hour," I replied.

"An hour, ok, sounds good. I'll have one of my security people meet you at the nurses' station in the emergency room in one hour," Pete told me.

"Ok, thanks, Pete," I said.

Pete replied, "No, thank you."

We ended the call, and I went back into Bill's cubicle. "I just spoke to the head of security; he is sending a security guard to meet us in an hour at the nurses' station. Bill, obviously you cannot participate."

Bill nodded.

"Sue and Tom, I want to do a basic investigation in the morgue area and around the lower level."

Tom asked, "Handheld video cameras, voice recorders, and EMF detectors?"

"Yes," I answered. "Bill, you will be getting your cast applied, and then you can either wait for us here or in the waiting room, depending on what the hospital policy is once you're finished being treated."

Bill replied, "Sure, no problem."

"This investigation should not take too long. The hospital administration is basically looking for evidence that will corroborate the reports of paranormal activity that have been made in the hospital. Tom, you can wait for us here. Sue and I will go to the vehicle and retrieve the necessary equipment."

Tom nodded. Sue and I left the cubicle and headed for the parking lot.

Sue and I walked past the emergency room nurses' station, where two nurses were talking. As we passed, one of the nurses pointed to us, and they both took a long look. Sue noticed the actions of the two nurses and asked, "What's that about?"

I answered, "They must have heard about your little EVP excursion. I guess news travels fast here."

Sue just shook her head and muttered, "Rude." I agreed.

We walked through the emergency room waiting area and out into the parking lot. Sue and I arrived at the vehicle. I opened the back door and started to shuffle the equipment cases around, searching for the cases that contained the equipment we needed.

"There's your case," Sue exclaimed.

I grabbed my personal equipment case, opened it, and removed my ghost box and digital voice recorder. Sue grabbed one of the portable equipment bags we used for carrying small equipment. I opened the equipment case containing the voice recorders, handheld video cameras, and digital cameras. Sue collected the needed equipment and placed it in the bag. I closed the equipment case and the vehicle doors. Being a gentleman, I asked Sue if I could carry the equipment bag.

Sue replied, "That's ok; it's not heavy. I got it," and hung the equipment bag over her shoulder. I carried my ghost box and voice recorder. We made our way back to Bill's cubicle in the emergency treatment area. We entered the cubicle to find Tom flipping through the channels on the small flat-screen TV that hung from the wall.

"I see they came to get Bill," I said.

"Yeah, right after you guys left."

"Ok, let's get started. It's just about time to meet that security guard at the nurses' station." Before we left the cubicle, I asked Tom, "Are you up for this, buddy?"

Tom answered, "Yeah, no problem; they gave me some painkillers. I feel great."

The three of us walked over to the nurses' station. The security person we were supposed to meet had not arrived yet. A nurse came over to the spot we were standing and asked, "Hi, can I help you with something?"

I answered, "No, thank you, we are waiting for a security officer to meet us here."

The nurse nodded and replied, "Oh, ok, well, if you need anything, just shout."

I thanked her, and she returned to her desk.

"So how do you want to do this?" Tom asked.

I told both Tom and Sue, "Let's keep it simple. Tom, you grab a video camera and a voice recorder. Sue, you take a voice recorder and the EMF detector. I'll have a voice recorder and my ghost box." I continued, "Once we get down to the lower level, I'll take a spot near the morgue. Tom, you go to one end of the level, and Sue, you go to the other end. Tom, you can take video and do an EVP session. Sue, you take EMF readings and do an EVP session as well."

Tom and Sue acknowledged my instructions.

"I will do a ghost box session near the morgue area. If we are going to capture anything, which I'm certain we will, it will be almost immediately. The whole investigation shouldn't last more than an hour or so."

Tom and Sue both agreed.

Our conversation was interrupted by the security guard who was sent to escort us to the lower level. "Hello, you must be the ghost people. I'm Jim."

"Yes, Jim, we are the ghost people. I'm Bruce; this is Tom and Sue," I replied.

"Are you ready?" asked the security officer Jim.

"Ready when you are," Tom answered.

"Ok, follow me," Jim said.

We grabbed our gear and followed the security guard out of the emergency room and down a corridor. We reached a freight elevator at the end of the corridor; Jim pushed a button on the wall. I could hear the elevator kick into gear below us, it stopped with a thud, and the heavy elevator door slid open. We all got into the elevator, and the guard Jim exclaimed, "So you guys are ghost hunters, huh?"

I replied, "Yes, I guess you could call us ghost hunters; the actual title would be paranormal investigators."

Sue added, "We don't hunt ghosts; we interact with spirits."

The security guard just smiled and nodded. The elevator jolted to a halt, and the door slid open. We all stepped off the elevator into another long hallway. There were doors on either side along its entire length, and at the other end, I could see two big double doors. We made our way down the long hallway; there were offshoot hallways that led left and right at quarter intervals along the way. As we approached the two double doors at the end of the hallway, I could see a sign above them that read Morgue Entrance.

The security guard swung open the two double doors, and we entered the morgue. "Never liked coming in here, it's creepy, but I guess you guys like that."

I smiled and walked over to a desk where a young man in scrubs was sitting. Before I could speak to the young man, the security guard exclaimed, "Ok, I guess you're all set, let the attendant there know when you're all done, and I'll come back to get you." He turned and left the morgue.

I addressed the young morgue attendant. "Hi, my name is Bruce, and these are my two associates, Tom and Sue."

The attendant nodded.

I continued, "I don't know if anyone notified you, but we are here to conduct a paranormal investigation."

The young man replied, "My name is Tim. I'm the morgue attendant on duty. Is there anything you need from me?"

"No, we pretty much have everything under control. Are there any restricted areas where we cannot go?"

Tim answered, "Nope, I was told you have complete access." He added, "Just holler if you need me."

I asked, "Is there a spot where we can put our equipment bags?"

Tim replied, "Yes, there's an empty table just inside that room."

I turned and looked; there was another room on the left side of the main morgue area. It was dark, which was probably why I did not notice it sooner. "Is there a light in there?" I asked Tim.

"Yes, the switch is on the left as you walk in."

I thanked Tim, and we headed for the dark room.

I reached for the light switch and flicked it on. The room was illuminated by three fluorescent light fixtures on the ceiling. There were two stainless-steel double-door cabinets and an empty stainless-steel table in the room with a single swivel chair. We walked over to the table and placed the equipment bags on it. I placed my ghost box down and turned to Tom and Sue.

"Tom, you take the east end of this level. Sue, you take the west end." I continued, "I want you both to do an EVP session. Also, Tom, you run the video camera from the time you walk out of here until you return, and Sue, you take some EMF readings on your way to your area and when you get there. Document any extraordinary anomalies. I'm going to stay here in the morgue and do a ghost box session." I checked my watch; it was 6:30 p.m. "It's 6:30; we will meet back here at 8:00 p.m.," I told them.

Tom and Sue acknowledged their instructions, grabbed the equipment they needed, and headed out of the morgue.

I grabbed the ghost box power cord from my equipment bag and placed it into a nearby electrical outlet. I attached the other end to my ghost box and sat down at the table. I reached into my equipment pouch and retrieved my voice recorder. I switched it on and stated the session information. I paused the recorder and placed it on the table next to the ghost box. There was an eerie feeling in the room, which I attributed to my subconscious aware-ness that I was sitting in a morgue. I got up and walked back into the main morgue area.

"Excuse me, Tim, do you mind if I ask you a question?"

Tim replied, "Of course not, shoot."

I asked, "Do you always work here in the morgue?"

"Yes," Tim answered.

"Have you ever experienced anything you would say was paranormal in nature, ever seen or heard anything?"

Tim hesitated for a moment, as all people not involved in the paranormal do, and then answered, "Well, yes, I have seen and heard some things I couldn't explain."

"Can you tell me about them?" I asked.

Tim began to tell me how on several occasions while working alone here in the morgue on a night shift, he had experienced the doors to the cadaver units, which were the drawers where the corpses were kept, open on their own. He went on to say that he had on many occasions heard whispery voices in the middle of the night when there was no one else on the whole lower level except him. Tim also stated that he had once seen the figure of a man walk across the morgue and through the doors, not opening them, just walking straight through them as if they were not there.

I listened to Tim's account of the paranormal experiences he'd had here in the hospital morgue. When he finished, I asked, "Do you believe there are spirits here?"

Tim answered, "I never believed in ghosts until I started to work here, now I can honestly say I do, and I'm not the only one. There are a lot of employees in the hospital who have seen and heard things."

"Ok, Tim, thanks. I'll let you get back to work, and I'll do the same."

Tim smiled and went back to what he was doing.

I returned to my seat in the adjacent room. I retrieved a K2 meter from my equipment pouch, turned it on, and placed it on the table. As soon as I did, it started to register, not a high reading, about midrange, which could just be normal electrical interference. My voice recorder was still running. I reached over and turned on my ghost box, fully expecting a less than stellar radio broadcast reception signal due to the fact we were on the lower level below ground and the abundant amount of electronic equipment that was in operation. After a few seconds, the ghost box began to emit sweep sounds. I was pleasantly surprised when I heard a relatively loud and clear sweep coming through.

Of course, the first thing I did, as in every live ghost box session, was to ask for my spirit technicians Mike and Lisa. "Mike, Lisa, are you guys there? Can you help with this session?" A few seconds went by, and the response, "Yes, Bruce," came through in a familiar male voice. "Hi, Mike, how are you, buddy?" I asked. "Good," Mike answered. "Lisa, are you there also?" The response, "Here, Bruce," was returned. "Great, hi, Lisa," I replied. I followed with, "Are there any entities here who would like to communicate?" The answer, "Yes," was delivered. "The spirit who answered yes, can you tell me your name?" A few seconds passed, and the response, "David," came through, followed by, "Cole." I heard this and asked, "I heard the name David, and did you say cold?" A short time passed without a response, and I repeated the question. "No," followed by, "Cole, Cole," came through. I heard this communication a bit more clearly and asked, "Did you say 'Cole'?" The answer, "Yes," came through immediately. "Ok, so your name is David Cole?" I asked. "Yes," was delivered again through the ghost box.

"Hello, David, thank you for communicating," I said. There was no response to my comment. I then asked, "David, are you the spirit who asked for help when the woman Sue was here asking questions?" Shortly the answer, "Yes, me," was delivered. "Do you need help, David?" I asked. "Please help," was the response through the ghost box. "Ok, David, I will try to help you. What do you need help with?" About twenty seconds passed, and the answer, "Lost here, help," came through. From the few communications I'd received from David, I surmised this was a common case of a spirit entity who was lost and confused and needed my and my spirit technicians' help to cross over to the spirit world.

"David, are you here with me now?" I asked the wayward spirit. "Yes, here," was returned. I looked over at the K2 meter; the indicator lights were fully and steadily lit up. "Mike, Lisa, are you aware of and in contact with the spirit David Cole, whom I am communicating with?" The response, "Yes, Bruce," came through immediately. "Ok, Mike, Lisa, I am going to leave the box for a moment. Please excuse me. I'll be right back." Lisa responded, "Yes, Bruce."

I rose to my feet and made my way back into the main morgue area. I walked over to the desk where Tim was seated. "Tim, I wonder if you could do me a favor. I have made contact and am communicating with a spirit who gave his name as David Cole. Is there any way you can search the hospital records for a patient with that name who died here in the hospital?"

Tim smiled and said, "Way ahead of you. I couldn't help but hear your interaction with the voices coming over your radio, so I took the liberty of searching the name before you asked."

I responded, "Oh, ok, did you find anything?"

"Hang on, the info is printing out now," Tim replied. As we waited for the printer to finish its task, Tim said, "I heard weird sounds coming from that radio you are using. I heard you clearly asking and answering questions, but I didn't hear any other people speaking. I heard what could have been voices but really didn't understand anything that might have been said."

I told Tim the device I was using was a ghost box, and it was used by paranormal researchers to communicate live in real time with spirit entities. I went on to tell him that it was not easy for someone, especially someone not familiar with a ghost box, to hear the spirit communication live as it was delivered. Tim nodded as if he understood. I told him that if he liked, I could send him some of the audio files from my session here after the review of the session recording. He affirmed that he would appreciate that and would be looking forward to receiving them.

Tim got up and went over to the printer and retrieved the papers that had been printed. "Here you go. I hope this is helpful. If you need anything else, let me know."

I took the papers from Tim and returned to my seat. The ghost box was still running smoothly. I sat down and read the information Tim had found. Most of the personal information about the patient had been redacted. The information that I was able to read told me the patient was David W. Cole, age fifty-nine, who had been admitted to the hospital in June of 1998 to have a cardiac procedure to implant a stent. During the relatively common procedure, David Cole had suffered a major heart attack, which resulted in cardiac arrest. The document went on to say that the patient could not be resuscitated and consequently died during the incident. The information also stated that David Cole's body had been kept here in the hospital morgue pending notification of his next of kin. It also stated that no next of kin could be located, and the body had been turned over to the county coroner three weeks after the time of death for subsequent burial.

I placed the papers in my bag before returning to the ghost box session. I thought to myself, *The reason David Cole has not moved on and remains here in the morgue, apparently lost and confused, is due to the untimely and unexpected circumstances of his death, which were compounded by the lack of any family or friends to claim his physical remains, and his unceremonial burial by the county.* These were classic catalysts for a spirit being grounded or lingering at the location where they spent their last moments of physical life.

I returned my focus to the live ghost box session still in operation. "Mike, Lisa, and David, please excuse me for making you wait," I stated. "Ok, Bruce," came through in Mike's familiar tone. I thanked my spirit techs and David Cole for their understanding. "David, I know what happened to you here in this hospital. I can help you. Are you willing to leave here?" I asked. The response, "Yes, please," came through the ghost box. I spoke to my spirit technicians. "Mike, Lisa, I need your help in crossing over the spirit David Cole. Can you help?" The answer, "Yes, Bruce," came through instantly. "Thank you, guys."

I asked the entity David, "David, I need you to follow my instructions; we are going to help you leave here and cross over to the spirit realm, where you will be happy and safe. Will you follow my instructions?" After a few seconds, the answer, "Yes," came through. "Ok, David, that's good." I continued, "David, can you see a bright light anywhere near you?" David responded, "Yes," followed by, "Very bright." I replied, "Ok, David, are you aware of the two spirit entities who are with you now? They are my friends and are there to help you." "Yes, here," was returned through the ghost box. "Ok, David, I want you to walk to the light. Mike and Lisa will help you."

A few seconds went by, and I asked, "Mike, Lisa, is David going toward the light?" The answer, "Yes," was received. I waited a moment and then asked, "David, are you at the bright light?" I waited for a response, and the answer, "Yes," came through, followed by, "See people," and then, "Warm." I replied, "Good, David. I want you to walk into the light; the people there will meet you and help you to cross into the spirit world." I sat and waited for any response through the ghost box. About a minute passed, and I became impatient, so I asked, "Mike, Lisa, was David able to make it across successfully?" The answer, "Yes, here with me," came through in Lisa's telltale tone of voice. "David is safely in the spirit world?" I asked. "Yes, Bruce, safe," was the answer received. I thanked my spirit technicians Mike and Lisa for their help.

I sat back in my chair and took a breath. I looked at my watch; it was 7:41 p.m. Tom and Sue should be returning in around fifteen minutes. I was about to inform my spirit techs that I was closing down the ghost box session when I noticed there were numerous random communications coming through the box. They consisted of single words and short phrases and were being delivered in different voices, male and female, at different volumes and different speeds. I paused and focused on trying to hear any of the communication that was being attempted. I could discern many different words of live spirit communication that were being delivered chaotically, so it was very difficult to isolate and recognize any single message or pinpoint repeated communication that was coming from a single entity. A ghost box in operation emits an energy signal that acts like a beacon in a fog, or a flame to a moth; it will attract any spirit entities in the surrounding area. They are instinctively drawn to the ghost box, somehow knowing that it is a conduit for them to deliver messages to and communicate with human beings in the physical world, which will, in turn, allow the spirit entity to send an often-times desperate message in the hopes that somehow it will reach the intended ears.

I spoke loudly. "Ok, all spirits trying to communicate, stop yelling and calm down. I cannot hear you all at once." My next statement was to my techs Mike and Lisa. "Mike, Lisa, please control the entities who are trying to communicate; one at a time, please." The loud response of, "Yes, Bruce, wait," was sent by Mike. "Ok, I'll wait." Over the next thirty seconds or so, I could hear that things were calming down dramatically, and then the ghost box sweep returned to its normal sound. Before I could speak, I heard, "Ok, Bruce, good now," in Lisa's tone. I replied, "Ok, great, thank you, guys." I knew there had to be more spirit entities here who would attempt to communicate; what I didn't expect was that there would be so many. Tom and Sue would be returning to the morgue to meet me at any minute, and Bill would be waiting in the emergency room.

From what I could discern, there were far too many spirit entities here for me to attempt any individual communication; we would have to devote much more time than we had if we were to attempt to help any and all spirits here who needed or wanted help. I had never really run into this exact scenario before. I had encountered multiple spirit entities during an investigation and even in a controlled ghost box session who required my assistance, but never at the level I had detected here. I decided to enlist my spirit technicians Mike and Lisa and ask them to do something that up to this point was unprecedented.

I called out, "Mike, Lisa, are you still with me?" The response, "Yes, here" came through. "Great, Mike, Lisa, I need you to do something we have never done before if you are willing." After a few seconds came the reply, "Yes, Bruce." "Ok, thank you," I answered. "Mike, Lisa, I have to end the ghost box session. I know you are aware of the many spirit entities who are here in this hospital." I continued, "Mike, Lisa, is it possible for you to help any spirits who are willing to cross over without my help?" I waited a few seconds, and the answer, "Yes, Bruce, yes," came across the ghost box speaker. "Mike, Lisa, thank you very much. I knew I could count on you." The response, "Yes," came through. "Ok, Mike, Lisa, I am going to shut down the session now. Thank you again." The last communication that came through the ghost box was, "Goodbye, Bruce." I returned the goodbye and turned off the ghost box and voice recorder.

I had a nagging feeling of guilt. I had never abandoned a ghost box session and left the sole responsibility of helping spirits in need to my spirit technicians; it did not sit well with me. I knew, however, that the circumstances at this time did not permit the lengthy investigation and ghost box session it would have entailed to complete the task. I stood up and unplugged my ghost box from the electrical outlet.

I put away my voice recorder and K2 meter and grabbed the ghost box. Just as I was walking into the main morgue area, Tom and Sue came through the large double doors. They walked over, and I asked, "How did it go?"

Tom replied, "Fine."

Sue answered, "Got a ton of EVP." She then asked, "How did the session go?"

I answered, "Very good. I'll explain on the drive home."

Both Tom and Sue nodded. I turned to the morgue attendant Tim. "Tim, thanks for all your help and cooperation."

Tim replied, "Anytime, nice meeting you."

I then asked Tim, "Can you please call the security officer and tell him we are ready to go?"

"Sure, no problem," Tim replied.

We headed out of the morgue and waited in the long hallway for Jim the security guard. As we stood there talking, we heard the elevator come to a stop, the door slid open, and there stood Jim. "Hey, folks, all done?" Jim asked.

"Yes, thanks, can you take us to the security administrator's office?" I replied.

"Sure, get in," Jim said with a smile. "So how did it go? Did you find any ghosts?" Jim asked.

"A few," I answered.

Jim displayed a condescending sort of smile. The elevator came to a stop on the main floor, and the doors opened. We exited the elevator and followed Jim to the head of security's office. Jim opened the door and stepped back, allowing us to enter.

The head of security, Peter Tuttle, raised his head from his paperwork, smiled, and asked, "Well, all finished?"

I answered, "Yes, Pete, all finished for now."

Pete replied, "For now, what do you mean for now?"

I went on to explain to Pete the events of our short investigation and informed him that we would like to return for a full and proper paranormal investigation. Pete listened intently to my recounting of the events without interrupting, and then said, "Well, I can't make that decision; that will be up to the hospital administrator." Pete followed with, "The administrator will want to review any type of evidence you have to back up your claims."

I assured Pete that we indeed had tangible evidence, definitely audio evidence and possibly photographic evidence, which we would not be able to confirm until we reviewed the pictures that were taken.

Sue broke in and said, "I happened to quickly check some of the images that were taken on the camera. I could see immediately that there were some captures made."

I informed Pete that we would be compiling a complete and thorough report, including any and all evidence that would be submitted to the hospital administration. Pete smiled and asked, "Hey, you think I could see a couple of those pictures?"

I answered, "We don't reveal any alleged evidence before we have had a chance to review it ourselves. I'm sure you understand."

Pete winked and nodded understandingly. "Ok, I'm sure you are all anxious to get started home. I'll make my report to the administrator and tell him to expect yours," Pete told us. We all shook hands with Pete and left the security office.

The security guard Jim was still standing outside the door. "You folks need an escort back to the emergency room?" he asked.

"No, thank you. I'm sure we can find our way there," I answered.

"Ok, you folks take care," he replied.

I thanked Jim for his help, and we headed for the emergency room. I walked up to the emergency room nurses' station and asked about Bill. The nurse on duty told me that Bill had been released about fifteen minutes earlier. We all headed to the waiting area to find Bill. As we walked into the waiting room, we saw Bill sitting on the far side near the hospital's main door. We walked over to Bill. He was sitting, holding a brand-new pair of wooden crutches, and had a white cast that covered his foot and ankle and went up to his knee.

"Hey, guys, how did it go?" Bill asked.

"It went well. I'll tell you about it on the way home," I told him.

Bill managed to get up, he tucked the crutches under his arms, and we headed out of the hospital. As we walked to the vehicle, I could not help but imagine that we resembled that old scene of the three American Revolutionary soldiers carrying the flag and playing a fife and drum, limping and bandaged, as they marched along. Tom and Sue loaded the equipment bags into the back of the vehicle, and I helped Bill into the passenger seat. We all got into the vehicle, and I started the engine. I took a deep breath as I fastened my seat belt. It was a relief to finally be heading home; we could all use a couple of days' rest. I exited the hospital parking lot onto the main road. I looked at the digital time display on the radio; it was 8:41 p.m.

As we drove, Sue asked, "Is anybody hungry?"

Tom answered, "I could eat."

Bill added, "Me too."

In the distance I could see the familiar golden arches of a McDonald's illuminated against the night sky. "McDonald's ok?" I asked, and everyone agreed. I drove to McDonald's and went through the drive-through. We parked in the fast-food restaurant's parking lot and began to devour the burgers and fries. I had not realized how long it had been since we all had eaten, or how hungry I really was. We finished our dinner, and I pulled out of the parking lot and back onto the road. We had quite a few hours of driving ahead of us and plenty of time to discuss all that had happened in the last two days.

Bill was still sipping his soda when he asked, "Can you tell me how the hospital investigation went?"

Before I started the story of the short hospital investigation, I glanced in the rearview mirror. Sue had nodded off, and Tom looked like he was just about to. I quietly started to recount the events of the hospital investigation for Bill. I had not gotten five minutes into the story when Bill let out a snore; so much for company and conversation on the long drive home. I drove down the straight and narrow highway. The broken yellow lines dividing the lanes of the highway whizzed by, illuminated by the vehicle headlights.

My thoughts drifted to the angels and my spirit technicians. I could not help but wonder how they would fare in their attempt to close the dark portal that remained in the Conjuring house. I also thought of the investigating team that was there now, in the middle of their investigation, and what they might be experiencing. Did any evil entities cross back into the Conjuring house after we left? As all these thoughts ruminated in my mind, I looked ahead into the ink-black darkness beyond the reach of the headlights and wondered what type of paranormal and supernatural experiences lay ahead for me, my ghost box, and my loyal paranormal investigating team.

CLOSING

Throughout the many years I have dedicated to the practice and research of live spirit ghost box communication, I have often wondered what it would have been like to conduct a paranormal investigation of some of the more celebrated haunted locations, such as the Amityville house and the Conjuring house, using a ghost box as the primary investigating tool. Finally, I decided to put pen to paper and convey my interpretation of what these paranormal investigations might have been like had the investigator used a ghost box as the primary tool and was able to communicate live in real time with the entities that dwelled in these haunted locations.

From its creation, live spirit ghost box communication has allowed physical human beings like me to communicate and interact live in real time with entities that are no longer a part of this physical realm with the use of a ghost box. The method of live spirit ghost box communication has spanned over twenty years now. It has afforded me the opportunity to accumulate the knowledge I have been so blessed to acquire from my daily research and from continuous communication with otherworldly entities that have been so dedicated and selfless in their efforts to accommodate the ongoing barrage of questions and requests that have come from me and other researchers in the field over these many years. It has allowed me to formulate and document many theories and practicing protocols adhered to in the field today.

The vast amount of knowledge and understanding of the spirit realm and its inhabitants that I have gathered over these many years has culminated in my burning desire to share what I have learned with the world. Over the course of my career in this field of research, I have always tried to be forthcoming with the data and knowledge I have acquired. I have tried to disseminate this knowledge and experience by way of written articles, live broadcast appearances, social media platforms, and personal interactions.

Because this unique method allows a physical human being to interact with spirit entities live and in real time, it has caused the interest in the field of live spirit ghost box communication to grow exponentially over the years, allowing the method to integrate itself into every aspect of paranormal research and investigation. I have always been fascinated by the paranormal, and through my many years of practicing and researching live spirit ghost box communication, I have often fantasized about what it would have been like had the individuals who were lucky enough to conduct investigations of historically haunted locations used a ghost box to establish live, real-time communication with the entities that inhabited those locations.

I finally decided to put my imaginings down on paper, which led me to the writing of this new book, *What If The Spirits Could Have Spoken*. In this writing, I have attempted to portray what it might have been like if a paranormal investigating team were to investigate two of the most celebrated hauntings in history, the Amityville house and the Conjuring house. I decided to split the book into two parts, the first is the account of a fictional paranormal investigating team that conducts a paranormal investigation of the Amityville house using the ghost box as the primary evidence-gathering tool. The second part follows the same team on an investigation of the infamous Conjuring house. Each story begins with the account of reports made by individuals who resided in the homes and who publicly reported incidents of horrific paranormal encounters with malevolent entities.

In this writing, as the stories progress, they go from reported factual accounts and meld into a fictional account of the respective paranormal investigations and how they might have unfolded. I have tried to convey my idea of what it might have been like for an investigating team consisting of a team leader, whom I based on myself, and three seasoned investigators to encounter and communicate live with the dark entities that inhabit these two locations. Both accounts will take you through the entire paranormal investigations, from beginning to end, and you will experience every harrowing moment of the encounters with the dark and vengeful entities that control these two houses. You will feel the evil, the darkness, and physical danger. You will also experience the emotion, compassion, and victory felt by the paranormal team members and the spirit beings they encounter. My intention with this book is to have the reader experience the actual paranormal investigations as they might have unfolded, and to feel every terror, as well as every heartwarming moment, as if they themselves were there, enveloped by the dark, ominous, and foreboding walls of the Conjuring house and Amityville house.

ABOUT THE AUTHOR

Bruce Halliday is a renowned paranormal researcher with over twenty years of experience and is known as one of the first people to create and develop live spirit ghost box communication research. Bruce is responsible for most, if not all, of the working theories and protocols accepted in the field of live spirit ghost box communication. He is the author of *When Spirits Speak: Live Spirit Ghost Box Communication,* his debut book, which details his long and expansive journey in live spirit ghost box communication research. It is the premier comprehensive reference guide on the subject. He has published many articles on the theories and workings of ghost box communication and has appeared on numerous radio shows and podcasts discussing his expertise in live spirit ghost box communication and ITC. Examples of his work with live spirit ghost box communication can be found on his personal Facebook page, as well as his Facebook group "Live Spirit Ghost Box Communication Sharing & Education." Bruce also has a popular YouTube Channel "Halliday Paranormal."

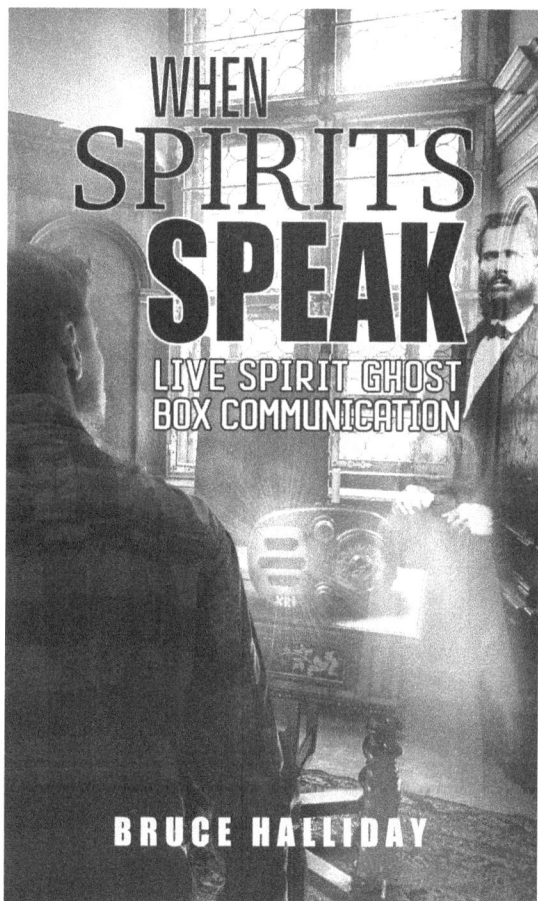

When Spirits Speak

www.ingramcontent.com/pod-product-compliance
Lightning Source LLC
Chambersburg PA
CBHW032343280326
41935CB00008B/432